An Educator's Guide to
SPECIAL EDUCATION LAW

Brenda Bowlby
Catherine Peters
Martha Mackinnon

Aurora Professional Press
a division of Canada Law Book Inc.
240 Edward Street, Aurora, Ontario, L4G 3S9

Cover Photograph:
Charles Thatcher/Tony Stone Images

National Library of Canada Cataloguing in Publication Data

Bowlby, Brenda J. (Brenda Jean), 1952-
    An educator's guide to special education law

(Educator's guides to the law)
Includes bibliographical references and index.
ISBN 0-88804-341-4

    1. Special education—Law and legislation—Ontario.
I. Mackinnon, Martha, 1948- II. Peters, Catherine III. Title.
IV. Series.

KEO771.4.B69 2001   344.713'0791   C2001-901713-8

To my husband, Rick Burgess, and my daughter,
Lindsay Burgess, who, with love and support, gave me
"their time" to write this book.

BJB

To my family, friends and colleagues, whose support
and encouragement have made this book possible.

CLP

For my family which has always valued education
and law and my work in each; for the students who
have taught me so much; and for the friends who
have cared about me, even through indexing.

MMM

Foreword

Never before has the pace of change had such a powerful impact on education. Over the past decade school boards have participated in enormous change focusing on significant reform and accountability structures. These changes have required educators to make connections, forge partnerships and design frameworks to bring meaning and direction for programs and services.

Special educators have taken these challenges seriously. Policies in special education are built on the premise that it is possible to respond to the strengths and needs of each student with special needs. Individual boards and schools are required to provide programs, services and processes to meet the needs of these students, within legislative requirements. While Ontario educators have long been recognized for their attention to the delivery of programs and services which comply with these requirements, an increased public awareness of the accountability structures and fewer resources has made it more difficult.

The creativity of committed teachers, principals and board personnel continues to be exemplary in Ontario. However, the reality of the new responsibilities, and increased parental and student rights leads educators to seek out resources and the guidance of experts focused on educational law. The need to be cognizant of the legislative requirements and to be confident that our programs are being delivered within the parameters of the law is essential. Hence, *An Educator's Guide to Special Education Law* is both valuable and timely.

Brenda, Catherine and Martha are applauded by educators across the province for their leadership in Special Education Law. Their experiences in managing the changes in special education legislation and supporting school boards in difficult times are unprecedented. All three have demonstrated sensitivity towards the needs and responsibilities of the boards, and the needs and rights of parents and students.

An Educator's Guide to Special Education Law will give educators the confidence to speak knowledgeably to parents and advocates about programs, services, processes and legislative requirements. The next best thing to having Brenda, Catherine and Martha on the other end of the telephone is having their book on the corner of your desk!

Suzanne Earle
Louise Moreau

Preface

This book has been written primarily for educators who, on a daily basis, are faced with increasingly complex legal issues in identifying and placing exceptional pupils. We also hope that the book will prove to be useful for parents and others who seek to understand the legal aspects of special education.

Our goal was to provide an overview of the legal framework, together with a practical analysis of the legal questions that arise on a day-to-day basis. In respect of the appeal process, our goal has been to provide a layperson's overview of how the process works and how hearings unfold, together with some explanation of the manner in which legal issues are handled along the way. Our firm belief is that an understanding of the overall legal process will permit better informed decision-making along the way.

Over the course of the past couple of years during which we have been working on this book, the Ministry of Education issued new guidelines and standards where none existed before. These new guidelines and standards have provided far greater definition of the obligations of school boards in the administration of special education than existed throughout the 1980s and 1990s, but also prompted "rewrites" of chapters along the way to incorporate summaries of these new requirements. We are grateful that most of these have been issued in time to permit references to them in the book. A new Special Education Handbook is expected to be released shortly and we regret that we could not delay this book any longer to permit reference to be made to it in its final form.

The authors would like to acknowledge their huge debt of gratitude to Deborah Goldberg who spent hours painstakingly reviewing much of the text in this book. Deborah challenged us, provided us with information, made many suggestions (most of which appear in the book) and, generally, improved this book significantly. We would also like to take this opportunity to publicly acknowledge Deborah as a treasure, residing within the Ministry of Education. We truly appreciate the opportunity we have had to access Deborah's wealth of knowledge and wisdom, which she generously shared with us with her usual even-handedness, common sense and, above all, her concern for and commitment to the school kids of Ontario.

We would also like to express our gratitude to Ruth Mattingly, Suzanne Earle, who both reviewed Chapter 6 and contributed real life insights and comments on the IPRC process. Thanks also go to Nancy Tully-Peever and Jeanette Schieck for providing unique opportunities to work through some of the issues we deal with in this book as well as their insights into these issues, and to Mary Anne Sanderson for her usual insightful analysis which assisted tremendously in dealing with a particularly difficult piece of the puzzle.

Thanks to Mary Nedovich and Anna Del Giudice who patiently typed whatever we gave them.

Finally, two of us wish to express our appreciation for the support from our partners and colleagues at Hicks Morley Hamilton Stewart Storie LLP in our writing of this book. The third expresses the same sentiments to her colleagues at Justice for Children.

Toronto, Ontario   Brenda Bowlby
July 2001   Catherine Peters
                                                   Martha Mackinnon

Table of Contents

3 The Administrator's Framework 17

4 Identification and Exceptionality 39

5 Placement   45

6 The Identification, Placement and Review Committee   59

7 The Individual Education Plan

8 Mediation

9 The First Stage of Appeal

10 The Final Appeal

11 Review by the Courts 151

12 Preparation and Presentation of Your Case 169

13   "Hard to Serve" Students and Other Legal Issues 179

1

Introduction

WHAT IS "SPECIAL EDUCATION LAW"?

We use the term "special education law" in this book to define the legal rights and obligations surrounding the education of students who are "exceptional" — that is, students whose educational needs are not met by the regular curriculum because of mental and/or physical disabilities or because of the high level of their intellectual needs (giftedness).

Special education law has its genesis in Bill 82[1] which introduced into Ontario in 1980 the process for the identification and placement of exceptional students which remains in place today, with only minor modifications. Since Bill 82 came into force, special education law has continued to develop, augmented by amendments to the legislation (both statutes and regulations), as well as interpretations of the legislation which have been provided by the Special Education Tribunals and the courts. Human rights and constitutional legislation have also come into play to shape this unique area of law.

In this book we will review the rights of exceptional students and their parents together with the obligations of school boards and the provincial government as provided for under the statutory framework which constitutes Ontario's blueprint for special education. In this chapter we will provide a brief overview of the most recent historical context of today's statutory framework, an overview of the legal process for identification, placement and appeal, and a general outline of the contents of this book.

BILL 82

Prior to the enactment of Bill 82, children with severe disabilities were often excluded from Ontario's school systems. In some localities parents set up "schools for the mentally retarded". In some cases, such schools were housed in buildings built for that purpose. In other cases, parents set up "schools" in community spaces

---

[1] *Education Amendment Act, 1980*, S.O. 1980, c. 61.

or church basements. And in some cases, children with disabilities simply remained at home and received no education or were placed in residential institutions.

Bill 82 was heralded as introducing "universal access" to publicly funded education to all Ontario's children.[2] It came with the recognition that in order for the right to an education to be meaningful for children with disabilities, special measures would have to be taken where those disabilities interfered with the ability of these children to learn from the normal curriculum. The Bill 82 amendments to the *Education Act* charged the Minister of Education, in the first instance, with the responsibility of ensuring that those measures were taken. Moreover, the Minister was also charged with the responsibility of setting up a process for parents[3] to appeal the appropriateness of special education placements provided for their children.

Bill 82 also imposed on each school board the obligation to provide special education programs and special education services for its exceptional pupils, either directly or through purchase of service agreements with another school board.[4]

The framework created by Bill 82 was supplemented by a number of regulations and Ministerial policies and directives. This framework, which was introduced in 1980, remains essentially intact today.

THE CURRENT PROCESS

At the outset, school boards were required to phase in special education programs and services over a four-year period[5] and to report to the Minister on their progress. The reporting obligation on the status of school board special education plans continues today.[6]

The process for identifying exceptional students has changed little over the past two decades. School boards are required by regulation[7] to establish at least one

---

[2]   The provisions of Bill 82 applied to both the public school board and Roman Catholic separate school boards. Private or independent schools are not subject to the special education provisions of the *Education Act*, R.S.O. 1990, c. E.2 (as amended to 2000, c. 26).

[3]   Throughout this book, the term "parent" includes both parents if they live together or are separated but have joint custody of the student, as well as the custodial parent if the parents are separated. It also refers to the student's legal guardian where a court has made an order naming an individual or individuals as the child's guardian. "Guardian" is defined by s. 1 of the Act as "a person who has lawful custody of a child, other than the parent of the child". Note that a child aged 18 years or older is an adult and that any guardianship order ceases to have effect once the child reaches the age of majority, unless the basis of the guardianship order is that the individual is not competent.

[4]   The language imposing this obligation remains unchanged today and is currently set out in s. 170(1), para. 7 of the *Education Act*.

[5]   *Special Education Programs and Services*, R.R.O. 1980, Reg. 274, as amended by O. Reg. 553/81.

[6]   See Chapter 3, "The Administrator's Framework".

[7]   *Special Education Programs and Services*, R.R.O. 1990, Reg. 306.

Identification, Placement and Review Committee ("IPRC") for the purpose of determining whether students are exceptional.[8] Where a student is determined to be exceptional, the IPRC must use the definitions of exceptionalities which have been prescribed by the Minister.[9] Once a student is identified as exceptional, the IPRC must determine the placement[10] for the student and, thereafter, must review the placement at least annually. This process must be carried out in consultation with parents and all IPRC decisions must be made in the presence of parents. Once a placement is implemented, an Individual Education Plan must be created by school staff, again in consultation with parents.[11]

In accordance with the directive to the Minister of Education to provide a process for parents to appeal the appropriateness of special education placements, parents have been given the right to request a review of the IPRC decision by a tripartite board (a Special Education Appeal Board)[12] comprised of a parent appointee, a school board appointee and a chair selected by the appointees. Following a meeting with all persons who might contribute to the matter, the Special Education Appeal Board must make a recommendation to the school board which will then reconsider the IPRC's decision.

Should the parents disagree with the school board's decision on placement, the parents are entitled as of right to appeal to the Special Education Tribunal.[13] This tribunal was initially established by the Bill 82 amendments to the *Education Act* and these statutory provisions continue today. The decision of the Special Education Tribunal is final and binding on the parents and the school board, subject only to review by the courts where the tribunal makes a legal error in its process or decision.[14]

Beyond the statutory scheme, parents and school boards are increasingly turning to mediation as an alternative forum for resolving their differences over identification and placement disputes. We have devoted a full chapter to this process because it provides a much more constructive approach to the resolution of disputes between parents and the school board than the appeal process itself.[15]

OTHER LEGISLATION

Legal recognition of the rights of persons with disabilities has existed in Canada for a scant two decades. It was not until 1982 that Ontario's *Human Rights Code, 1981*,[16] was proclaimed in force and added "handicap" as a protected

---

[8] See Chapter 6, "The Identification, Placement and Review Committee".
[9] See Chapter 4, "Identification and Exceptionality".
[10] See Chapter 5, "Placement".
[11] See Chapter 7, "The Individual Education Plan"
[12] See Chapter 9, "The First Stage of Appeal".
[13] See Chapter 10, "The Final Appeal".
[14] See Chapter 11, "Review by the Courts".
[15] See Chapter 8, "Mediation".
[16] S.O. 1981, c. 53; proclaimed in force June 15, 1982.

ground. The right to equal treatment under the law for persons with disabilities in the *Canadian Charter of Rights and Freedoms*[17] did not come into force until 1985. It is significant to note that Bill 82, which entrenched in Ontario's *Education Act* the right of students with disabilities to an education in Ontario's schools, was passed in 1980, prior to both of these enactments.

Because human rights law also deals with the rights of persons with disabilities,[18] it was foreseeable that once "handicap" was added as a ground of discrimination, parents of students with disabilities might also access the complaint procedure under the *Human Rights Code* as a means of seeking resolution of disputes involving their children with disabilities.[19] Similarly, the *Canadian Charter of Rights and Freedoms* guarantees equal treatment under the law without discrimination on certain grounds, including mental and physical disability. Both pieces of legislation have played a role in the development of special education law.[20]

OTHER ISSUES

In addition to the issues which arise in the process of identifying and placing exceptional students, and the appeal process, unique challenges arise daily for school staff in attempting to meet the needs of exceptional pupils. Dealing with students whose disabilities give rise to violent behaviour or students who are medically fragile, can raise challenging legal issues which can, on occasion, involve balancing the rights of the student in question with the rights of others. In the final chapter of this book we deal with several of these issues.[21]

---

[17] Part I of the *Constitution Act, 1982*, being Schedule B of the *Canada Act 1982* (U.K.), 1982, c. 11.

[18] It should be noted that giftedness is not a disability under the *Human Rights Code.* However, where a gifted student also has a disability, such as a learning disability or other physical or mental disability, the Code would have application in respect only of that disability. Similarly, the Code would apply to the behavioural exceptionality only where the student's behavioural problems arise or are perceived to arise from a mental or physical disability.

[19] The earliest special education case to reach a Human Rights Board of Inquiry was *Lanark, Leeds and Grenville Roman Catholic Separate School Board v. Ontario (Human Rights Commission)* (1986), 7 C.H.R.R. D/3546 (Ont. Bd. Inq.), revd 8 C.H.R.R. D/4235, 40 D.L.R. (4th) 316, 60 O.R. (2d) 441, 24 O.A.C. 11 (Div. Ct.), affd 67 O.R. (2d) 479n, 57 D.L.R. (4th) 479n, 10 C.H.R.R. D/6336 (C.A.), where the complaint centred on three students, all identified as "trainable mentally retarded" (now called "developmental disability"), who were enrolled as students in a separate school board but received most of their education in a school operated by the co-terminus public board of education under a purchase of special education services agreement. Ultimately, the complaint was dismissed by the Divisional Court on the basis of a provision of the *Human Rights Code* which has since been removed.

[20] See Chapter 2, "The Legal Framework".

[21] See Chapter 13, " 'Hard to Serve Students' and Other Legal Issues".

2

The Legal Framework

INTRODUCTION

Special education law is a unique discipline, drawing upon principles derived from a number of separate, overlapping and sometimes competing legal regimes. This complex legal framework provides the context for understanding the structure and functioning of Ontario's special education scheme, which is described in detail in later chapters of this book.

In this chapter, we have described in general terms four of the key sources of special education law: administrative law; education law; human rights law; and child welfare law.

ADMINISTRATIVE LAW

Special education law is part of the broader discipline of administrative law. Administrative law can be described in very general terms as the body of legal principles which regulates the manner in which the government exercises its authority vis-à-vis its citizens. "Government" in this context includes the Cabinet, government ministries, the Legislature and the judiciary. However, it also covers a wide range of governmental and quasi-governmental decision-makers, boards and tribunals that carry out statutory functions and/or exercise statutory authority to make decisions affecting the lives of members of the public.

The special education regime imposes duties and obligations on a number of different administrative decision-makers. The most important of these are the Minister of Education, school boards and the adjudicative bodies involved in special education decision-making, particularly the Special Education Tribunal.

The Minister of Education

Under the *Education Act*,[1] some very specific obligations are placed on the Minister of Education with respect to special education. Section 8(3) of the *Education Act* sets out the Minister's obligations:

> The Minister shall ensure that all exceptional children in Ontario have available to them, in accordance with this Act and the regulations, appropriate special education programs and special education services without payment of fees by parents or guardians resident in Ontario, and shall provide for the parents or guardians to appeal the appropriateness of the special education placement, and for these purposes the Minister shall,
>
> (a) require school boards to implement procedures for early and ongoing identification of the learning abilities and needs of pupils, and shall prescribe standards in accordance with which such procedures be implemented; and
>
> (b) in respect of special education programs and services, define exceptionalities of pupils, and prescribe classes, groups or categories of exceptional pupils, and require boards to employ such definitions or use such prescriptions as established under this clause.

Pursuant to these obligations, the Ministry of Education has established regulations governing the special education process.[2] The Ministry has also developed and implemented a number of guidelines and policy documents which set out the standards the Ministry expects school boards to meet in implementing the special education scheme.[3] In addition, the Ministry has developed a complex funding scheme, pursuant to which the funding available to school boards for special education programs and special education services is determined.[4]

School Boards

School boards are also administrative decision-makers. They too have specific obligations with respect to special education under the *Education Act*. In particular, pursuant to s. 170(1), para. 7, every school board is required to:

> 7. provide or enter into an agreement with another board to provide in accordance with the regulations special education programs and special education services for its exceptional pupils . . .

---

[1] R.S.O. 1990, c. E.2 (as amended).

[2] *Identification and Placement of Exceptional Pupils*, O. Reg. 181/98; *Special Education Programs and Services*, R.R.O. 1990, Reg. 306; *Special Education Advisory Committees*, O. Reg. 464/97.

[3] See, for example, "The Special Education Appeal Board", *Special Education Monograph No. 1* (Ontario, Ministry of Education: March, 1985); "Identification, Placement and Review Committees", *Special Education Monograph No. 2* (Ontario, Ministry of Education: October, 1985); *Draft Special Education Information Handbook* (Ontario, Ministry of Education: 2000); *Individual Education Plans: Standards for Development, Program Planning and Implementation* (Ontario, Ministry of Education: 2000).

[4] See, for example, *Student Focused Funding — Legislative Grants for the 2000-2001 School Board Fiscal Year*, O. Reg. 170/00, ss. 14 to 20.

Pursuant to this obligation, school boards must establish and maintain a special education plan, and review the plan annually.[5] Any amendments to the plan must be submitted to the Ministry for review and the Ministry may, at any time, require the school board to make amendments to its special education plan.[6] School boards must also report every two years to the Ministry on their provision of special education programs and special education services.[7]

School boards are also required to establish Identification, Placement and Review Committees (IPRCs) and Special Education Appeal Boards (SEABs), consider their recommendations concerning the identification and placement of exceptional pupils and review of identification and/or placement, and make decisions based on those recommendations.[8] This obligation includes an obligation to publish a parent's guide explaining the IPRC and SEAB processes,[9] and an obligation to require the development of an individual education plan (IEP) where placement in a special education program has been implemented.[10]

The Special Education Tribunal

The Special Education Tribunal is also an administrative decision-maker. Under s. 57 of the *Education Act*, the Tribunal is given the statutory authority to hold a hearing and decide parents' appeals of school board decisions concerning the identification and placement of exceptional pupils.[11]

Administrative Law Requirements

The principles of administrative law provide an important set of "checks and balances" on the manner in which all of the administrative decision-makers identified above carry out their functions under the special education scheme. All administrative bodies must conform to certain basic procedural and substantive requirements in carrying out their functions. If they do not, the courts may judicially review their decisions and set their decisions aside or otherwise direct them to comply with their statutory responsibilities.

Administrative law requirements are discussed further in Chapter 11. Some of the basic legal requirements which govern special education decision-makers are outlined below.

The Canadian Charter of Rights and Freedoms

The Ministry of Education, school boards, the IPRC, the SEAB and the Special Education Tribunal are all subject to the *Canadian Charter of Rights and*

---

[5] Regulation 306, s. 2(2) to (4).
[6] *Ibid.*, s. 2(4) and (5).
[7] *Ibid.*, s. 3. These requirements are discussed further in Chapter 3.
[8] O. Reg. 181/98.
[9] *Ibid.*, s. 13.
[10] *Ibid.*, s. 6. For further discussion, see Chapters 6 to 9.
[11] *Education Act*, s. 57(3), (4). For further discussion, see Chapter 10.

Freedoms. Their actions, recommendations and decisions must all be consistent with the Charter; if they are not, they will be set aside.

The provision of the Charter which arises most often in the special education context is s. 15, the equality rights provision, which states:

> (1) Every individual is equal before and under the law and has the right to the equal protection and equal benefit of the law without discrimination and, in particular, without discrimination based on race, national or ethnic origin, colour, religion, sex, age or mental or physical disability.

> (2) Subsection (1) does not preclude any law, program or activity that has as its object the amelioration of conditions of disadvantaged individuals or groups including those that are disadvantaged because of race, national or ethnic origin, colour, religion, sex, age or mental or physical disability.

The equality rights guarantee in s. 15 is subject to s. 1 of the Charter, which provides:

> 1. The *Canadian Charter of Rights and Freedoms* guarantees the rights and freedoms set out in it subject only to such reasonable limits prescribed by law as can be demonstrably justified in a free and democratic society.

During the 1990s, there was considerable debate and litigation over the question of whether Ontario's special education regime was consistent with s. 15 of the Charter. Parents, aided by advocacy groups for persons with disabilities, argued that s. 15 required a presumption in favour of integrated education. School boards and the Ministry of Education argued that s. 15 required a more individualized approach, involving a consideration in each case of the educational setting in which the student's best interests could be met. This issue was ultimately resolved in the seminal case of *Eaton v. Brant County Board of Education*,[12] in which the Supreme Court of Canada preferred the latter approach and upheld the constitutionality of Ontario's special education scheme.

Since *Eaton*, there have been a number of other examples where the Charter has been invoked to challenge special education decision-making.[13] Moreover, even in the absence of a Charter challenge, administrative bodies are expected to respect "Charter values" in carrying out their statutory functions. Thus, special education decision-makers must be vigilant to ensure that their actions and decisions are consistent with both the Charter, and the social values underlying it.

Procedural Fairness and Natural Justice

All administrative decision-makers are required to comply with basic rules of "natural justice" and "procedural fairness". These court-made rules are designed to ensure that persons who may be affected by administrative decisions receive fair

---

[12]   [1997] 1 S.C.R. 241, 142 D.L.R. (4th) 385, 31 O.R. (3d) 574*n*, 97 O.A.C. 161, 41 C.R.R. (2d) 240, 207 N.R. 171.

[13]   See, for example, *Adler v. Ontario* (1996), 140 D.L.R. (4th) 385, [1996] 3 S.C.R. 609, 30 O.R. (3d) 642*n*, 40 C.R.R. (2d) 1, 204 N.R. 81; *Concerned Parents for Children with Learning Disabilities Inc. v. Prince Albert (Various Boards of Education)* (1998), 27 C.P.C. (4th) 304, 170 Sask. R. 200, 56 C.R.R. (2d) 76 (Q.B.).

treatment. Among other things, these rules require notice of the information being considered by the decision-maker and an opportunity to respond to it. They also require that the decision in question be made by an unbiased and impartial decision-maker.

All of the administrative bodies involved in special education decision-making — the Ministry, school boards, IPRCs, SEABs and the Special Education Tribunal — are bound by these court-made procedural rules. The specific procedural rules which are applicable will vary from case to case depending on, among other things, the statutory and regulatory requirements, the decision-maker involved and the decision under consideration.[14]

In addition to the court-made rules of natural justice and procedural fairness, some administrative decision-makers are governed by the *Statutory Powers Procedure Act*,[15] which sets out a code of minimum procedural rules which must be followed by the decision-maker. In the special education context, only the Special Education Tribunal is governed by the SPPA.

If an administrative body does not comply with the procedural rules applicable to it — whether the court-made rules of "procedural fairness" and "natural justice" or the statutory rules of the SPPA — its decisions can be overturned by a court. Accordingly, it is necessary both to understand the basic procedural rules and to ensure that they are followed, in order to immunize the decision from judicial intervention.

Review of Administrative Decisions

An administrative decision-maker may be given the statutory authority to exercise a discretion or to hold a hearing, adjudicate factual and legal issues, and reach a decision on a matter. An example of discretionary authority is the school board's discretion to accept or reject the recommendations of the SEAB with respect to identification and/or placement.[16] An example of adjudicative authority is the Special Education Tribunal's statutory authority to hear and decide special education appeals under s. 57 of the *Education Act*.

The courts generally defer to the decisions of administrative bodies. However, the degree of deference will depend on a number of factors. As in the case of procedural rules, these factors will include the statutory and regulatory requirements, the decision-maker involved and the nature of the decision in question. Where deference is at its highest, the administrative decision will only be set aside if it is "patently unreasonable"; where deference is at its lowest, the decision will be set aside if it is "incorrect"; in intermediate cases, the decision may be set aside if it is "unreasonable".

---

[14] *Baker v. Canada (Minister of Citizenship and Immigration)*, [1999] 2 S.C.R. 817 at pp. 837-41, 174 D.L.R. (4th) 193, 14 Admin. L.R. (3d) 173, 1 Imm. L.R. (3d) 1, 243 N.R. 22.

[15] R.S.O. 1990, c. S.22 ("SPPA").

[16] O. Reg. 181/98, s. 30.

Conclusion

The three broad categories of administrative review discussed above provide the context within which all of the various administrative bodies involved in the special education scheme carry out their statutory functions. They inform both the procedures followed and the decisions made by these bodies. As such, they comprise an important part of the legal framework for special education in this province.

EDUCATION LAW

Special education law is also part of the discipline of education law. Education law is part of the broader discipline of administrative law. However, education law is also its own unique discipline, and the source of many important legal principles applicable to the public education system. These principles are an important part of the legal framework within which special education decisions are made.

Constitutional Requirements

Our Constitution protects both denominational, separate and dissentient school rights and minority language instruction rights in certain contexts.

Section 93 of the *Constitution Act, 1867,* preserves denominational, separate and dissentient school rights which existed at the time of Confederation:

> 93. In and for each Province the Legislature may exclusively make Laws in relation to Education, subject and according to the following Provisions: —
>
> (1) Nothing in any such Law shall prejudicially affect any Right or Privilege with respect to Denominational Schools which any Class of Persons have by Law in the Province at the Union:
>
> (2) All the Powers, Privileges, and Duties at the Union by Law conferred and imposed in Upper Canada on the Separate Schools and School Trustees of the Queen's Roman Catholic Subjects shall be and the same are hereby extended to the Dissentient Schools of the Queen's Protestant and Roman Catholic Subjects in Quebec:
>
> (3) Where in any Province a System of Separate or Dissentient Schools exists by Law at the Union or is thereafter established by the Legislature of the Province, an Appeal shall lie to the Governor General in Council from any Act or Decision of any Provincial Authority affecting any Right or Privilege of the Protestant or Roman Catholic Minority of the Queen's Subjects in relation to Education:
>
> (4) In case any such Provincial Law as from Time to Time seems to the Governor General in Council requisite for the due Execution of the Provisions of this Section is not made, or in case any Decision of the Governor General in Council on any Appeal under this Section is not duly executed by the proper Provincial Authority in that Behalf, then and in every such Case, and as far only as the Circumstances of each Case require, the Parliament of Canada may make remedial Laws for the due Execution of the Provisions of this Section and of any Decision of the Governor General in Council under this Section.

These rights are further reinforced in s. 29 of the Charter, which provides:

> 29. Nothing in this Charter abrogates or derogates from any rights or privileges guaranteed by or under the Constitution of Canada in respect of denominational, separate or dissentient schools.

The Charter also protects the right of certain Canadian citizens to have their children educated in English or French, where that language is the minority language in the province in which they reside:

> 23 (1) Citizens of Canada
> (a)   whose first language learned and still understood is that of the English or French linguistic minority population of the province in which they reside, or
> (b)   who have received their primary school instruction in Canada in English or French and reside in a province where the language in which they received that instruction is the language of the English or French linguistic minority population of the province,
> have the right to have their children receive primary and secondary school instruction in that language in that province.
>
> (2) Citizens of Canada of whom any child has received or is receiving primary or secondary school instruction in English or French in Canada, have the right to have all their children receive primary and secondary school instruction in the same language.
>
> (3) The right of citizens of Canada under subsections (1) and (2) to have their children receive primary and secondary school instruction in the language of the English or French linguistic minority population of a province
> (a)   applies wherever in the province the number of children of citizens who have such a right is sufficient to warrant the provision to them out of public funds of minority language instruction; and
> (b)   includes, where the number of those children so warrants, the right to have them receive that instruction in minority language educational facilities provided out of public funds.[17]

Like any form of publicly funded education, special education programs and services must be provided in a way which is consistent with and respectful of these important constitutional rights.[18] In other words, special education programs and

---

[17]   Section 59 of the *Constitution Act, 1982* provides that s. 23(1)(*a*) will only come into force in Quebec where proclamation is authorized by the legislative assembly or government of Quebec. That authorization has never been given. Accordingly, s. 23(1)(*a*) is not in force in the Province of Quebec.

[18]   In Ontario, this principle is reinforced in the *Education Act*, s. 1(4) and (4.1), which provide:
> (4) This Act does not adversely affect any right or privilege guaranteed by section 93 of the *Constitution Act, 1867* or by section 23 of the *Canadian Charter of Rights and Freedoms*.
> (4.1) Every authority given by this Act, including but not limited to every authority to make a regulation, decision or order and every authority to issue a directive or guideline, shall be exercised in a manner consistent with and respectful of the rights and privileges guaranteed by section 93 of the *Constitution Act, 1867* and by section 23 of the *Canadian Charter of Rights and Freedoms*.

services must be available in both the English and French languages, at both public and separate school boards.

Other Statutory Requirements

Quite apart from the constitutional requirements with respect to education which are described above, the *Education Act* and other applicable legislation impose a wide variety of obligations on school boards. A full discussion of all of these requirements is beyond the scope of this work. However, some examples which will be relevant to special education include the following:

- the establishment of the school calendar[19] and the school day;[20]
- class size requirements;[21]
- enrolment limitations in special education classes;[22]
- compulsory school attendance requirements and resident pupil requirements;[23]
- requirements with respect to transportation of students;[24]
- requirements governing the holding of school board meetings and the keeping of school board records;[25]
- restrictions on the use and disclosure of information in the Ontario School Record;[26]
- requirements governing access to, and collection, use and disclosure of, students' personal information under the *Municipal Freedom of Information and Protection of Privacy Act;*[27]
- the provincial code of conduct, and requirements concerning behaviour, discipline and safety in the schools;[28] and
- *Occupational Health and Safety Act*[29] requirements with respect to persons working on school property.

In providing special education programs and services to exceptional pupils, school boards must comply not only with the specific requirements of the special education regime, but with the myriad obligations and requirements listed above.

---

[19]   *School Year Calendar*, R.R.O. 1990, Reg. 304.
[20]   *Operation of Schools — General*, R.R.O. 1990, Reg. 298, s. 3.
[21]   *Education Act*, s. 170(1) to (2.1); *Class Size*, O. Reg. 118/98.
[22]   Regulation 298, ss. 30 and 31.
[23]   *Education Act*, ss. 18 to 49.
[24]   *Ibid.*, s. 190.
[25]   *Ibid.*, ss. 200 to 209; *Electronic Meetings*, O. Reg. 463/97.
[26]   *Ibid.*, s. 266.
[27]   R.S.O. 1990, c. M.56.
[28]   *Education Act*, ss. 300 to 316; Regulation 298, s. 23.
[29]   R.S.O. 1990, c. O.1.

HUMAN RIGHTS LAW

Special education law is also subject to the discipline of human rights law.

The Ontario *Human Rights Code*[30] prohibits discrimination in the provision of services (including educational services) because of handicap. The term "handicap" is broadly defined in s. 10(1) of the Code as follows:

> "because of handicap" means for the reason that the person has or has had, or is believed to have or have had,
>
> (a) any degree of physical disability, infirmity, malformation or disfigurement that is caused by bodily injury, birth defect or illness and, without limiting the generality of the foregoing, including diabetes mellitus, epilepsy, any degree of paralysis, amputation, lack of physical coordination, blindness or visual impediment, deafness or hearing impediment, muteness or speech impediment, or physical reliance on a guide dog or on a wheelchair or other remedial appliance or device,
> (b) a condition of mental retardation or impairment,
> (c) a learning disability, or a dysfunction in one or more of the processes involved in understanding or using symbols or spoken language,
> (d) a mental disorder, or
> (e) an injury or disability for which benefits were claimed or received under the insurance plan established under the *Workplace Safety and Insurance Act, 1997.*

Most students identified as "exceptional pupils" — with the exception of those who are gifted — will have a "handicap" for the purpose of this definition. However, not every difference in treatment with respect to these students related to the handicap will constitute discrimination. Rather, as the Supreme Court of Canada recognized in the *Eaton*[31] case, in some cases, differences in treatment will be necessary and appropriate in order to ensure equal treatment of persons with disabilities:

> The principal object of certain of the prohibited grounds is the elimination of discrimination by the attribution of untrue characteristics based on stereotypical attitudes relating to immutable conditions such as race or sex. In the case of disability, this is one of the objectives. The other equally important objective seeks to take into account the true characteristics of this group which act as headwinds to the enjoyment of society's benefits and to accommodate them. Exclusion from the mainstream of society results from the construction of a society based solely on "mainstream" attributes to which disabled persons will never be able to gain access. Whether it is the impossibility of success at a written test for a blind person, or the need for ramp access to a library, the discrimination does not lie in the attribution of untrue characteristics to the disabled individual. The blind person cannot see and the person in a wheelchair needs a ramp. Rather, it is the failure to make reasonable accommodation, to fine-tune society so that its structures and assumptions do not result in the relegation and banishment of disabled persons from participation, which results in discrimination against them. The discrimination inquiry which uses "the attribution of stereotypical characteristics" reasoning as commonly understood is

---

[30] R.S.O. 1990, c. H.19 (as amended to 1999, c. 6) ("the Code") ss. 1 and 11.

[31] *Eaton v. Brant County Board of Education*, [1997] 1 S.C.R. 241 at pp. 272-3, 142 D.L.R. (4th) 385, 31 O.R. (3d) 574*n*, 97 O.A.C. 161, 41 C.R.R. (2d) 240, 207 N.R. 171.

simply inappropriate here. It may be seen rather as a case of reverse stereotyping which, by not allowing for the condition of a disabled individual, ignores his or her disability and forces the individual to sink or swim within the mainstream environment. It is recognition of the actual characteristics, and reasonable accommodation of these characteristics which is the central purpose of s. 15(1) in relation to disability.

Although the above statements were made in the context of the equality rights provisions of the Charter, they apply equally under the Code. Where the treatment of a student with a handicap gives rise to an inference of discrimination, the Code imposes on the school board a duty to accommodate the pupil to the point of undue hardship.[32] "Accommodation" and "undue hardship" are very complex legal concepts; a full discussion of these concepts is beyond the scope of this chapter. For present purposes, it will suffice to note that the Supreme Court of Canada is placing increasing emphasis on the need to accommodate persons with disabilities, in order to increase the inclusiveness of our social institutions.[33]

Section 14(1) of the Code also provides for the implementation of a "special program" which is "designed to relieve hardship or economic disadvantage or to assist disadvantaged persons or groups to achieve or attempt to achieve equal opportunity or that is likely to contribute to the elimination of [discrimination]".

The special education regime is, at its essence, a form of legislated "special program" directed at students with disabilities. The regime recognizes that, without accommodation, students with disabilities would have a lesser ability to profit from the service of education than their non-disabled peers. They would, to use the language of *Eaton*, be left to "sink or swim" in the mainstream environment. In response to this problem, the Legislature established a process for identifying students with special educational needs, and determining the placement which will best serve those needs. The placement — and the special education programs and services provided in the placement — are all means of accommodating the special needs arising from the student's disability.

Thus, it can be seen that the special education regime parallels the requirements of the Code in several significant respects. In addition, the implementation of the special education regime can be reviewed under the Code, to ensure that the standards of the Code are maintained.[34] Thus, the Code is an important part of the legal framework governing Ontario's special education scheme.

---

[32] Code, ss. 17 and 11.

[33] *British Columbia (Public Service Employee Relations Commission) v. B.C.G.S.E.U.*, [1999] 3 S.C.R. 3 at p. 38, 176 D.L.R. (4th) 1, [1999] 10 W.W.R. 1, 207 W.A.C. 161, 66 B.C.L.R. (3d) 253, 46 C.C.E.L. (2d) 206, 99 C.L.L.C. ¶230-028, 35 C.H.R.R. D/257, 68 C.R.R. (2d) 1, 244 N.R. 145.

[34] Section 47(2) of the Code provides:

 Where a provision in an Act or regulation purports to require or authorize conduct that is a contravention of Part I, this Act applies and prevails unless the Act or regulation specifically provides that it is to apply despite this Act.

CHILD WELFARE LAW

Finally, special education law has important links to the discipline of child welfare law. Although parents generally have the right to make important life decisions on their child's behalf, including schooling decisions, the courts retain a general supervisory jurisdiction to intervene to ensure that the child's best interests are protected.[35] In the *Eaton* decision, the Supreme Court of Canada held that the essence of the identification and placement process under the *Education Act* is to determine the educational "best interests" of the child from the child's own perspective.[36] While parental preference will ordinarily be given some weight, it will not always be determinative of the issue.[37]

CONCLUSION

As the above discussion illustrates, special education law draws upon and is influenced by a vast body of overlapping — and sometimes competing — legal principles. This complex legal framework lies beneath many of the specific legislative and court-made requirements comprising the special education regime, which are discussed in the upcoming chapters of this book.

---

[35] See, for example, *E. (Mrs.) v. Eve*, [1986] 2 S.C.R. 388, 31 D.L.R. (4th) 1, 61 Nfld. & P.E.I.R. 273, 8 C.H.R.R. D/3773, 13 C.P.C. (2d) 6, 71 N.R. 1; *B. (R.) v. Children's Aid Society of Metropolitan Toronto*, [1995] 1 S.C.R. 315, 122 D.L.R. (4th) 1, 21 O.R. (3d) 479n, 78 O.A.C. 1, 26 C.R.R. (2d) 202, 9 R.F.L. (4th) 157, 176 N.R. 161 *sub nom. Sheena B. (Re)*.

[36] *Eaton, supra*, footnote 31, at pp. 277-8.

[37] *Ibid.*, at pp. 278-9.

3

The Administrator's Framework

INTRODUCTION

The *Education Act*[1] and regulations impose on school boards specific requirements concerning the manner in which special education programs and services are planned for and delivered to exceptional students. These requirements create a framework based on which a school board, its superintendents, principals and teachers will carry out the school board's obligations under the *Education Act* in respect of its exceptional students.

In the first instance, the school board must set out, in a Special Education Plan ("SEP"), an outline of the special education placements and the special education programs and services it will be providing for its exceptional pupils. This plan will be subject to review by the Minister of Education who may require that the school board amend the plan. This document will also serve to inform parents and the public about the manner in which the board is carrying out its special education responsibilities.[2]

In order to ensure that school boards receive input from parents of exceptional pupils in developing and delivering special education programs and services, each school board is required to establish a Special Education Advisory Committee ("SEAC") comprised of representatives of parent advocate groups together with trustees.[3]

To ensure that parents are fully informed as to their rights in the identification and placement process, school boards must produce a Parent Guide which details the process whereby students are identified and placed, and parental rights to appeal identification and/or placement.[4]

In planning for special education classes, limits are placed on maximum class sizes based on the exceptionality which each class is designed to deal with.

---

[1] R.S.O. 1990, c. E.2 (as amended), s. 170(1), para. 7.
[2] *Special Education Programs and Services*, R.R.O. 1990, Reg. 306.
[3] *Education Act*, s. 57.1.
[4] *Identification and Placement of Exceptional Pupils*, O. Reg. 181/98.

Two other critical parts of the "Administrator's Framework", are the Identification Placement and Review Committee (which is dealt with in Chapter 6) and the Individual Education Plan (which is dealt with in Chapter 7).

In this chapter we will canvas the legal obligations underlying the creation and review of the SEP and the operation of the SEAC. We will also outline the obligation of a school board to create a Parent Guide. Finally, we will set out the maximum limits on the size of special education classes established for particular exceptionalities.

THE SPECIAL EDUCATION PLAN

Historical Context: The Multi-Year Plans

When Bill 82[5] ushered in Ontario's present scheme of special education in 1980, some school boards already had in place relatively sophisticated arrays of special education services and programs. Others did not.

In recognition of the disparity in the level of special education programs and services available at school boards throughout Ontario prior to 1980, Bill 82 provided for a five-year "phase-in" period. The deadline by which all school boards were expected to have put the necessary special education programs and services in place to meet the needs of their exceptional pupils was September 1, 1985. (In the case of special education programs and services for the "trainable retarded" designation, the target date was December 31, 1985.)[6]

During the phase-in period leading up to the full implementation date, each school board was required to prepare and file, annually, a "multi-year" plan outlining the blueprint for proceeding to put into place the special education programs and services which would be needed to comply with its statutory obligation to provide special education programs and services for all its exceptional pupils by the target date.[7] The culmination of this process of preparing and filing multi-year plans was the preparation and filing of a SEP for the 1985-86 school year which disclosed all the special education programs and services which the school board had put into place to address the needs of the school board's exceptional pupils.[8]

Following the filing of the 1985-86 SEP, each school board was required to file a report on its special education programs and services, commencing in 1987, and every two years thereafter. Until recently, no policy or directive specified the form

---

[5] *Education Amendment Act, 1980*, S.O. 1980, c. 61.

[6] *Special Education Programs and Services*, R.R.O. 1980, Reg. 274, as amended by O. Reg. 53/81.

[7] During this period, students were entitled to receive only those special education programs or services which, under the terms of the multi-year plan, had been put into place at the particular point in time: *Dolmage v. Muskoka Board of Education* (1985), 49 O.R. (2d) 546, 15 D.L.R. (4th) 741, 6 O.A.C. 389 (Div. Ct.).

[8] *Special Education Programs and Services*, Reg. 274.

or contents of a school board's special education plans. However, in 1999, the Ministry of Education required school boards to submit a full new SEP instead of a biannual report and stipulated the criteria which would be used to review the plans.[9]

Current Requirements

In the Fall of 2000, the Ministry of Education issued a new policy document, entitled *Standards for School Boards' Special Education Plans* (the "*Standards*").[10] This policy sets out precise requirements for SEPs and advises school boards of the standards against which their SEPs will be measured. While the policy does not have the force of law, the Minister does have the power to "require a board to amend its special education plan in a manner that the Minister considers necessary so as to ensure that the board provides special education programs and special education services that meet the current needs of the exceptional pupils of the board".[11] The *Standards* reflect what the Minister considers to be necessary to meet the current needs of exceptional students, and the Minister may require boards to amend their SEPs to comply with them.

The issuance of the *Standards* marks a change in the role and function of the SEP. Previously, the SEP was primarily a reporting document which allowed the Minister to monitor the manner in which each board was providing special education programs and services for its exceptional pupils. The *Standards* contemplate, however, that the purpose of the SEP is not only to inform the Minister but also the public about the manner in which the school board is carrying out its special education responsibilities. Each school board must make its SEP available to the public and inform the public how to access the document. If the school board maintains an Internet website, the board must include information on how the SEP may be accessed. It is not necessary for the board to include the SEP on the website, but the Ministry encourages that this be done.[12]

Maintenance and Review of the SEP

The SEP, as a document, is subject to the ultimate approval of and adoption by resolution of the board of trustees.

School boards are required to keep their SEPs current. In addition to ongoing review of SEPs, which may result in *ad hoc* amendments, each school board must annually review its SEP. This review must be completed by May 15th each year[13] and the SEP must be amended to ensure that it continues to address the needs of the school board's exceptional pupils. Review of the SEP will normally fall, in the first

---

[9] Ministry of Education, Memorandum to Directors of Education, Re: Report to the Minister/Annual Review of Special Education Plans (dated April 5, 2000.)

[10] Ministry of Education, *Standards for School Boards' Special Education Plans* (2000).

[11] Regulation 306, s. 2(5).

[12] The *Standards*, at p. 17.

[13] *Special Education Programs and Services*, Reg. 306, s. 2(3).

instance, to special education staff, although the SEAC will also play a role in ensuring that the SEP is maintained and updated.[14]

The *Standards* impose an obligation on school boards to "consult" with members of the community, including parents of children who are receiving special education programs and services and school councils, as part of the process of developing and modifying their SEPs.[15]

Ministerial Review of SEPs and Amendments to SEPs

It is the responsibility of the Minister of Education to ensure that all exceptional children in Ontario have available to them appropriate special education programs and services without payment of fees.[16] In order to carry out this statutory mandate, the Minister has been given a broad power of review and the power to require school boards to amend their SEPs where the Minister is of the view that the plans are deficient. Specifically, the Minister may require a school board to amend its SEP "in a manner that the Minister considers necessary so as to ensure that the board provides special education programs and special education services that meet the current needs of the exceptional pupils of the board".[17]

In order to facilitate the Minister's ongoing review of SEPs, each board is required to forward any amendments which it has made to its SEP to the Minister of Education for review. Amendments include any modifications, addition or deletion of programs, services and/or personnel (*i.e.,* positions) approved by the board following a review of the special education plan.[18] Any amendment made in the preceding 12 months must be submitted to the Minister by May 15th in each year.[19]

Every two years, a school board must submit to the Minister a report on the provision by the school board of special education programs and special education services. This report must be prepared in accordance with procedures stipulated by the Minister and approved by the board of trustees. As already noted, the deadline for submission of the first report was May 15, 1987. Reports have been required every two years since the first report.[20] As also noted, in 1999, the Ministry of Education required school boards to submit a full new SEP which complied with stipulated criteria.[21] Henceforth, the Minister will require that SEPs comply with the *Standards* it has specified as a matter of policy.

---

[14] *Special Education Advisory Committees,* O. Reg. 464/97.
[15] The *Standards,* at p. 4.
[16] *Education Act,* s. 8(3).
[17] Regulation 306, s. 2(5).
[18] *Ibid.,* s. 2(2).
[19] *Ibid.,* s. 2(4).
[20] *Ibid.,* s. 3.
[21] *Education Act,* s. 170(1), para. 7.

Contents of the Special Education Plan

The SEP must disclose the methods by which a school board will comply with its obligation under s. 170(1), para. 7 of the *Education Act* to "provide or enter into an agreement with another board to provide in accordance with the regulations special education programs and special education services for its exceptional pupils".

A "special education program" is defined as "an educational program [in respect of an exceptional pupil] that is based on and modified by the results of continuous assessment and evaluation and that includes a plan containing specific objectives and an outline of educational services that meets the needs of the exceptional pupil".[22]

"Special education services" are defined as "facilities and resources, including support personnel and equipment, necessary for developing and implementing a special education program".[23]

Implicit in the requirement that the school board disclose the methods it will use to comply with its obligation to provide special education services and programs for its exceptional pupils is a requirement that the school board will also disclose the various placements in which these special education services and programs will be provided. Accordingly, the SEP must also set out the range of placements which the school board will make available for its exceptional pupils. The Ministry of Education has made this one of the standards which a school board must comply with in its SEP.[24]

Standards for Special Education Plans

The *Standards* provide a very detailed set of requirements of what must be included in each school board's SEP. Indeed, the *Standards* go beyond a requirement that certain information be contained in the SEP and reflect an expectation that each board will have set up certain mechanisms, procedures and policies as a precondition to meeting the *Standards* for the SEP. Thus, the *Standards* not only require that descriptions of policies and procedures be included in the SEP, but actually dictate the policies and procedures which must be put into place by the school board in order to comply with the *Standards*.

We have summarized below the requirements imposed on school boards by the *Standards*.

The School Board's Consultation Process

The *Standards* contemplate the existence in each school board of a process for public consultation, undertaken with the assistance of the SEAC, to allow the school board to receive continuous feedback on special education issues from the community. This process must be described in the SEP. The SEP must also

---

[22] *Ibid.*, s. 1(1).
[23] *Ibid.*
[24] The *Standards*, at p. 9.

describe how the school board ensures the SEAC's involvement in the annual plan review; describe majority and minority reports which have been received from the SEAC, together with the school board's response to those reports; state how community members, and particularly parents of children receiving special education programs and services, are given an opportunity to provide input (including timelines and methods for providing opportunities); and include a summary of the feedback received from the community. Finally, the SEP must set out the results of any internal or external reviews of the school board's special education programs and services undertaken in the prior or current school year, and list any planned reviews.

Special Education Programs and Services

The School Board's General Model for Special Education

The SEP must include a detailed outline of the school board's general philosophy and service-delivery model for the provision of special education programs and services. The SEP must comply with the *Canadian Charter of Rights and Freedoms,* the Ontario *Human Rights Code,*[25] the *Education Act* and the Regulations[26] and include a statement confirming this.

Roles and Responsibilities

The SEP must include a description of the roles and responsibilities of the Ministry of Education, the school board, the SEAC, principals and teachers, parents or guardians, and students.[27]

Early Identification Procedures and Intervention Strategies

School boards have long been required by Policy/Program Memorandum No. 11, "Early Identification of Children's Learning Needs", to put into place "procedures to identify each child's level of development, learning abilities and needs and to ensure that educational programs are designed to accommodate these needs and to facilitate each child's growth and development".[28] The *Standards* require that the SEP must explain these procedures in detail, including an outline of the school board's guiding principles or philosophy, the types of assessment tools/strategies used to gather information on students for the purpose of developing educational programs and the types of early intervention strategies used to support students before they are referred to an Identification, Placement and Review Committee (IPRC).

---

[25]   R.S.O. 1990, c. H.19.

[26]   *Special Education Programs and Services,* Reg. 306; *Identification and Placement of Exceptional Pupils,* O. Reg. 181/98; *Special Education Advisory Committees,* O. Reg. 464/97.

[27]   See Appendix A of the *Standards,* which sets out in detail the information necessary to meet this requirement.

[28]   Ministry of Education, Policy/Program Memorandum No. 11, "Early Identification of Children's Learning Needs" (Revised, 1982) at p. 1.

The SEP must also set out the role of teachers and parents in early identification, as well as the school board's policies and procedures on screening, assessment, referral, identification and program planning for students who may be in need of special education programs and services. In addition, the SEP must disclose the school board's procedures for notifying parents that their child is having difficulty; procedures for referring children for assessment and the manner in which parents will be notified about and be involved in this process; and procedures for notifying parents that their child might be referred to an IPRC or might be provided with special education programs and services without a referral to an IPRC.

Finally, the SEP must include a statement that "these procedures are a part of a continuous assessment and program planning process which should be initiated when a child is first enrolled in school or no later than the beginning of a program of studies immediately following Kindergarten and should continue throughout a child's school life".[29]

The IPRC Process and Appeals

The SEP must set out a description of the school board's IPRC process and include a copy of the school board's Parent Guide. In addition, the SEP must set out statistics concerning the number of IPRC referrals, reviews and appeals within the school board during the previous school year.

Educational and Other Assessments

The SEP must set out the types of educational assessment tools used within the school board and, for each assessment tool, must set out the qualifications of staff administering the tool and the legislation governing the staff (*e.g., Education Act, Regulated Health Professions Act, 1991,*[30] *Health Care Consent Act, 1996,*[31] and other applicable legislation). In addition, for each assessment tool, the SEP must note the average waiting time for assessments and the criteria for managing waiting lists; an acknowledgement that requirements for obtaining parental consent are met prior to conducting the assessment; an explanation of how assessment results are communicated to parents; a description of the protocols in place for sharing information with staff and outside agencies; and an explanation of how the privacy of information is protected.

Specialized Health Support Services in School Settings

The *Standards* require that the SEP disclose information on each type of specialized health support service which is provided to the school board's students (*i.e.,* nursing, occupational therapy, physiotherapy, nutrition, speech and language therapy, speech correction and remediation, administering of prescribed medications, catheterization, suctioning, lifting and positioning, assistance with

---

[29] *Ibid.*
[30] S.O. 1991, c. 18 (as amended to 2000, c. 26, Sch. H.).
[31] S.O. 1996, c. 2, Sch. A (as amended to 2000, c. 9).

mobility, feeding, toiletting and others). This information must be set out under stipulated headings that include the following:

- agency or position of person who performs the service (*i.e.,* Community Care Access Centre, board staff, parent, student);
- eligibility criteria for students to receive the service;
- position of person who determines eligibility to receive the service and the level of support;
- criteria for determining when the service is no longer required; and
- procedures for resolving disputes about eligibility and level of support (if any).

Categories and Definitions of Exceptionalities

The categories and definitions of exceptionalities prescribed by the Minister in accordance with his or her authority under s. 8(3) of the *Education Act,*[32] must be set out in the SEP. In addition, the SEP must describe the ways in which the IPRC applies the categories and definitions when making identification and placement decisions.

Special Education Placements Provided by the School Board

The SEP must describe how the SEAC is involved in providing advice on the range of placements offered by the school board.

In addition to setting out the range of placement options available for each category of exceptionality, the SEP must set out the admission criteria and the admission process for each placement option. As well, a description of the process for determining the level of support provided in each placement and the school board's criteria for assigning intensive support for students who are in need of a great deal of assistance must be set out in the SEP. The alternatives provided when the needs of a student cannot be met within the range of placements and how those options are communicated to the parents must also be disclosed in the SEP.

Reflecting the IPRC's obligation to consider a regular class placement prior to considering placement of an exceptional pupil in a special education class,[33] the *Standards* require that the SEP acknowledge that a regular class placement for an exceptional student is the first option considered by an IPRC. Further, the SEP must set out the different ways in which a student can be integrated into the regular classroom when regular class placement can meet the student's needs. The SEP must also list the criteria used to determine if there is a need to change a student's placement.

Finally, the SEP must set out maximum class size for each type of special education class.

---

[32] See Chapter 4.
[33] O. Reg. 181/98, ss. 17(1) and 23(6).

Provincial Demonstration Schools in Ontario

The *Standards* set out information[34] on the programs and services offered by the Provincial and Demonstration Schools and require this information to be included in each school board's SEP. In addition, the SEP must set out, by program, the number of students who are otherwise qualified to be resident pupils[35] and who are attending Provincial and Demonstration schools. Information must also be provided on how transportation is provided for students to and from Provincial and Demonstration Schools.

Special Education Staff

The *Standards* include a form[36] which must be included in the SEP and which sets out information on the types of staff (teachers, educational assistants, other professional resource staff and paraprofessional staff) involved in providing special education programs and services.

Staff Development

The SEP must make reference to the school board's plans for the professional development of its special education personnel, including the overall goal of these plans. The SEP must set out specifics on courses, in-service training and other types of professional development activities provided by the board for its staff, together with an outline of the manner in which staff is trained on legislative requirements and Ministry policy. In addition, the SEP must set out how the board makes its staff aware of the SEP and of professional development opportunities.

The *Standards* impose an obligation on school boards to seek input from staff and to consult the SEAC in creating professional development plans. The SEP must disclose how this obligation has been met.

Finally, the SEP must outline details of the board's budget allocation for staff development in special education, together with any cost-sharing arrangements with other ministries or agencies for staff development.

---

[34] The *Standards*, Appendix E.

[35] A person is qualified to be an elementary resident pupil when the person is aged six years to the end of June in the year in which the person reaches 21 years of age, the person resides in the jurisdiction of the school board and the person's parent or guardian is a tax supporter of the school board. A person is qualified to be a secondary resident pupil if the person and the person's parent or guardian live in the jurisdiction of the board, or the person is an owner or tenant of residential property separately assessed in the jurisdiction of the board and lives in the jurisdiction of the board, or if the person is over the age of 18 years and has lived in the jurisdiction of the board for the 12 preceding months. At the secondary school level, a resident pupil may also be a student who would otherwise be a resident pupil of another board but who is enrolled in a secondary school under "open access" or pursuant to an agreement for the provision of education services between the board providing the services and the board where the student would, otherwise, have been a resident pupil (*Education Act*, ss. 33, 36 and 37). A secondary student is entitled to attend a secondary school or secondary schools without payment of fees for a maximum of seven years (*Education Act*, s. 38).

[36] The *Standards*, Appendix F.

Equipment

The SEP must include an explanation on how the school board determines student needs for individualized equipment and the criteria for purchasing individualized equipment. In addition, the manner of allocation of the board's budget for equipment must be set out in the SEP.

Accessibility of School Buildings

The *Standards* contemplate that school boards will develop a multi-year capital expenditure plan for improving accessibility to their buildings and facilities, including schools, school grounds and administrative offices. The SEP must include a summary of this multi-year capital expenditure plan, including an outline of the resources which are dedicated to providing barrier-free access in future years. Further, the SEP must report on the board's progress in implementing the capital expenditure plan and include a statement advising how the public can obtain a complete copy of the multi-year capital expenditure plan.

Transportation

The *Standards* stipulate that certain students are eligible to receive transportation, including: students in special education programs (whether in special education classes or regular classes); students in educational programs in care, treatment and correctional facilities and in Provincial and Demonstration Schools; and students requiring transportation to attend summer school programs.

The SEP must also describe the process used by the school board to decide whether it is in the best interests of a student with special needs to be transported with other children or transported separately. As well, the SEP must set out the criteria for determining safety which are used in the board's tendering process in selecting transportation providers for exceptional students.

The School Board's Special Education Advisory Committee

The *Standards* require the school board to outline, in its SEP, the manner in which the SEAC has fulfilled its responsibilities as outlined in the Regulation.[37]

The SEP must include the names of SEAC members and indicate the basis of their membership on SEAC — whether they are trustees or representatives of parent associations. If the latter, the names of the associations with which they are affiliated must be set out. In addition, a contact address, telephone number and/or e-mail address for each member must be set out. Where applicable, the SEP must indicate that the SEAC includes membership representing Native students. The SEP must set out the process for selecting SEAC members and the meeting times and locations of the SEAC.

The SEP must describe how the SEAC has fulfilled its responsibilities during the school year in which the plan was developed and must set out the

---

[37] O. Reg. 464/97. (See under heading "The Special Education Advisory Committee", *infra*, for discussion of SEAC.)

documentation provided by the school board to the SEAC to enable it to fulfil its responsibilities.

Finally, the SEP must set out the ways in which the public, including parents, can make their views known to the SEAC.

Coordination of Services with Other Ministries or Agencies

The *Standards* contemplate that the school board will have developed strategies to ensure a smooth transition for students with special needs who are entering or leaving a school. The SEP must disclose specific details of the planning which is done in advance for students with special needs who are arriving at one of the board's schools from other programs; including pre-school programs (whether nursery, speech and language programs, or programs for the deaf); care, treatment and correctional programs; and programs provided by other boards of education.

The school board must indicate in its SEP whether it is the board's policy or practice to accept assessments of incoming students from the program which the student has been attending or whether the board requires its own assessment of incoming students. If the board does its own assessment, the estimated waiting time for completing the assessment must be set out in the SEP.

For students leaving to attend other programs offered by other school boards or by care, treatment or correctional facilities, the school board must detail in its SEP the way in which it shares information about the departing students.

Finally, the school board must identify in the SEP the position of the board employee who is responsible for ensuring the successful transition of students who are leaving the board to transfer into other programs or who are being admitted to the board from other programs.

Addressing Placements for Persons Not Enrolled as Students

Although not referenced in the *Standards*, school boards are required by regulation to address in their SEP placements two categories of students who are not actually attending schools.[38]

School boards are required to ensure that the SEP provides for the enrolment and placement of each "trainable retarded" child[39] who is qualified to be a

---

[38] O. Reg. 181/98, ss. 4 and 5.

[39] All references to "trainable retarded" and "educable retarded" were removed from the *Education Act*, by the *Education Statute Law Amendment Act, 1993*, S.O. 1993, c. 11. The definitions of exceptionalities provided by the Minister of Education were similarly amended. Students who were once identified as "trainable retarded" are now identified as having a "developmental disability". Students who were once identified as "educable retarded" are now identified as having a "mild intellectual disability". However, a corresponding amendment was not made to Regulation 306, or *Operation of Schools — General*, R.R.O. 1990, Reg. 298, which, in s. 30, establishes the maximum class size for "trainable retarded" and "educable retarded" students.

"resident pupil"[40] of the school board and is attending a day nursery, licensed under the *Day Nurseries Act,*[41] in a program for developmentally handicapped children.

Similarly, SEPs must make provision for the enrolment and placement of certain persons under the age of 21 years who are qualified to be resident pupils of the school board and who reside in licensed facilities, such as a hospitals, group homes, institutions or young offenders' facilities, within the jurisdiction of the school board where no educational program is provided by the Ministry of Education or the Ministry of Correctional Services.[42] In this case, the school board must make provision in its SEP for the enrolment and placement of each person under the age of 21 years who resides in the licensed facility and who is qualified to be a resident pupil or would be qualified to be a resident pupil if the person's parents resided within the area of jurisdiction of the board. (Accordingly, a public school board would not be required to include provision in its SEP for a pupil who was a separate school supporter and vice versa.)

THE SPECIAL EDUCATION ADVISORY COMMITTEE

In order to ensure that parents have input into the school board's special education planning process, the *Education Act* requires each school board to create a Special Education Advisory Committee ("SEAC").[43] School authorities, other than those established on lands which are owned by the Crown in right of Canada or Ontario or an agency of either, and which are exempt from taxation for school purposes, are also required to establish a SEAC.[44]

The SEAC is charged with the responsibility of making recommendations to the board "in respect of any matter affecting the establishment, development and delivery of special education programs and services for exceptional pupils of the board".[45] The SEAC is also obliged to participate in certain school board functions relating to special education which will be discussed under the heading "Role of the SEAC".

The special education policy issues on which the Ministry expects SEACs to advise school boards are as follows:

- philosophy and goals;
- organizational structures;
- policies and procedures;
- role of personnel;
- delivery of systems;

---

[40] See discussion in footnote 35.
[41] R.S.O. 1990, c. D.2.
[42] Regulation 306, s. 5.
[43] *Education Act*, s. 57.1(1).
[44] *Special Education Advisory Committees*, O. Reg. 464/97, s. 3; *Education Act*, s. 68.
[45] *Special Education Advisory Committees*, O. Reg. 464/97, s. 11(1).

- staffing (teaching, administration, professional support, paraprofessional support);
- program development (types, location);
- identification of special needs assessment;
- transportation policies/practices;
- special needs;
- interaction with other board committees in related areas;
- any other matter in special education.[46]

Parents are represented on the SEAC by "local associations". A "local association" is defined as "an association or organization of parents that operates locally within the area of jurisdiction of a board and that is affiliated with an association or organization of professional educators but that is incorporated and operates throughout Ontario to further the interests and well-being of one or more groups of exceptional children or adults".[47]

Role of the SEAC

The SEAC is given a general power to make recommendations to a school board "in respect of any matter affecting the establishment, development and delivery of special education programs and services for exceptional pupils of the board".[48] These recommendations may be presented to the board of trustees. Before the board, or a committee of the board, makes any decision on the recommendation — whether to accept the recommendation with or without amendments, to reject the recommendation or send the matter back to the SEAC — the board of trustees, or the committee, first must provide the SEAC with "an opportunity to be heard".[49] This requirement can be met by providing the opportunity for one or more representatives of SEAC to present the recommendation in person, together with supporting submissions, to the board or a committee. Alternatively, the recommendation might be forwarded by the SEAC, together with a written submission explaining the purpose of the recommendation. The SEAC might be "heard" by way of a written submission where the circumstances legitimately preclude the opportunity to make submissions personally or where the recommendation is expected to be agreed to by the board or committee. In some cases, the SEAC may decide that the recommendation is sufficiently straightforward that no personal presentation is required.

In addition to its authority to make recommendations on special education programs and services, the SEAC plays a significant role in the review of the

---

[46] Ministry of Education, *Special Education Information Handbook, 1984*. Although many parts of this *Handbook* are now out of date, and the *Handbook* is likely to be replaced shortly, this list continues to be applicable.

[47] O. Reg. 464/97, s. 1.

[48] *Ibid.*, s. 11(1).

[49] *Ibid.*, s. 11(2).

SEP and in that part of the annual budget process which relates to special education.[50]

School boards are specifically directed to ensure that the SEAC is given the opportunity to "participate" in the school board's annual review of its SEP.[51] This does not mean that the SEAC may direct that the board make amendments to its plan. However, the SEAC may recommend changes to the SEP during the review process and, as noted previously, the board is obliged to provide an opportunity to the SEAC to be heard on this issue before it accepts, rejects or makes some other decision on the recommendation. The *Standards*[52] require that a description of any majority or minority reports from the SEAC concerning the board's SEP which have been received from SEAC members must be included in the SEP. Moreover, any motions or recommendations from the SEAC related to the school board's approval of the SEP must be submitted to the Ministry of Education with the SEP.[53]

School boards must also ensure that their SEACs have the opportunity to "participate" in the school board's annual budget process of preparing estimates of revenues and expenditures, as that process relates to special education.[54] This means that the school board must provide, at the very least, an opportunity for the SEAC to be heard on any recommendations which it makes on budget issues which touch on special education programs and services before any final decisions are made on special education expenditures. Indeed, the entitlement to "participate" in budget decisions suggests that the SEAC should be involved actively in the special education budget process, which might be achieved through meaningful consultation in the budget planning process.

In addition, a school board must provide its SEAC with the opportunity to review the financial statements it prepares annually for submission to the Ministry of Education, as those financial statements relate to special education.[55] This will allow the SEAC's participation in the budget process to be more meaningful.

Composition of the SEAC

SEACs are composed, generally, of representatives of local associations and trustees. In addition, if the school board, or school authority, has entered into an agreement with the Crown or a band or council of the band (as defined by the *Indian Act*),[56] or an educational authority authorized by the federal government to provide education for Native students, persons must also be appointed to represent Native interests.[57]

---

[50]   *Ibid.*, s. 12.
[51]   *Ibid.*, s. 12(1).
[52]   Ministry of Education, *Standards for School Boards' Special Education Plans* (2000) at p. 4.
[53]   The *Standards*, at p. 17.
[54]   O. Reg. 464/97, s. 12(2); *Education Act*, s. 231.
[55]   O. Reg. 464/97, s. 12(3); *Education Act*, s. 252.
[56]   R.S.C. 1985, c. I-5.
[57]   *Education Act*, s. 188.

School Board SEACs

School board SEACs are comprised of:

- **Representatives of Local Associations**: There must be one representative from each of up to 12 local associations which operate within the school board's jurisdiction. If there are more than 12 local associations operating within the school board's jurisdiction, the board must select the 12 local associations which will be represented on the SEAC.[58] No criteria are imposed on the school board in making this selection, but a selection of local associations which represent a broad spectrum of exceptionalities will result in a more credible SEAC than will a narrower selection of local associations representative of only a few exceptionalities.

  Once the school board has selected the local associations, it is up to each local association to nominate the person who will represent the local association on the SEAC; the school board must appoint the local association's nominee to the SEAC. In addition, an "alternative" member must be nominated by the local association and appointed by the school board.[59] Nominees for SEAC membership and alternates selected by local associations must be qualified to vote for trustees of the board (*i.e.,* they must have directed their taxes to the board, be at least 18 years of age[60] and they must be a Canadian citizen),[61] and they must be resident in the area of the school board's jurisdiction.[62] A local association may not nominate a person to the SEAC, either as a member or as an alternate, who is an employee of the school board.[63]

- **Board of Trustees**: From amongst its own members, the board of trustees is required to appoint to the SEAC three trustees, unless the board of trustees is comprised of fewer than 12 trustees. In the latter case, the number of trustees to be appointed to the SEAC is 25% of the total number of trustees rounded down to the nearest whole number. Where a board is limited to fewer than three members on the SEAC, the board must also appoint an alternate member for each member it appoints to the SEAC.[64]

- **Representatives of Interests of Native Students**: Where a school board has entered into an agreement to provide accommodation, instruction and special services to Native students and a trustee has been appointed to the school board's board of trustees to represent the interests of Native students,[65] the SEAC must include one person to represent the interests of Native students. Where more than one trustee has been appointed to represent the interests of

---

[58] O. Reg. 464/97, s. 2(1)(a), (2) and (3).

[59] *Ibid.,* s. 2(1)(b).

[60] *Education Act,* ss. 58.6, 58.7 and 58.9; *Municipal Elections Act, 1996,* S.O. 1996, c. 32, s. 1(1), Sch. (as amended to 2000, c. 25).

[61] *Education Act,* ss. 1(10) and 58.9.

[62] O. Reg. 464/97, s. 5(1).

[63] *Ibid.,* s. 5(3).

[64] *Ibid.,* s. 2(1)(c), (d) and (4).

[65] *Education Act,* s. 188; *Native Representation on Boards,* O. Reg. 462/97.

Native students, the SEAC must include two persons to represent the interests of Native students. In addition, alternates are to be appointed for each person appointed to the SEAC to represent the interests of Native students. In each case, the representatives and alternates must be nominated by the band councils with whom the school board has entered into the agreement. The board of trustees must appoint the persons nominated by the band council.[66] A person nominated by the band council need not be qualified to vote for trustees of the school board nor must the person reside in the area of the school board's jurisdiction to be eligible to be nominated and appointed to the SEAC.[67]

- **Additional Members**: The board of trustees may appoint an unlimited number of additional members to the SEAC who are not representatives of local associations or trustees of the board or members of any other committee of the school board. (Examples might include representatives of medical associations, or associations which do not meet the definition of "local association".) Employees of the board are not eligible to be appointed as members of the SEAC and additional members must be eligible to vote for trustees of the school board and must reside in the area of the jurisdiction of the board.[68] The Regulation does not limit the ability of additional members to vote on SEAC motions or otherwise participate fully in the SEAC.

School Authority SEACs

In the case of school authorities, SEAC representatives are to be comprised of the following:

- **Local Associations**: Two representatives must be appointed from amongst all of the local associations which operate locally within the area of jurisdiction of the board. If there are more than two local associations within the area of jurisdiction of the board, the local associations should agree on the two persons they will nominate as their representatives and the school authority must appoint these nominees. In addition, two alternates nominated by the local associations must be appointed by the school authority. However, if no local associations have been established in the area, then the school authority must appoint two persons as SEAC members and two persons as alternates who are not trustees or employees of the Board. The persons appointed to the SEAC, whether as representatives of local associations or otherwise, must be qualified to vote for trustees of the school authority and must be resident of the area of the jurisdiction of the school authority.[69]
- **Board of Trustees**: One trustee must be appointed as a member of the SEAC, together with one alternate.[70]

---

[66] O. Reg. 464/97, s. 4.
[67] *Ibid.*, s. 5(2).
[68] *Ibid.*, ss. 2(1)(f), (5), 5(1) and (3).
[69] *Ibid.*, ss. 3(1)(a), (b), (2) and 5.
[70] *Ibid.*, ss. 3(1)(c) and (d).

- **Representatives of the Interests of Native Students**: Where the school authority has entered into an agreement to provide accommodation, instruction and special services to Native students, and one trustee has been appointed as a trustee to the board of the school authority to represent the interests of Native students, one person nominated by a band council must be appointed by the school authority to the SEAC. Where two trustees or more have been appointed to the school authority to represent the interests of Native students, two persons nominated by the band council (or band councils) must be appointed to the SEAC.[71]

Term of Office of SEAC Members

Members of the SEAC are appointed for a term of office which corresponds with the three-year term of office of the board of trustees. Members are appointed following the election of a new board and membership in the SEAC continues until a new board is organized following an election.[72]

A SEAC member (or alternate) is deemed to "vacate" his or her position if he or she

- is convicted of an indictable offence;
- is absent from three consecutive regular SEAC meetings without the authorization of a SEAC resolution which has been entered in the minutes (provided that, in the case of the alternate, he or she had notice of the meeting); or
- no longer holds the qualifications to be appointed to the committee (*e.g.*, he or she ceases to be a member of the local association which nominated him or her or moves away from the area over which the school board/school authority has jurisdiction).[73]

Where a member or alternate vacates his or her position on the SEAC, either by way of resignation or because he or she is deemed to have vacated his or her position, the school board must appoint a qualified replacement for the remainder of the vacating member's term. The process which the board followed in the first instance in appointing the member or the alternate who has vacated his or her position must be followed by the board in appointing a replacement. For example, if the member or alternate who vacates his or her position is the representative of a local association, then the local association must nominate the person whom the board will appoint as a replacement.[74] Where the member or alternate is deemed to have vacated his or her position as a consequence of being convicted of an indictable offence, his or her replacement cannot be named until either the time for taking an appeal from the conviction has passed and no appeal has been taken or, if

---

[71] *Ibid.*, ss. 3(1)(e) and 4.
[72] *Ibid.*, s. 6.
[73] *Ibid.*, s. 7(1) and (2).
[74] *Ibid.*, s. 8.

an appeal is taken, until the final determination of the appeal. If the appeal is successful and the conviction is quashed, the member or alternate is deemed not to have vacated his or her seat.[75]

Role of SEAC Alternates

Where a member cannot attend a meeting, the member is obliged to advise his or her alternate. Once notified that the member for whom he or she is appointed cannot attend a meeting, the alternate is obliged to attend the SEAC meeting and to act in the place of the member.[76]

As well, where a member has vacated his or her position and the position has not yet been filled, the alternate, if any, is authorized to act in the member's place on the SEAC.[77]

Since SEAC meetings are open meetings, alternates are able to attend SEAC meetings as observers when not acting in place of a member. Although alternates may not participate in a meeting unless acting in place of an absent member, it is prudent for them to attend as many meetings as possible in order to keep abreast of the business being conducted at the SEAC, so that the alternate can participate more meaningfully if called upon to attend in place of an absent member.

Conduct of SEAC Meetings

A majority of the SEAC's members (or alternates attending on their behalf) constitutes a quorum.[78] The SEAC must meet at least 10 times a year and may meet by teleconference, in accordance with the board's policy on teleconferencing.[79]

At the first meeting of the SEAC following its appointment, the members must elect a chair and a vice-chair from among their members. The chair will preside at all meetings, assisted by the vice-chair, unless the chair is absent. In that event, the vice-chair will preside at the meeting. Should both the chair and the vice-chair be absent from a meeting, the members present are required to select a chair for that meeting.[80]

---

[75] *Ibid.*, s. 7(4).

[76] *Ibid.*, s. 9(9) and (10). While not specified in the Regulation, it may be inferred that the alternate would also act in place of a SEAC member who has a conflict of interest. This might occur in circumstances where a parent, who is a SEAC member, has an exceptional student enrolled with the board and is appealing a placement issue. In such circumstances, the SEAC member could be in a conflict of interest when the SEAC deals with any matters which touch on the issues between the parent and the board.

[77] *Ibid.*, s. 8(3).

[78] *Ibid.*, s. 9(1) and (8).

[79] Section 208.1 of the *Education Act* permits the government to make regulations respecting the conduct of electronic meetings by boards. *Electronic Meetings*, O. Reg. 463/97 has been introduced under this section. This Regulation requires each school board to develop and implement a policy providing for the use of electronic means for the holding of meetings of the board and of committees of the board. Members who participate in a meeting in accordance with this policy will be deemed to be present at the meeting.

[80] O. Reg. 464/97, s. 9(3), (4), (5) and (6).

Decisions of the SEAC are made based on a vote of the majority of the members present. Every member (or alternate sitting in the member's place), including the chair, has one vote. In the event of a tie vote, the motion is lost.[81]

Support for the SEAC

A school board is required to provide the SEAC with the administrative support, including personnel and facilities, which the school board considers necessary for the proper functioning of the committee. This will include secretarial support and professional support from the school board's special education experts. It will also mean providing technical support in the form of both equipment and personnel in order to allow for meetings to be held by way of teleconferencing or videoconferencing.[82] This is particularly important in the case of school boards with geographic jurisdiction over large areas where members may be able to attend meetings only if they are able to do so through electronic means.

Beyond administrative assistance, the school board is obliged to educate all SEAC members and their alternates about the role of the SEAC and of the school board in relation to special education and about the special education policies of both the Ministry of Education and the school board. Specifically, the school board is required to provide to the SEAC members and their alternates "information and orientation" on these matters.[83]

THE PARENT GUIDE

A guide specifically designed to explain the special education process to parents must be prepared and made available to parents by every school board. The Parent Guide must include the following information:[84]

- an explanation of the function of the IPRC where a student is referred to the IPRC for the purposes of identification and placement in the first instance, or for review of identification and/or placement;
- an outline of the procedures which the IPRC must follow, as set out in O. Reg. 181/98, together with an outline of any procedures established for the IPRC by the school board respecting the identification and placement of exceptional students;
- an explanation of the IPRC's duty both to describe the student's strengths and needs and to include in its statements of decision the categories and definitions of any exceptionalities identified by the IPRC;

---

[81] *Ibid.*, s. 9(1), (2) and (7).
[82] *Ibid.*, s. 10(1).
[83] *Ibid.*, s. 10(2).
[84] *Identification and Placement of Exceptional Pupils*, O. Reg 181/98, s. 13.

- an explanation of the function of a Special Education Appeal Board ("SEAB") and the right of a parent to appeal decisions of the IPRC to an SEAB;
- a list of those parent organizations of which the school board is aware which are "local associations" — that is, associations or organizations of parents which operate locally within the board's jurisdiction and which are associated with incorporated associations or organizations which operate throughout Ontario to further the interests and well-being of one or more groups of exceptional children or adults;[85]
- a list of the names, addresses and telephone numbers of the provincial and demonstration schools in Ontario;
- an indication of the extent to which the school board provides special education programs and special education services and the extent to which it purchases those programs and services from another school board;
- an explanation that no IPRC placement can be implemented unless either a parent has consented to the decision in writing, or the time limit for filing an appeal in respect of the decision has expired and no appeal has been filed or, if an appeal has been filed, the appeal has been abandoned.

A sample Parent Guide is attached to the *Standards* and the guide prepared by the school board must also contain the information set out in this sample.[86]

Copies of the Parent Guide prepared by the school board must be made available at each school in the board's jurisdiction and at the board's head office. In addition, the board must provide a copy of its Parent Guide to the Ministry of Education.[87]

Where a principal refers a pupil to the IPRC for the first time, either on the request of the parent or at the principal's initiative, the principal must provide a copy of the Parent Guide to the parents within 15 days after notifying the parents of the student's referral to the IPRC.[88]

Where a parent or pupil requests the school board to provide a copy of the Parent Guide in a braille, large print or audio-cassette format, the school board must supply the guide in that format.[89]

LIMITS ON CLASS SIZE

In setting up special education classes, school administrators must be mindful of limits which have been placed on the maximum number of students who can be placed in specific special education classes.[90] The maximum class size limit for

---

[85] O. Reg. 464/97, s. 1.
[86] The *Standards*, Appendix B.
[87] O. Reg. 181/98, s. 13(2).
[88] *Ibid.*, s. 14(6).
[89] *Ibid.*, s. 13(3).
[90] *Operation of Schools — General*, R.R.O. 1990, Reg. 298, s. 31.

special education classes is dependent on the definition of the exceptionality[91] of the students in the class. Unfortunately, the language of the regulation which sets these limits is quite dated and the terms used to describe the exceptionalities does not always coincide with the current definition of exceptionalities.

There is no specific reference to the "behaviour" exceptionality in the regulation. However, the maximum size for classes for students who are "emotionally disturbed or socially maladjusted" — which categories would appear to be most applicable to the behaviour exceptionality — is eight pupils.[92]

The maximum class size for a special education class for autistic students is six students.[93]

A class for students who are deaf is limited in size to a maximum of 10 students.[94] The maximum size of a special education class for children with hearing impairment (which corresponds to the current "hard of hearing" exceptionality) who are younger than compulsory school age is eight students.[95] Otherwise, a special education class for students who have hearing impairment is limited to 12 students.[96]

A special education class for students with "speech and language disorders" (which correlates to the current exceptionalities of language impairment and speech impairment) can have a maximum of 10 students.[97]

The maximum size for a class of students with "severe learning disabilities" is eight students.[98] There is no limit on a special education class for students whose learning disabilities are not "severe". Where a special education class for "aphasic" students is established, the size is limited to six students.[99]

The exceptionality, now called "mild intellectual disability" was formerly called "educable retarded", and some reference to this previous term continues in the regulation which defines class-size limits. The maximum size for a special education class comprised of students "who are educable retarded" is 12 students in the primary division and 16 students in the junior and intermediate divisions.[100]

The exceptionality now called "developmental disability" was formerly called "trainable retarded". A special education class established for "trainable retarded" students has a size limit of 10 students.[101]

The maximum size for a class of gifted students in elementary school is 25 students.[102] There is no limit on the number of grade levels which can be included

---

[91] See Chapter 4, "Identification and Exceptionality", for definitions of exceptionalities.
[92] Regulation 298, s. 31(a).
[93] *Ibid.*, s. 31(f).
[94] *Ibid.*, s. 31(b).
[95] *Ibid.*, s. 31(a).
[96] *Ibid.*, s. 31(c).
[97] *Ibid.*, s. 31(b).
[98] *Ibid.*, s. 31(a).
[99] *Ibid.*, s. 31(f).
[100] *Ibid.*, s. 31(d).
[101] *Ibid.*, s. 31(b).
[102] *Ibid.*, s. 31(e).

in the class. There are no limits imposed on the size of any gifted class which might be established at the secondary level.[103]

The maximum size of a special education class established for students with "orthopaedic or other physical handicaps" is 12 students.[104]

The maximum size for a class established for blind students is 10 students.[105] Where a class is established for students with limited vision (now "low vision"), the size is limited to 12 students.[106]

The maximum class size for a special education class established for students with "multiple handicaps for whom no one handicap is dominant" (now "multiple exceptionalities") is six pupils.[107]

Where a special education class is established for students with different exceptionalities, the maximum class size is 16 students.[108] Where students with exceptionalities are placed in regular classes, the normal class-size limits will apply.[109]

---

[103] It should be noted that the limits imposed on the size of regular classes do not apply to classes for exceptional students: *Class Size*, O. Reg. 118/98, s. 3(1), definition of "class".

[104] Regulation 298, s. 31(c).

[105] *Ibid.*, s. 31(b).

[106] *Ibid.*, s. 31(c).

[107] *Ibid.*, s. 31(f).

[108] *Ibid.*, s. 31(g).

[109] *Education Act*, s. 170.1.

4

Identification and Exceptionality

INTRODUCTION

The rationale for the provision of special education to students in Ontario is the acknowledgement in the *Education Act,*[1] that some students require modification to the regular curriculum and program in order to access fully their opportunity to learn. The Ministry of Education's *Policy/Program Memorandum No. 11* directs school boards to have procedures to identify each student's level of development, learning abilities and needs from the time the student is first enrolled in school.[2] This policy of early identification ensures that educational programs are designed to accommodate each student. The process results in the identification of students who are called "exceptional pupils" under the *Education Act.* An "exceptional pupil" is defined as:

> . . . a pupil whose behavioural, communicational, intellectual, physical or multiple exceptionalities are such that he or she is considered to need placement in a special education program . . .[3]

Although there is significant overlap between the concept of an "exceptional pupil" under the *Education Act* and a student with a "handicap" under the *Human Rights Code,*[4] the two concepts are not identical. "Exceptional" students are exceptional because they need placement in a special education program. A student with a handicap is entitled to be accommodated and to receive educational services free of discrimination because of handicap.

Thus, a student might have a physical disability and use a wheelchair, but not require a special education program. A student might be gifted and require a special education program, but not have a condition of mental impairment. School boards are required both to provide appropriate special education programs for exceptional students and to accommodate students with handicaps. This book

---

[1] R.S.O. 1990, c. E.2 (as amended), s. 1.
[2] Ministry of Education, *Policy/Program Memorandum No. 11 — Early Identification of Children's Learning Needs* (Revised 1982).
[3] *Education Act,* s. 1.
[4] R.S.O. 1990, c. H.19, s. 10(1) (as amended to 1999, c. 6).

focuses on special education, although a school board is subject to both legal regimes.[5]

This chapter will canvas the specific exceptionalities which will apply when a student is "identified".

CATEGORIES OF EXCEPTIONALITY

The categories of exceptionality recognized in the *Education Act* are:

(a) behaviour;
(b) communication;
(c) intellectual;
(d) physical; and
(e) multiple.[6]

The Minister of Education has been directed by the *Education Act* to,

> . . . in respect of special education programs and services, define exceptionalities of pupils, and prescribe classes, groups or categories of exceptional pupils, and require boards to employ such definitions or use such prescriptions as established under this clause.[7]

The Minister has, for some of the categories listed above, defined additional subcategories. For each category or subcategory, the Minister has prescribed an outline of the characteristics, from an educational perspective, which will define the exceptionality. The definitions originally provided by the Minister[8] were updated in 1999.[9] Because the wording of the definition of each exceptionality is critical in determining whether a student falls within that exceptionality, we have set out in each case the precise language from the Ministry of Education document which establishes the definition.

Behaviour

Not every incident of inappropriate behaviour indicates a behavioural exceptionality. The key will be whether the behavioural problems interfere in the student's ability to learn. The specific definition which the Minister of Education has given to the exceptionality of "behaviour" is as follows:

---

[5] See *An Educator's Guide to Human Rights* (Aurora, Ont.: Aurora Professional Press — a division of Canada Law Book, 1998), another publication in the Educator's Guides to the Law series of which this book is a part.

[6] *Education Act*, s. 1(1), definition of "exceptional pupil".

[7] *Ibid.*, s. 8(3)(b).

[8] Ministry of Education, *Special Education Information Handbook*, 1981.

[9] Ministry of Education, *Standards for School Boards' Special Education Plans* (2000), Appendix D (the "Standards"). © Queen's Printer for Ontario, 2000. Reproduced with permission.

A learning disorder characterized by specific behaviour problems over such a period of time, and to such a marked degree, and of such a nature, as to adversely affect educational performance, and that may be accompanied by one or more of the following:

    (a)   an inability to maintain interpersonal relationships;

    (b)   excessive fears or anxieties;

    (c)   a tendency to compulsive reaction;

    (d)   an inability to learn that cannot be traced to intellectual, sensory or other health factors, or any combination thereof.[10]

Communication

Communication exceptionalities include a wide range of special needs, including deafness and hearing impairments, learning disabilities, and speech disorders. Autism is also usually characterized as a communication exceptionality. Accordingly, the Minister has defined several subcategories for this category. The definition of each subcategory follows.

Autism

Pervasive developmental disorder (PDD) and autism are characterized by difficulty with communication and interactional skills, often accompanied by difficulty relating to others and adapting to the environment. The Ministry's definition of the exceptionality of autism is as follows:

A severe learning disorder that is characterized by:

    a)   disturbances in:
          — rate of educational development;
          — ability to relate to the environment;
          — mobility;
          — perception, speech and language;

    b)   lack of the representational symbolic behaviour that precedes language.[11]

Deaf and Hard-of-Hearing

A unique feature about special education for young children with hearing difficulties is that: "A hearing-handicapped child who has attained the age of two years may be admitted to a special education program for the hearing-handicapped."[12]

This provision is relatively dated and was most likely written at a time when most children with hearing disabilities were enrolled in schools for the deaf. The current definition of the exceptionality is as follows: "An impairment characterized by deficits in language and speech development because of a diminished or non-existent auditory response to sound."[13]

---

[10] *Ibid.*, at p. 32.

[11] *Ibid.*

[12] *Operation of Schools — General*, R.R.O. 1990, Reg. 298, s. 30.

[13] The "Standards", Appendix D, at p. 32.

Language Impairment

This subcategory of the communication exceptionality is defined as follows:

> A learning disorder characterized by an impairment in comprehension and/or use of verbal communication or the written or other symbol system of communication, which may be associated with neurological, psychological, physical, or sensory factors, and which may:
>
> a) involve one or more of the form, content, and function of language in communication; and
> b) include one or more of the following:
>   — language delay;
>   — dysfluency;
>   — voice and articulation development, which may or may not be organically or functionally based.[14]

Speech Impairment

The educational exceptionality of speech impairment is defined as follows:

> A disorder in language formulation that may be associated with neurological, psychological, physical, or sensory factors; that involves perceptual motor aspects of transmitting oral messages; and that may be characterized by impairment in articulation, rhythm, and stress.[15]

Learning Disability

The definition of learning disability is as follows:

> A learning disorder evident in both academic and social situations that involves one or more of the processes necessary for the proper use of spoken language or the symbols of communication, and that is characterized by a condition that:
>
> a) is not primarily the result of:
>   — impairment of vision;
>   — impairment of hearing;
>   — physical disability;
>   — primary emotional disturbance;
>   — cultural difference; and
> b) results in a significant discrepancy between academic achievement and assessed intellectual ability, with deficits in one or more of the following:
>   — receptive language (listening, reading);
>   — language processing (thinking, conceptualizing, integrating);
>   — expressive language (talking, spelling, writing);
>   — mathematical computations;
> c) may be associated with one or more conditions diagnosed as:
>   — a perceptual handicap;
>   — a brain injury;
>   — minimal brain dysfunction;
>   — dyslexia;
>   — developmental aphasia.[16]

---

[14] *Ibid.*
[15] *Ibid.*, at p. 33.
[16] *Ibid.*

Intellectual

The intellectual category has been broken down into three subcategories: giftedness, mild intellectual disability and developmental disability.

Giftedness

The definition of this subcategory of intellectual is as follows:

> An unusually advanced degree of general intellectual ability that requires differentiated learning experiences of a depth and breadth beyond those normally provided in the regular school program to satisfy the level of educational potential indicated.[17]

Mild Intellectual Disability

The definition of mild intellectual disability is as follows:

> A learning disorder characterized by:
>
> a) an ability to profit educationally within a regular class with the aid of considerable curriculum modification and supportive services;
> b) an inability to profit educationally within a regular class because of slow intellectual development;
> c) a potential for academic learning, independent social adjustment, and economic self-support.[18]

Developmental Disability

This exceptionality is defined as follows:

> A severe learning disorder characterized by:
>
> a) an inability to profit from a special education program for students with mild intellectual disabilities because of slow intellectual development;
> b) an ability to profit from a special education program that is designed to accommodate slow intellectual development;
> c) a limited potential for academic learning, independence, social adjustment, and economic self-support.[19]

Physical

The physical category of exceptionality is broken into two subcategories: physical disability, and blind and low vision.

Physical Disability

The definition of the physical disability exceptionality is as follows:

> A condition of such severe physical limitation or deficiency as to require special assistance in learning situations to provide the opportunity for educational achievement equivalent to that of pupils without exceptionalities who are of the same age or developmental level.[20]

---

[17] *Ibid.*

[18] *Ibid.*

[19] *Ibid.*, at p. 34.

[20] *Ibid.*

Blind and Low Vision

This subcategory is defined as follows: "A condition of partial or total impairment of sight or vision that even with correction affects educational performance adversely."[21]

Multiple

The definition of multiple exceptionalities is as follows:

> A combination of learning or other disorders, impairments, or physical disabilities, that is of such nature as to require, for educational achievement, the services of one or more teachers holding qualifications in special education and the provision of support services appropriate for such disorders, impairments, or disabilities.[22]

---

[21]   *Ibid.*
[22]   *Ibid.*

5

Placement

INTRODUCTION

Placement has proved to be the focal point of litigation between parents and school boards, not only in cases before the Special Education Tribunal ("Tribunal") but also in cases before boards of inquiry and the courts under the *Human Rights Code*[1] and the *Canadian Charter of Rights and Freedoms*. The decisions arising in these various fora have defined the standards which those responsible for determining placement must apply in making placement decisions.

To complicate matters, placement has not been defined by the legislation, however, the legislation has made clear that it is distinguishable from special education services and programs, neither of which can be appealed.

In this chapter we will consider the meaning of placement, examine the distinction between placement and special education programs and services, and review the standards which are to be used in making placement decisions.

WHAT IS PLACEMENT?

While the *Education Act* defines "special education programs"[2] and "special education services",[3] there is no definition of "placement". The absence of a statutory definition suggests that the legislature intended that the normal usage of the word would apply. In normal usage, "placement" means a situation, site or location. The usage of the word in the context of special education does not generally extend to a specific geographic location (*e.g.*, a particular school);

---

[1] R.S.O. 1990, c. H.19 (as amended to 1999, c. 6).

[2] "Special education program" means, in respect of an exceptional pupil, an educational program that is based on and modified by the results of continuous assessment and evaluation and that includes a plan containing specific objectives and an outline of educational services that meets the needs of the exceptional pupil: *Education Act*, R.S.O. 1990, c. E.2 (as amended), s. 1(1).

[3] "Special education services" means facilities and resources, including support personnel and equipment, necessary for developing and implementing a special education program: s. 1(1).

rather, placement is generally a description of a generic setting (or settings) where the appropriate special education programs and services can be delivered to the student.

The Ministry of Education has directed school boards to provide "as full a range of placements as possible to meet the needs of exceptional pupils".[4]

Placements can extend from a regular class placement with monitoring to full-time placement in a provincial or demonstration school, to a whole range of placements in between.[5] Some of the placements in between include: regular classroom with consulting support to the classroom teacher and/or direct support to the student; regular classroom with withdrawal for direct one-on-one assistance; part-time regular classroom and part-time special education classroom; full-time special education classroom; special day school.

Placements can also include various combinations or permutations of the above placements. For example, a student in a special education class might be withdrawn for a portion of each day for one-on-one support with a special education teacher or aide. A regular classroom or special education class placement might include modification of regular curriculum for the student.

In addition, in at least one case, the Tribunal has approved a placement of home instruction.[6] "Home instruction" was defined in the school board's Special Education Plan ("SEP") to mean a modified school day with individual instruction that could be carried out in a location other than a school. The *Eady* case involved an exceptional student diagnosed with autism, who displayed aggressive conduct and outbursts of unacceptable behaviour which prompted the school board to conclude that special education services could not be provided for him at a school. The specific placement proposed was modified home instruction which would be provided in one of the school board's buildings with the parent hired as an assistant for two and one-half hours per day and another assistant working three and

---

[4] Ministry of Education, *Special Education Information Handbook, 1984*, at p. 48. A revised version of this document is expected imminently, as of the date of writing.

[5] Ontario Schools for the Blind and Deaf are generally referred to as "provincial schools". They include: The W. Ross Macdonald School (blind and deaf students), The Sir James Whitney School (deaf students) and The Ernest C. Drury School (deaf students). (Ministry of Education, Policy/Program Memorandum No. 1 — "Ontario Schools for the Blind and Deaf as Resource Centres", April 2, 1986.) Demonstration schools are also provincially operated schools which are geared to students with severe learning disabilities who require the facilities of a residential school. There are three demonstration schools in Ontario: Robarts School, the Sagonaska School and the Trillium School. School boards can refer students to a demonstration school upon the recommendation of an Identification, Placement and Review Committee (IPRC). However, decisions regarding admission are made by the Provincial Committee on Hearing Disabilities. Where the school board or parents (or the student if aged 18 years or more) disagree with the Committee's decision and request an appeal, the Director of the Special Education and Provincial Schools Branch will appoint a review committee to hear the appeal. (Ministry of Education, Program Memorandum No. 89, "The Residential Demonstration Schools for Students With Learning Disabilities: General Information and Details of the Referral Process", February 6, 1990.)

[6] *Eady v. Dryden Board of Education* (unreported, January, 1998) (Tompkins).

one-half hours per day. A home instruction teacher would provide seven hours per week to assist with the academic program. The principal of the secondary school the student otherwise would have attended was to be responsible to supervise the placement.

PLACEMENT VERSUS SPECIAL EDUCATION PROGRAMS AND SERVICES

While special education programs and services and placement do seem to be closely linked, they are treated as quite separate issues under the *Education Act*. For example:

- Section 8(3) of the *Education Act* requires that the Minister of Education ensure that all exceptional students in Ontario have "appropriate special education programs and special education services", but the section deals quite distinctly with placement by requiring the Minister to "provide for the parents or guardians to appeal the appropriateness of the special education placement".[7]
- Section 11(1), para. 5 of the *Education Act* empowers the Minister of Education to make regulations respecting special education programs and services, while para. 6 empowers the Minister to make regulations governing procedures for parent appeals of "identification and placement of exceptional pupils into special education programs".
- O. Reg. 181/98[8] permits the IPRC to make decisions on placement, but limits the IPRC to making recommendations on special education programs and services. Indeed, the IPRC is not obliged to discuss special education programs and services unless the parents request them to.[9] Similarly, the Regulation provides for parent appeals of IRPC decisions on placement but not on IPRC recommendations on special education programs and services.[10]

Similarly, the *Education Act* provides in s. 57(3) that:

> Where a parent or guardian of a pupil has exhausted all rights of appeal under the regulations in respect of the identification or placement of the pupil as an exceptional pupil and is dissatisfied with the decision in respect of the identification or placement, the parent or guardian may appeal to a Special Education Tribunal for a hearing in respect of the identification or placement.

---

[7] The subsection reads: "The Minister shall ensure that all exceptional children in Ontario have available to them, in accordance with this Act and the regulations, appropriate special education programs and special education services without payment of fees by parents or guardians resident in Ontario and shall provide for the parents or guardians to appeal the appropriateness of the special education placement . . .".

[8] *Identification and Placement of Exceptional Pupils*, O. Reg. 181/98.

[9] *Ibid.*, s. 16(1).

[10] *Ibid.*, s. 26(1).

The section makes no reference to an appeal of special education programs or services.

Nevertheless, from the outset, the Tribunal has made clear that the determination of placement must include some consideration of the programs and services which will be delivered in the placement. In *Dolmage v. Muskoka Board of Education*,[11] the first decision by the Tribunal made during the "phase-in" period,[12] the following comment was made:

> While the nature and content of the program that is provided to an exceptional pupil pursuant to a placement may be considered in order that the rationale for the placement can be understood, opinions in respect of the course content, the staffing allocated to the program, the adequacy of a teacher's capabilities to communicate in sign language, and the means by which the program could or should be enhanced or improved, tend to obscure those other matters that have to be considered in trying to decide whether a placement that has been recommended is right or wrong.

The *Dolmage* decision was reviewed by the Ontario Divisional Court,[13] which commented as follows:

> In considering the placement of a child in the phase-in period, the first step is to ascertain the needs of the child. This must include a consideration of such things as the nature and content of the programme and the services required to accomplish this purpose. When turning to placement, one must be sought which is suitable to the needs of the pupil. In doing so, however, it is essential to consider what programmes and services are available and perhaps even the degree of availability.[14]

These comments were made in the context of a case which arose during the "phase-in" period, which lasted from 1980 to September 1, 1985. However, the comments may also have application to the post "phase-in" period to the extent that they suggest that a consideration of placement includes a consideration of the programs and services which are provided in the particular placement.

A good example of the manner in which the Tribunal has considered programs and services is *Razaqpur v. Carleton Roman Catholic Separate School Board.*[15] In this case, the Ontario Special Education (English) Tribunal found that the placement of a student identified as gifted did not meet the student's needs for the following reasons: the frequency and intensity of special education activities designed and provided for the student were insufficient to meet the needs of someone with his level of giftedness; the nature of the special education placement did not address the discrepancy between the achievement level customarily expected of a student of his age and what he was capable of doing; and, finally, there was a lack of school board impetus in coming to grips with and managing the student's case. The Tribunal determined that the student's needs would be best met

---

[11] (unreported, February 28, 1984) (Houghton) at p. 17.

[12] See Chapter 3, "The Administrator's Framework".

[13] *Dolmage v. Muskoka Board of Education* (1985), 49 O.R. (2d) 546, 15 D.L.R. (4th) 741, 6 O.A.C. 389 (Div. Ct.).

[14] *Supra*, at p. 555.

[15] (unreported, undated) (Houghton).

in a congregated class comprised of his gifted peers and ordered a placement in a congregated class. Since the school board did not have such a class, it was directed to purchase the placement from its co-terminus board.

There have been other cases where the Tribunal has given consideration to the programs and services which can be provided in a particular placement and has even given directions with respect to programs or services to be provided in a particular placement:

- In *Stutt v. Carleton Board of Education*[16] the Tribunal ordered that all future Individual Education Plans include a statement that the student was described by a physician as being environmentally sensitive.
- In *Ormerod v. Wentworth County Board of Education*[17] the student was identified as deaf. The appeal involved the decision by the school board to maintain the student's placement in a regular class with resource withdrawal, but to change the identity of the resource teacher, who was fluent in cueing and to provide an aide fluent in cueing in the resource classroom as well as in the regular class. The Tribunal ordered that the student continue in a regular class for about 50% of the day with a cueing aide, but that the school board provide a teacher of the deaf for the balance of the day and ensure that an effective mechanism was established to co-ordinate the various aspects of the student's program and provide for continuous assessment of the student and evaluation of his program.

Since these cases were decided, the Regulation governing IPRCs and Special Education Appeal Boards (SEABs) has been replaced. The current Regulation requires an IPRC to "consider whether placement in a regular class, with appropriate special education services . . . would meet the pupil's needs".[18] This provision makes clear that, at the very least, the IPRC must consider special education programs and services which could be provided in the placement, but the IPRC may only make recommendations on special education programs and services.[19] It follows that an SEAB and the Tribunal must also consider special education programs and services.

It would appear, then, that a determination of placement will involve a consideration of programs and services to be provided in the placement. Further, while IPRCs and SEABs are limited to making recommendations on special education programs and services, it is likely that the Tribunal will be prepared to give directions on programs and services where it finds that programs or services are so intrinsically entwined in the placement as to form part of the placement.

---

[16] (unreported, April 2, 1993) (Weber).
[17] (unreported, June 5, 1987) (Houghton).
[18] *Identification and Placement of Exceptional Pupils*, O. Reg. 181/98, s. 17(1).
[19] *Ibid.*, s. 16.

STANDARDS AGAINST WHICH PLACEMENTS ARE TO BE MEASURED

The only guidance provided by the *Education Act* for measuring the adequacy of a placement is found in s. 8(3). This section requires the Minister to "provide for the parents or guardians to appeal the *appropriateness* of the special education placement".[20]

This somewhat imprecise language was considered by a court in an application for judicial review of the first Tribunal decision. In *Dolmage v. Muskoka Board of Education*,[21] the Divisional Court stated as follows:

> I cannot help but think that the language of s. [8(3)] should not be read in any more absolute sense than the words reasonably require. To do so would ignore the practicalities previously adverted to. The idea of an "appropriate" special education programme, and the "appropriateness" of the placement of the pupil, surely involves the idea of suitability, and is not to be confused with a placement which amounts to perfection.

These comments are still applicable today.

Over the past two decades, disputes over the standard to be used for measuring placement have arisen most often in the context of parents seeking "integrated" placements for their severely developmentally disabled children. The litigation resulting from these disputes has called into play the *Human Rights Code* and the *Canadian Charter of Rights and Freedoms* and has resulted in decisions which have served to define the criteria to be used by school boards in making placement decisions.

A review of the historical context gives focus to the criteria which are currently used to determine the appropriateness of a special education placement.

Historical Context: The Integration Movement

At the point Bill 82[22] was introduced, a debate had begun amongst the academics in the education community over the issue of "segregated"[23] placements versus "integrated" placements, especially in respect of students with developmental disabilities. Bill 82 was introduced at a time when children with severe developmental disabilities (then referred to as "trainable retarded" or "trainable mentally retarded") were excluded from the mainstream of education in Ontario. It was heralded as legislation which established universal access to all Ontario students. It did so by incorporating into the *Education Act* a definition of "exceptional pupil" which included all students, including those identified as "trainable retarded", and by removing admissibility requirements which had

---

[20] Emphasis added.
[21] *Supra*, footnote 13, at p. 554.
[22] *Education Amendment Act, 1980*, S.O. 1980, c. 61.
[23] At the time, the word "segregated" was used to denote a placement outside the regular class in a special education class which might be located in regular school or in a school for the "trainable retarded".

applied to these students.[24] It also required all school boards to provide, either directly or through purchase of services from other school boards, special education programs and services for their exceptional students.

Bill 82 removed a number of barriers which had existed for students with developmental disabilities in accessing the education system, but it also required that segregated schools and classes be provided for "trainable retarded pupils".[25] While a few school boards in Ontario, primarily Roman Catholic separate school boards, put fully integrated placements into place, the requirement that separate facilities be created and maintained for "trainable retarded pupils" was seen by many as a big step forward from the days when youngsters with severe developmental delays were excluded, for the most part, from the educational system. Prior to Bill 82, if the student was not in one of the few school board jurisdictions where educational services were being provided by the local board, the only educational services available were provided by local parent groups (*e.g.*, local Associations for the Mentally Retarded, now called Associations for Community Living), sometimes in special schools, sometimes in settings such as church basements.

The movement towards integration of all students into regular classes was occurring across Canada and the United States, driven in large part by parent advocacy groups. In Ontario, those spearheading this movement turned to legal forums to push for fuller integration of students identified as "trainable retarded", often supplying counsel for parents to represent them to fight for full regular class placements for their children.

Initially, the focus of parents seeking to achieve fuller integration for their children in the education system was on the Special Education Tribunal. The Tribunal heard appeals from a number of parents seeking to have their children placed in regular classes instead of segregated classes, based on arguments which increasingly drew on human rights principles. However, early on, the Tribunal made clear that it would examine the circumstances of each individual child, and would make decisions on placement issues based on the educational needs and best interests of that individual child. This usually meant a placement in a self-contained class.[26] The comments of one Tribunal summarized the approach taken by all:

---

[24] Anne Keeton Wilson, *A Consumer's Guide to Bill 82: Special Education in Ontario* (Toronto: OISE Press, 1983), at p. 9.

[25] In fact, the manner of the funding at the time encouraged the use of specialized settings particularly in respect of students with developmental disabilities.

[26] In *Lewis v. York Region Board of Education* (unreported, September 10, 1985) (Houghton), the Tribunal rejected placement in both a "class for the trainable retarded" (supported by the school board) or the regular class requested by the parents, and ordered placement in a "class for multi-handicapped pupils". In *Fripp v. Nippissing Board of Education* (unreported, July 18, 1986) (Duchesneau-McLachlan), the IPRC's determination of placement in a class for the trainable retarded was upheld, rejecting the parents' position that the student should be re-identified as "educable" and placed in a regular classroom with a teacher's aide for 50% of the day with remaining time spent with a speech pathologist and occupational therapist or alternatively in a basic learning skills program in a neighbourhood school. In *Murray v. Brant County Board of*

It is the firm opinion of this Tribunal that the wholesale integration of exceptional pupils into regular classes, solely on the basis of philosophical principle, untempered by due and informed consideration of each individual situation, is directly counter to the best interests of all pupils. Further, it is the conviction of the Tribunal that the assumption of rigid, doctrinaire positions on the issue, not only threatens the very future of integration as a desirable practice, but specifically, in cases such as Jaclyn's, serves only to erode the good will and reason that must obtain if all parties are to act in her best interests.[27]

In the meantime, parents sought other avenues to pursue fuller integration for their children — through complaints to the Ontario Human Rights Commission and through the courts under the Charter.

However, the case which finally determined the issue started with an appeal of placement to the Special Education Tribunal.

Eaton v. Brant County Board of Education,[28] started with an appeal of the placement of Emily Eaton. The appeal focused directly on the issue of self-contained (segregated) class versus integrated placement in a regular class. Emily had no established communication system and, additionally, had severe developmental delays including a severe intellectual handicap. She had originally been placed in a regular kindergarten class and then in a regular Grade 1 class with a full-time aide. At the end of her Grade 1 year, the IPRC recommended that Emily be placed in a self-contained class. Her parents appealed, resulting in a stay of placement in the regular class, so that by the time the case reached the Tribunal, Emily was in the regular Grade 2 class. At the hearing, the parents squarely put their arguments in support of a fully integrated placement on the footing of equity principles under the *Human Rights Code* and under the Charter. They argued that a placement outside the regular class discriminated against Emily on the basis of her disability and violated her equality rights under the Charter.

The Tribunal heard evidence that:

- in the Grade 2 class, Emily often fell asleep and this falling asleep seemed to be her way of shutting down if she was overstimulated;
- Emily would on occasion vocalize in a loud and disturbing way until she was taken out into the hall where her aide would walk her up and down the hall, an activity which she appeared to enjoy;

Education (unreported, July 17, 1985) (Houghton), the Tribunal upheld the IPRC's determination of placement in a "school for trainable retarded pupils", rejecting the parents' proposed placement in a Grade 8 class in the student's neighbourhood school "with an individually adapted curriculum and the support of a teacher's aide", or alternatively, a "trainable retarded class" in a public school. In *Rowett v. York Region Board of Education* (unreported, September, 1986) (MacDonald), the Tribunal confirmed the IPRC's determination of placement in a "primary, self-contained class for slow learners", with a direction that the fullest possible opportunities for integration be provided, and rejected the parents' argument of placement in an age-appropriate class in the neighbourhood school with a diagnostician and resource teacher's assistance in the classroom or resource withdrawal, or a teacher's aide.

[27] *Rowett v. York Region Board of Education, supra,* at p. 46.
[28] (unreported, November 19, 1993) (Weber).

- during group activities, the other children were increasingly interacting with the aide instead of Emily despite the aide's efforts (in short, Emily's interaction with her peers was limited);
- if not watched carefully, Emily would put small things in her mouth.

The Tribunal concluded that the regular class placement was not meeting Emily's needs and stated,

> . . . the nature and extent of immediate adult intervention and care essential to meet her profound intellectual, physical and emotional needs, even minimally, has the counter-productive effect of isolating her, of segregating her in the theoretically integrated setting.[29]

The test which the Tribunal applied in upholding the decision of the IPRC on placement, was what placement best met Emily Eaton's special needs.[30]

The parents brought an application for judicial review of the Tribunal's decision to the Ontario Divisional Court,[31] which dismissed the application. The parents appealed to the Court of Appeal where they were successful in getting the decision of the Tribunal quashed.

The Court of Appeal held that the normal placement for a student is in the regular class and that the reason Emily was excluded from the regular class was because she had a disability. The Court of Appeal found that this was discriminatory, unless her parents consented to the placement outside the regular class. The Court of Appeal concluded that since the *Education Act* did not include a presumption in favour of the regular class, the *Education Act* was contrary to s. 15 of the Charter. The Court of Appeal held that s. 15 of the Charter required that all reasonable efforts should be made to integrate the disabled into the regular class. The Court stated: "In short, the Charter requires that, *regardless of its perceived pedagogical merit*, a non-consensual exclusionary placement be recognized as discriminatory and not be resorted to unless alternatives are proven inadequate."[32]

The school board appealed to the Supreme Court of Canada which reversed the Court of Appeal's decision and restored the decision of the Special Education Tribunal. While the Court of Appeal had focused on the location of the placement (*i.e.*, a regular class versus a "segregated" class), the Supreme Court of Canada focused on the pedagogical reasons for the placement. The Supreme Court of Canada recognized that the pedagogical principles underlying the placement in a special class were directed towards ameliorating those disadvantages which prevented Emily from benefiting from an education in a regular class. The Supreme Court of Canada stated:

---

[29] *Supra*, at p. 66.

[30] *Supra*, at p. 58.

[31] *Eaton v. Brant County Board of Education* (1994), 71 O.A.C. 69 (Div. Ct.), revd 123 D.L.R. (4th) 43, 22 O.R. (3d) 1, 77 O.A.C. 368, 27 C.R.R. (2d) 53 (C.A.), revd [1997] 1 S.C.R. 241, 142 D.L.R. (4th) 385, 31 O.R. (3d) 574n, 97 O.A.C. 161, 41 C.R.R. (2d) 240, 207 N.R. 171.

[32] *Supra*, at p. 65 D.L.R. (C.A.) (emphasis added).

In some cases, special education is a necessary adaptation of the mainstream world which enables some disabled pupils access to the learning environment they need in order to have an equal opportunity in education. While integration should be recognized as the norm of general application because of the benefits it generally provides, a presumption in favour of integrated schooling would work to the disadvantage of pupils who require special education in order to achieve equality. Schools focussed on the needs of the blind or deaf and special education for students with learning disabilities indicate the positive aspects of segregated education placement. Integration can be either a benefit or burden depending on whether the individual can profit from the advantages that integration provides.[33]

The Supreme Court of Canada went on to say:

A decision-making body must determine whether the integrated settings can be adapted to meet the special needs of an exceptional child. Where this is not possible, that is, where aspects of the integrated setting which cannot be reasonably changed interfere with meeting the child's special needs, the principle of accommodation will require a special placement outside of this setting. For older children and those who are able to communicate their wishes and needs, their own views will play an important role in the determination of best interest. For younger children, and those like Emily, who are either incapable of making a choice or have a very limited means of communicating their wishes, the decision maker must make this determination on the basis of other evidence before it.[34]

As a result, while consideration must be given to whether an exceptional pupil's needs can be met in a regular class, the educational needs of the student must be given a primary focus in determining placement. Where reasonable modifications cannot be made to a regular class placement to make that placement work, a placement outside the regular class will not be discriminatory, so long as the placement is in the student's best interests.

The Supreme Court of Canada also confirmed the standard of review adopted by the Tribunal in the *Eaton* case in determining appeals on placement, namely, which placement meets the pupils' best interests.[35]

The Regulatory Standard

Shortly after the release of the Supreme Court of Canada's decision in the *Eaton* case, the Ontario government established a new test which IPRCs must consider in making placement decisions:[36]

17. (1) When making a placement decision . . . the committee shall, before considering the option of placement in a special education class, consider whether placement in a regular class, with appropriate special education services,

---

[33] *Supra*, at p. 274 S.C.R.

[34] *Supra*, at p. 278.

[35] This standard was reconfirmed by the Ontario Divisional Court in *Pokonzie v. Sudbury District Roman Catholic Separate School Board* (1997), 104 O.A.C. 367.

[36] O. Reg. 181/98, ss. 17 and 23(6). It should be noted that this Regulation had been drafted prior to the decision of the Supreme Court of Canada, and in fact was put before the Supreme Court of Canada as part of the Ministry of Education's case.

(a)   would meet the pupil's needs; and

(b)   is consistent with parental preferences.

(2) If, after considering all of the information obtained by it or submitted to it under s. 15 that it considers relevant, the committee is satisfied that placement in a regular class would meet the pupil's needs and is consistent with parental preferences, the committee shall decide in favour of placement in a regular class.

The requirements set out in this provision meet the standards imposed by the Supreme Court of Canada in the *Eaton* case. It should be noted that while parent wishes must be considered, those wishes are not determinative of what the placement will be. This is in keeping with the Supreme Court of Canada's view that the IPRC has the authority to make the final decision on placement, based on the "best interests" test.

IMPLEMENTING A PLACEMENT

Once a placement has been determined, it cannot be implemented by a school board unless one of the following events occurs:

- the parent has given written consent to the placement;
- the parent has failed to appeal a placement decision by the IPRC within 30 days of receipt by the parent of notice of the decision;[37]
- where the parent has appealed to an SEAB, the parent has failed to appeal a placement decision by the school board, following the receipt of the recommendations of the SEAB, within 30 days of receipt by the parent of notice of the decision;[38] or
- where the parent has appealed to the Special Education Tribunal, the parent has abandoned the appeal or the appeal has been dismissed.[39] The decision of whether the appeal has been abandoned will be made by either the Tribunal or the Secretary of the Tribunal.

Where a school board is able to implement a placement, it must do so as soon as possible after the occurrence of the event which permits the school board to proceed to make the placement.[40] Where the parent has not consented to the placement, written notice must be provided by the school board of the implementation of the placement.[41]

---

[37]   See Chapter 6, "The Identification, Placement and Review Committee".

[38]   See Chapter 9, "The First Stage of Appeal".

[39]   O. Reg. 181/98, ss. 20(1), 25(1) and 31(1).

[40]   *Ibid.*, ss. 20(2) and 25(2).

[41]   *Ibid.*, ss. 20(3) and 25(3).

Where the Tribunal orders a placement different than that argued for by either of the parties to the appeal — as was the case in *Ormerod* and *Lewis*[42]— that placement must be implemented.[43]

PLACEMENTS PENDING AN APPEAL AND TRANSITIONAL PLACEMENTS

Placements Pending an Appeal

If a student is already in a special education placement, and the parents are appealing the decision, the placement is effectively stayed during the period of the appeal unless the parties agree otherwise, or unless the appeal is abandoned. This is the case whether the appeal is to the SEAB or the Tribunal.

An interesting situation arises where the IPRC decision being appealed from relates to the transition from elementary school to secondary school; for example, when the secondary school placement differs from that provided in the elementary school and the parents prefer the latter. Promotional decisions, which are made by the principal,[44] are distinct from placement decisions, although the promotion of a student from elementary school to secondary school has been at the heart of at least two appeals to the Tribunal.[45] In such a case, the precise placement which was in effect for Grade 8 may not be available for Grade 9. In that event, if the parent appeals the placement which the IPRC has determined for Grade 9, the choices include the following: the student may remain in the elementary school in the same placement as he or she was in for Grade 8 placement but receive a program based on Grade 9 material; the student may be given a placement in the secondary school which as closely as possible approximates the Grade 8 placement; or the parent and the school board may agree to a compromise placement pending determination of the parents' appeal. This might be done on a "without prejudice" basis by the parties, such that the compromise placement is not seen as a concession against the position which either party is taking on the appeal.

Transitional Placements

No student can be denied an education program pending a meeting of the IPRC or a decision under s. 9 of O. Reg. 181/98. In such a case, the program provided must be appropriate to the pupil's apparent strengths and needs. It must also be consistent with the principles underlying s. 17 of O. Reg. 181/98, discussed

---

[42]   *Ormerod v. Wentworth County Board of Education* (unreported June 5, 1987) (Houghton); *Lewis v. York Region Board of Education* (unreported, September 10, 1985) (Houghton).

[43]   *Education Act*, s. 57(4).

[44]   *Ibid.*, s. 265(g).

[45]   *McLean v. Simcoe County Board of Education* (unreported, April 2, 1993) (Weber); *Irvine v. Timmins Board of Education* (unreported, May, 1997) (Tompkins).

previously under the heading "The Regulatory Standard". That is, consideration must first be given to a regular class placement and a placement outside the regular class may only be made where a placement in a regular class with appropriate special education services would not meet the student's needs. Parental preferences should be considered by the principal in determining a transitional education program. Appropriate education services must be provided to meet the student's apparent need.[46]

---

[46] O. Reg. 181/98, s. 9.

6

The Identification, Placement and Review Committee

INTRODUCTION

The responsibility for identifying a student as an exceptional pupil and determining a placement rests, in the first instance, with the Identification, Placement and Review Committee (the "IPRC"). In this chapter, we discuss the composition of the IPRC, the scope of its powers, the manner in which it carries out its responsibilities and the implementation of the IPRC's decision.

ESTABLISHMENT OF THE IPRC

Every school board is required to establish at least one committee for the identification and placement of exceptional pupils. No upper limit is placed on the number of IPRCs which a school board may establish.[1] Nor is there any definition of the types of IPRCs that may be set up. Therefore, school boards have flexibility in setting up IPRCs to meet their needs. A school board may decide to establish IPRCs which are dedicated to dealing with only elementary or secondary school students. Alternatively, IPRCs may be established to deal solely with the students who reside in a particular geographic area. A separate IPRC may be established for each school or for a group of schools. IPRCs may also be established to deal with particular exceptionalities. Such an IPRC could be composed of members who have expertise in a particular exceptionality in order to permit more in-depth recommendations to be made about the special education programs and services that might be appropriate in a particular case.

Each IPRC must consist of three or more members. It is mandatory that at least one member of the committee be either:

- a principal employed by the school board;
- a supervisory officer employed by the board; or

---

[1] *Identification and Placement of Exceptional Pupils*, O. Reg. 181/98, s. 10(1).

- a supervisory officer employed by another school board whose services are provided under a Minister-approved agreement with another school board.[2]

This mandatory appointee may designate another person to act in his or her place. It is not necessary to obtain the school board's approval for such a designation. The only limitation on this power to designate a replacement is that the person designated must also be either a principal or supervisory officer employed by the school board or a supervisory officer employed by another school board whose services are provided under a Minister-approved agreement with another school board.[3]

In appointing the other members of an IPRC, a school board is limited only in that the school board may not appoint one of its trustees to sit on an IPRC.[4] While, normally, the balance of the committee will be made up of teachers, special education consultants or other special education professionals employed by the school board, a school board is not limited to appointing employees of the school board. It may be helpful in some circumstances to appoint outside professionals such as medical doctors, social workers, psychologists or counsellors to an IPRC. However, where a school board appoints a non-employee to an IPRC, parental consent (or the consent of the student if aged 16 years or older) is necessary in order for the non-employee to have access to the student's personal information.[5]

A chair must be appointed for each IPRC and the manner of selection of the chair is left to the school board to determine in its discretion.[6] The school board may direct that the principal or supervisory officer which it appoints to the committee serve as the chair of the committee or it might delegate the responsibility for the selection of the chair for each IPRC to a supervisory officer or a principal. A further option would be for the school board to direct that the committee itself agree on a chair. Since the opportunity to sit as chair can provide an opportunity for leadership experience, the school board may decide that, rather than establishing a permanent chair, the position will be rotated amongst the members of the committee. Whatever procedure a school board decides will be used to select an IPRC chair, that procedure should be set out in a board policy.[7]

---

[2] *Ibid.*, s. 11(1) and (2).

[3] *Ibid.*, s. 11(3) and (4).

[4] *Ibid.*, s. 11(5).

[5] *Municipal Freedom of Information and Protection of Privacy Act*, R.S.O. 1990, c. M.56 (as amended to 2000, c. 26, Sch. J), ss. 32 and 54.

[6] O. Reg. 181/98, s. 10.

[7] Presumably a school board will establish one policy which covers the jurisdiction of IPRCs, the procedure for selecting an IPRC chair and any other procedures which the board has determined will be followed by IPRCs pursuant to its authority under s. 12(1) of O. Reg. 181/98.

REFERRAL OF STUDENTS TO THE IPRC

There are two different routes by which a student who has not previously been identified as an exceptional pupil may be referred to an IPRC. There is also a separate route of referral to an IPRC for students who are transferring into a school board from a demonstration school. Once a student has been identified and placed by an IPRC, there are several routes by which a student's identification or placement can be referred back for review by an IPRC.

Referral of a Student Who Has Not Been Identified as Exceptional

A principal of a school at which a student is enrolled may decide to refer the student to an IPRC to determine whether the student should be identified as an exceptional pupil and, if so, what the placement of the student should be. This route will generally be used where the student's teacher(s) in consultation with the principal have determined that the student appears to have an exceptionality which has not been formally identified and that the student would benefit from special education programs or services.[8]

In this process, the principal must provide to the student's parents[9] written notice of the referral of the student to the IPRC. It should be noted that whenever a written communication must be provided to a parent (or to the student), the parent (or student) may require the school board representative providing the communication to use braille, large print or audio-cassette format for the communication.[10]

---

[8] O. Reg. 181/98, s. 14(1)(a). It is not necessary to identify a student as exceptional before providing special education programs and services to the student, although the absence of a formal identification would preclude the school board from claiming additional funding where funding was otherwise available in the circumstances. (Currently, special education funding generally is based on overall enrolment rather than the number of identified students, and "per student" claims for Intensive Support Amount funding are not limited to identified students.) In addition, the requirement for annual reviews and the availability of a parent appeal are lost. However, where the parents do not wish the student to be identified, where there is no dispute as to needs and where no additional funding hinges on the identification, some school boards will agree not to identify the student. Even in the absence of a formal identification, the school board is obliged to provide "reasonable accommodation" to a student whose disability precludes the student from benefiting from the normal curriculum delivered in the normal manner. In almost every case, reasonable accommodation in such circumstances would look like the special education programs and services which the student would receive if identified. See Chapter 1, "Introduction".

[9] Throughout this chapter, a "parent" means either parent, if they live together or have joint custody of the student, the custodial parent if the parents are separated, or the legal guardian of a student under the age of 18 years. If the student is 18 years of age or older, the word "parent" should be read to mean the student, since at 18 years of age the student is, legally, an adult. It should be noted, however, that notices which are to be sent to parents are also to be sent to students 16 years or older. Indeed, students aged 16 or older have the right to be equal participants at an IPRC.

[10] O. Reg. 181/98, s. 4. This same provision applies to any communication which must be provided to parents or students under the Regulation.

Within 15 days of the date on which the principal gave written notice of referral to the parents, the principal must provide to the parents a written statement setting out approximately when the principal expects the IPRC to meet to discuss the pupil. Along with this written statement, the principal must also send a copy of the Parent Guide (see Chapter 3, "The Administrator's Framework").[11]

Alternatively, a parent may ask the principal to refer the student to an IPRC. This request must be made in writing and, upon receipt, the principal must refer the student to an IPRC.[12]

Within 15 days of receiving the parents' request for referral, the principal must provide the student's parents with a written statement acknowledging receipt of their request and advising approximately when the principal expects the IPRC will meet to discuss the student. A copy of the Parent Guide must also be sent to the parents.[13]

Referral from a Demonstration School

Where an exceptional pupil has been enrolled in a demonstration or provincial school[14] and a decision is made that the student will leave the demonstration school and enroll in a school within the jurisdiction of a school board at which the student is a "resident pupil", the superintendent of the demonstration school must notify the director of education of the school board (or the secretary or equivalent in a school board which does not have a director).[15]

Upon receipt of the notice from the demonstration school, the director of education (who will presumably delegate this responsibility to a supervisory officer or special education administrator) must ensure that the student is referred to the school board's IPRC or, if more than one IPRC has been established by the school board, to the IPRC which is most "appropriate" for the student.[16] Which IPRC is the most "appropriate" IPRC will depend on the manner in which the school board has set up its IPRCs. If IPRCs are set up by geographic area, the IPRC which deals with students from the area in which the student resides or in which he or she would likely attend school will be the most appropriate. If IPRCs have been established to deal with particular exceptionalities, then the IPRC which deals with the exceptionality of the student who is leaving the demonstration school may be the most appropriate.

There is an obligation upon both the director of education of the board and the superintendent of the demonstration school to use their best efforts to ensure that

---

[11] *Ibid.*, s. 14(6).

[12] *Ibid.*, s. 14(1)(b). Although some school boards have developed a practice of not referring students in junior kindergarten or kindergarten to an IPRC, or of waiting until a student is in Grade 3, these limitations are not found in the legislation or any regulation; therefore, a parental request must lead to an IPRC for a student of any age.

[13] *Ibid.*, s. 14(6).

[14] See Chapter 5, footnote 5.

[15] O. Reg. 181/98, s. 14(2).

[16] *Ibid.*, s. 14(3) and (5).

the IPRC meets as soon as possible after the decision is made to move the student from the demonstration school to a school within the jurisdiction of the school board where the student is a "resident pupil".[17] There is no requirement that the student must be enrolled with the school board prior to the meeting of the IPRC and it makes sense that the IPRC determination respecting placement be made in such a case before the student is actually moved from the demonstration school to the school that the student will attend.

Within 15 days of receipt of the notification from the demonstration school that the student will be leaving the demonstration school to enter a school within the jurisdiction of the school board, the director of education of the school board must provide the student's parent with a copy of the notice received from the demonstration school, a copy of the Parent Guide and a written statement which indicates approximately when the IPRC is expected to meet for the first time to discuss the student.[18]

Referral for Review

Where a student has been previously identified as an exceptional pupil, the student's identification and/or placement must be referred back to an IPRC for review at least once in each school year.

In fact, a responsibility is imposed upon the director of education of the school board to ensure that a review is held at least once in each school year, *unless* there has been an IPRC review held during the school year *or* the parents of the pupil have provided written notice to the principal dispensing with the annual review.[19]

Usually school boards have policies about annual reviews which require the principal at the school where the student is receiving his or her special education program to refer the student to the committee each year. However, the principal may refer the student back to an IPRC at any time, on written notice to the student's parents.[20]

Alternatively, the student's parents may require the student to be referred back to the IPRC by providing a written request to the principal. However, time constraints are imposed on the parents in making this request. A parent may not request a referral for review before a placement has been in effect for three months and may not make a request for review more often than once in every three-month period.[21] A parent's only possible avenue around these time constraints would be to persuade the principal, whose referral powers are not temporally limited, to request an earlier review. There is, however, no obligation on the principal to accede to the parent's request where the request is made sooner than three months after the last review or placement change.

---

[17] *Ibid.*, s. 14(4).
[18] *Ibid.*, s. 14(7).
[19] *Ibid.*, s. 21(3) and (4).
[20] *Ibid.*, s. 21(1)(a) and (b).
[21] *Ibid.*, s. 21(2).

Where the student is receiving his or her special education program from another school board under an agreement permitted by s. 170(1), para. 7 of the *Education Act*, the student's review will be conducted by an IPRC of the school board which is providing the special education program. This review may be initiated in one of three ways:

- by referral from the principal of the school that is providing the special program;
- by written request of the parent to the principal; or
- by written request of the director of education of the school board that is providing the special program to the principal.[22]

In each case where the student is referred back to an IPRC for review and the school board has established more than one IPRC, the principal must determine the IPRC that is most appropriate to conduct the review, having regard to the expertise and specific mandate of the various IPRCs.[23] In this respect, administrative procedures may be established by the school board which directs a principal in making this determination. Further, the principal must provide the parent with a written statement of the approximate time when the review meeting will take place.[24]

CONDUCT OF THE IPRC PROCEEDING

The Regulation which governs IPRCs sets out some rules concerning the manner in which the IPRC is to carry out its mandate, but leaves many of the procedural details to be determined by the school board or the IPRC itself.[25] While the IPRC is not subject to the rigorous procedural obligations of the *Statutory Powers Procedure Act*,[26] the IPRC is obliged to comply with the basic tenets of procedural fairness in dealing with parents and students.[27] Parents must be

---

[22] *Ibid.*, s. 21(2) to (4).

[23] *Ibid.*, s. 22(1).

[24] *Ibid.*, s. 21(5).

[25] *Ibid.*, s. 12.

[26] R.S.O. 1990, c. S.22 ("SPPA"). The SPPA is a code of minimum procedural rules applicable to administrative decision-makers that exercise a "statutory power of decision".

[27] While the IPRC is charged with making decisions, it would appear that it does not exercise a "statutory power of decision" within the meaning of the SPPA. The Ontario Divisional Court has found that very specific statutory language is required to create a "statutory power of decision" (*Poulten v. University of Toronto* (1975), 59 D.L.R. (3d) 197, 8 O.R. (2d) 749 (Div. Ct.)). Among other things, the statute must require the tribunal to hold a hearing. The language of O. Reg. 181/98, requires the IPRC to collect information and to meet and discuss, which falls short of the requirement to hold a hearing. Although the common law duty of fairness can also impose an obligation to hold a hearing, which would bring the SPPA into play, it would be unlikely that the circumstances in any case before an IPRC would raise this obligation. Nevertheless, the common law does impose obligations of procedural fairness, which will be outlined in this chapter.

provided with all information which the IPRC intends to consider in making its decision and are entitled to attend, with a representative or advocate, all meetings of the IPRC where there are discussions about their child or where decisions are being made about their child.[28] Parents and 16 year olds may be present at and participate in all discussions about the student. They are also entitled to be present when the IPRC makes its decision on identification and placement.

Consistency in Membership of IPRC

The need to ensure consistency in membership of the IPRC making the decision on a particular student arises from the principle of fairness. If one of the decision-makers does not participate in all of the meetings, the perception — and reality — may be that he or she is not capable of making a fully informed decision.

Therefore, it will be important to ensure that those IPRC members who make the determinations in each case have participated throughout all stages of that case. This means that, where the IPRC will not complete its deliberations in one meeting, the composition of the IPRC dealing with a particular student should be fixed as of the first meeting concerning the student. No new members may be added to the IPRC until the process involved with that student is completed, including any requests by the parent to meet to discuss the IPRC's decision.[29] If the IPRC begins its process and a member is unable to attend a subsequent meeting, then that member should not participate in further deliberations of the committee in respect of that particular referral. It is not appropriate, once the IPRC has begun to consider a matter, for substitution of committee members to be made.

Participants in an IPRC Meeting

The necessary participants in an IPRC meeting will include a parent of the student, the student (if the student is aged 16 years or older) and the referring principal.

Ontario Regulation 181/98 gives the parent of the student who is referred to the IPRC and the student, if he or she is 16 years of age or older, the right to attend and participate in all IPRC discussions about the student and the right to be present when the IPRC's identification and placement decisions are made.[30] This imposed transparency in decision-making may limit the candour with which IPRCs discuss particular situations, especially in those rare situations where there are hostile feelings between the parents and school board staff. However, the intent behind this provision is to encourage school board staff to form a partnership with parents so that parents are included in the process right through to the final decision, and to promote open communication between parents and school staff.

---

[28] O. Reg. 181/98, ss. 5 and 15(8).
[29] See discussion under the heading "Parental Request to Discuss the IPRC's Decision", *infra.*
[30] O. Reg. 181/98, s. 5.

While a student who is under the age of 16 years is not given a right of participation under the *Education Act* or its regulations, the Supreme Court of Canada has recognized that for "older children and those who are able to communicate their wishes and needs, their own view will play an important role in the determination of best interests".[31] Accordingly, an IPRC may also permit a student younger than 16 years to attend and participate in a meeting.

It is important to note that the parental/student right to attend and participate in discussions extends only to those situations where members of the IPRC are meeting as a committee. It would not appear that the provision precludes individual members of the IPRC from holding discussions about administrative matters related to setting up meetings.[32]

There may be an issue about which parent has party status where a student's parents are separated or divorced. In this situation, normally the parent with whom the student resides (the "custodial parent") has the right to make decisions respecting the student's schooling.[33] Only a custodial parent has the right to be notified of a referral to an IPRC or a request to review identification and placement, to participate in the IPRC process and to receive IPRC decisions. However, if a separation agreement or a court order gives joint custody to parents, both parents will continue to have the right to make decisions about the student and to participate in IPRC meetings.

Even where parents are separated and one has custody of the student, a court order or separation agreement may give limited rights to the non-custodial parent to have a say in the student's schooling. In any event, the non-custodial parent will continue to have the right to be given information about the education of the student and, accordingly, the school will be obliged to provide information to the non-custodial parent upon request.[34] If the custodial parent agrees, or where the IPRC believes the non-custodial parent has relevant information to contribute and his or her presence would contribute to a better determination of identification and placement, the non-custodial parent may attend IPRC meetings.

Where a dispute arises between separated parents concerning the rights of each to provide input into the student's schooling, the principal might request a copy of any court order or the portion of the separation agreement which outlines the custodial arrangements.

The principal who referred the student is entitled to be a participant in the IPRC proceedings, although he or she may delegate a vice-principal or teachers more familiar with the student to act in his or her stead. In the case of a student being transferred to the school board from a demonstration school, the superintendent of the demonstration school who initiated the process and the director of education of

---

[31]   *Eaton v. Brant County Board of Education*, [1997] 1 S.C.R. 241 at p. 278, 142 D.L.R. (4th) 385, 31 O.R. (3d) 574*n*, 97 O.A.C. 161, 41 C.R.R. (2d) 240, 207 N.R. 171.

[32]   O. Reg. 181/98, s. 5.

[33]   *Children's Law Reform Act*, R.S.O. 1990, c. C.12 (as amended to 1999, c. 6), s. 20(4).

[34]   Where a custody order is made under the *Divorce Act*, R.S.C. 1985, c. 3 (2nd Supp.), s. 16 (as amended to 1999, c. 3), similar principles apply.

the school board to which the student is being transferred would both be entitled to be participants in the IPRC process. However, in the latter circumstance, it is likely that responsibility for dealing with the process of the transfer, including attendance at IPRC meetings, would be delegated to another official — in the case of the superintendent of the demonstration school, the principal of the demonstration school, and in the case of a director of education of the receiving school, a superintendent or special education administrator.

As well, the student's teachers will often be participants. Consultants and other professionals who have worked with the student may also participate in IPRC proceedings.

Where a school board provides special education programs to a student of another school board under an agreement for purchase of services entered into pursuant to s. 170(1), para. 7 of the *Education Act*, the student's identification and placement will be reviewed by an IPRC of the school board which is providing the special program. In such a case, in addition to the other usual participants — parents/student, principal, teachers — the school board providing the special education program must invite a representative of the purchasing board to be present at and participate in all committee discussions about the student and to be present when the IPRC makes decisions about the identification or placement of the student.[35]

IPRC Meetings

Procedures

Ontario Regulation 181/98, which requires the establishment of IPRCs, imposes few requirements for the conduct of IPRC meetings. A school board may develop additional procedures to be followed by the IPRC, but may not mandate any procedures which are in conflict with those set out in the Regulation.

It is, in fact, quite appropriate for a school board to establish a policy which sets out the procedures to be followed in conducting IPRCs and IPRC reviews. This will help to ensure consistency in the conduct of IPRCs across the school board. Items which can be included in a policy on IPRC procedures include the quorum for the IPRC where the number of committee members is greater than three; the forms to be used by all IPRCs and review IPRCs and the format of their meetings. *Special Education Monograph No. 2*, which was issued in October 1985, and is now dated in certain respects, still contains some sage advice.[36] It suggests, for example, that school boards design a form to record the IRPC's decision. This form should record at least the following information:[37]

- the name, date of birth and grade of the student;
- the names of the committee members present;

---

[35] O. Reg. 181/98, s. 22(2).
[36] At the time of this writing, the Ministry was in the process of updating the *Special Education Information Handbook* which would, in part, replace this dated document.
[37] Based, in part, on the requirements in O. Reg. 181/98, ss. 18 and 23.

- the names of the parent and their representatives, if any;
- the names of any other persons who present information on behalf of the parents;
- the names of all school board staff who present information or participate in the discussion;
- the names of any persons from outside the school board who present information or participate in the discussion;
- an outline of the strengths and needs of the student;
- the decision on identification, including the categories and definitions of any exceptionality identified by the committee;
- if the student is identified as exceptional, the decision on placement;
- if the student is to be placed in a special education class, the reasons for that decision;
- recommendations, if any, on special education programs and services.

In addition, in the case of a review IPRC, the form could include:

- where the decision is to change identification, the reasons for that decision;
- where the decision is to change placement, the reasons for that decision.

The school board may also determine in its policy dealing with IPRC procedures, the format for providing notice to parents and the procedures to be followed in sending out the notice. If parents in all areas of the school board are treated in the same manner, this may substantially reduce the possibility of a perception by some parents that they have been treated inequitably in comparison with other parents with whom they have compared notes. An exception exists, of course, for the parent who wishes to receive notices in braille or on audiotape.

The school board may also determine the procedures to be used by the IPRC in decision-making — *e.g.*, consensus, majority or unanimity. Any decision reached by the IPRC must be consistent with the school board's Special Education Plan.[38]

Beyond any procedures set out in the Regulation or mandated by the school board, each IPRC has an inherent power to determine its own processes. The exercise of this power must not result in conflict with those requirements imposed by the Regulation or by the school board, or with the basic tenets of fairness to the persons who are entitled to participate in the meetings. A fair opportunity must be given to the parents, the principal and teachers to provide information; however, the IPRC may direct any person, who in providing information has become repetitious, to move on to a new point. Moreover, if the tenor of the meeting becomes heated, the chair may recess the meeting for a few minutes or longer in order to allow emotions to subside. If a person presenting information becomes abusive and the person is not a necessary participant (the parent and the principal are both necessary participants), the person may be directed to leave the meeting. It is prudent, however, to warn the person first that if they do not change their

---

[38] O. Reg. 181/98, s. 12.

conduct, they will be asked to leave the meeting. If one of the necessary parties to the IPRC meeting becomes verbally abusive towards others, the committee may consider giving a warning to the person that the meeting will be adjourned unless the conduct which prompts the warning ceases. If the conduct continues, the IPRC chair may adjourn the meeting. In short, the IPRC is entitled to insist that all participants treat each other with respect and civility.

Notice

An effort should be made to set up IPRC meetings at a time most convenient to all parties. Through this process, participants will typically know the date of the meeting. Nevertheless, written notice of every IPRC meeting, including the date, time and place of the meeting, should be provided to any person who has a right to attend the meeting. In the case of the parents and student (if aged 16 or older), notice must be given at least 10 days in advance of the IPRC's meeting;[39] however, a parent may agree to an earlier meeting. A copy of the notice should also be given to the principal. In the case of a student transferring from a demonstration school, the superintendent of the demonstration school who initiated the process should be given notice, as well as the director of education of the school board to which the student is being transferred — *i.e.*, the school board which has established the IPRC. In the case of an IPRC review of a student to whom a special education program is being provided under a purchase of services agreement, the director of education of the purchasing board should be provided with notice.

There is no specified method of delivery of the notice and, accordingly, in addition to regular mail, the notice may be delivered personally, by courier or by facsimile. Electronic mail is also a possibility, although proof of delivery to the intended recipient may be troublesome; for this reason e-mail should be used only with caution.

If the notice is sent by mail, it will be deemed to be received by the person to whom it is addressed on the fifth day after the day on which it is mailed, unless the fifth day is a school holiday within the meaning of the regulation which defines school holidays; in this latter case, the date of deemed delivery will be the next day following which is not a school holiday.[40] The notice must be received by the parent 10 days in advance of the meeting date. Accordingly, if it is to be sent by mail, it must be sent by at least the fifteenth day preceding the day on which the meeting is to be held.

---

[39] *Ibid.*, s. 5(5).

[40] *Ibid.*, s. 3; *School Year Calendar*, R.R.O. 1990, Reg. 304, as currently written, defines "school holidays" to include the following: every Saturday and Sunday; Canada Day; Labour Day; Thanksgiving; the school break over Christmas and New Year's; March break, Good Friday, Easter Monday and Victoria Day. The summer vacation period is not designated by the Regulation as a school holiday. However, it was not likely the intent of the Ministry that the summer vacation period would be treated as other than a "school holiday" for the purposes of O. Reg. 181/98. Accordingly, until the matter is clarified by way of an amendment to the regulation, a school board should carefully consider the position it will take where a time limit expires during the summer vacation period.

The notice may indicate that the meeting may proceed in the absence of the addressee of the notice. For example, the letter setting out the notice of time, date and location of the IPRC meeting might include the statement: "Please note that the IPRC's meeting to discuss [student] may proceed in your absence should you not attend at the appointed time and place." However, the school board should demonstrate some flexibility in altering the date and time of the meeting if parents advise, after receiving the notice, that they cannot attend at the appointed date and time, particularly if the parents have not been consulted in setting the date and time for the meeting.[41]

Agenda

The IPRC is responsible for setting the agenda for each meeting. A meeting will normally start with a statement of welcome to the participants, introductions and a short statement of the purpose of the meeting. The matters which should be canvassed through the process include:

- the strengths and needs of the student;
- the definition or definitions of any exceptionalities which the student may have;
- placement.

The agenda should ensure that all of these matters are canvassed and that an opportunity is provided to the parents/student, if participating, to provide input into the discussion.

The agenda may also include a discussion of special education programs and services. Certainly, if a parent requests, there must be a discussion of special education services and programs and a school board may provide in a policy that such a discussion will be a regular part of each IPRC.[42] Alternatively, the IPRC of its own volition may decide to discuss and make recommendations regarding special education services and programs.[43]

Parent Representatives

Some parents and students over 16 years may wish to bring along a "representative" to IPRC meetings. They are specifically given the right to have a representative present at any IPRC discussions about the student, either to speak

---

[41] As a practical matter, where a parent misses the IPRC meeting which the parent wished to attend, the parent is not without recourse: the parent may request a meeting to discuss the decision (see "Parental Request to Discuss the IPRC's Decision", *infra*) or may refuse to consent to the placement decided by the IPRC in the parent's absence and initiate an appeal of the IPRC's decision (see Chapter 9). Alternatively, the parent may request a new IPRC meeting after three months have elapsed (see section entitled "Review of an Identified Student's Identification and Placement", *infra*). Accordingly, an IPRC may wish to adjourn a meeting which the parent fails to attend where it is known that the parent did wish to be present.

[42] O. Reg. 181/98, s. 16(1).

[43] *Ibid.*, s. 16(2).

on behalf of the parent/student or simply to be present to provide support.[44] Parents and students over 16 years also have a right to have a representative present to support them when the IPRC makes its decision. Where students are 16 years of age or older, they are entitled to their own representative, separate from any representative their parents might have.

The choice of who will act as the representative of the parents or student rests with the parents or student; their choice may include legal counsel, a representative of a parent advocacy group or a friend. The presence of counsel or a parent advocate can, on occasion, introduce a note of adversity to the process or otherwise impose a filter on direct dialogue between the committee members and the parents; however, at the same time, some parents can feel overwhelmed by the number and expertise of school board staff and believe that bringing legal counsel or a parent advocate will provide protection for them. Parents will be less likely to feel the need for protection provided by representatives if they are encouraged to feel that their views and information are respected as much as the views and information provided by school board staff. A genuinely respectful IPRC climate will go a long way to reduce parental perceptions that formal representation is necessary in order to be heard at an IPRC.

On the other hand, discouraging the attendance of persons on whom parents may feel dependent to ensure the enforcement of their rights can only serve to alienate the parents and create an atmosphere of distrust. It is wise, therefore, that any discussion with parents and students about the possible presence of representatives acknowledge the legal right to representation.

Adjournments

Generally, the date and time of an IPRC meeting will be set in consultation with parents. Where that is not possible, as much advance notice as possible should be provided to parents. After the notice of the IPRC meeting has been sent out, there may be occasions where either school staff or a parent may seek an adjournment of the meeting. Such requests may be made in advance of the IPRC meeting or at the meeting itself.

The request for an adjournment should be directed to the chair of the IPRC. Where school board policy so provides, decisions on adjournment requests may be made by the chair of the IPRC alone. In the absence of a school board policy which gives the chair the authority to decide adjournment requests, the IPRC may determine its own procedure and may assign to the chair the responsibility to make decisions on adjournment requests. Alternatively, all members of the IPRC should be involved.

Assuming that the request for adjournment is made in good faith and for legitimate reasons, the adjournment will normally be agreed to by the IPRC. However, if adjournment requests become excessive or agreement on a mutually acceptable meeting time is not forthcoming, then the IPRC may proceed to set a

---

[44] *Ibid.*, s. 5(3).

date and time which appears to be the most reasonable in the circumstances and to send notice, well in advance of the meeting, to all participants. In this situation, care should be taken *not* to set the meeting at a time and date on which it is known the parent will not be able to attend.

Closed Meetings

The question of whether an IPRC meeting should be "closed" only becomes an issue where persons other than those directly interested (*i.e.,* custodial parents, the student, school staff involved with the student and members of the IPRC) seek to attend the meeting. The issue may arise where a non-custodial parent seeks to attend and the custodial parent objects. While a non-custodial parent may have information to contribute to a meeting, he or she does not have the same rights as a custodial parent to be present throughout the IPRC's discussions.

The school board may set out procedural rules about who may or may not attend IPRC meetings, provided that the rights of persons who are entitled to attend are protected. Should the school board not establish any such rules, then the IPRC, itself, may determine who may and who may not attend a meeting.

The IPRC has the power to control its own process and may exclude any person from attending the meeting where it deems it appropriate to do so. Moreover, in light of the fact that the student's personal information will be disclosed during the meeting, the requirements of the *Municipal Freedom of Information and Protection of Privacy Act* would likely require the IPRC to exclude persons, other than school board staff, the parent and the student, from the meeting unless the parent (or student if aged 16 or older) consented to the presence of the person.

Information to be Considered

An IPRC which has received a referral is obliged to consider certain information in its deliberations.

The IPRC must obtain and consider an educational assessment of the student.[45] This assessment will normally be prepared by the student's teachers and any special education teachers who have worked with the student. In the case of a student who is just entering the school system from a program outside the school system, information should be obtained from the educators and staff involved in that program. Parental consent will usually be required before the program will release information.

The IPRC must consider any information about the student submitted to it by a parent or, where the student is 16 years of age or older, by the student. In addition, the IPRC must consider any other information which is provided to it which it considers to be relevant.[46] This includes any information provided by teachers,

---

[45]   O. Reg. 181/98, s. 15(1).

[46]   *Ibid.*, s. 15(7). Information is relevant if it is specific to the student and helps the IPRC to understand the student's strengths and needs. On occasion, parents may object to information on the basis that the information either is not relevant or is prejudicial — for example, information that a student with a behavioural exceptionality has engaged in

consultants and other school board personnel who have interactions with the student, as well as information from persons who have provided information to the IPRC at the suggestion of the parents. The IPRC is not limited to information which others choose to provide to it about the student; it may actively seek out any other information which it considers might be relevant,[47] subject only to obtaining any written consents which may be required (*e.g.*, as in the case of medical or psychological information).

While the IPRC may not have the power to compel attendance at its meetings by way of summons, the IPRC may invite the attendance of persons who may provide relevant information which might assist the IPRC in its deliberations. This will include any teachers, consultants and other professionals (*e.g.*, psychologists, speech and language pathologists, or occupational therapists) who have worked with the student. In the case of a student entering the school system for the first time, it may also include early childhood educators or others who have worked with the student up to that point in time. Such persons may decline to attend an IPRC meeting without parental consent and it is wise to secure parental agreement before inviting them.

The IPRC must "obtain and consider" a health assessment of the pupil by a qualified medical practitioner and/or a psychological assessment, if the IPRC is of the view that a health or psychological assessment is necessary in order to make a correct decision on identification or placement.[48] The IPRC may request that parents obtain the assessment from a doctor or psychologist who has been treating the student, or may suggest that the student be seen by a different doctor or psychologist.[49] However, this requirement is subject to parental consent and specifically makes the IPRC's obligation to obtain an assessment subject to the *Health Care Consent Act, 1996*.[50] This Act requires the consent of the student, if capable of understanding the nature of the assessment and the implication of the consent, and if not, the consent of the parent, to undergo the health assessment.[51]

---

violent conduct outside the school. The test of relevance will be whether the information relates to the pupil and assists in the determination of identification and/or placement. Where parents argue that information should not be considered or received because of its prejudicial effect, the IPRC must balance the degree of relevance of the information with the degree of the prejudice inherent in the information. If the information would be of minimal assistance only in making a decision on identification or placement, the IPRC may decide not to consider the information.

[47] *Ibid.*, s. 15.

[48] *Ibid.*, s. 15(2) and (3).

[49] While the Regulation is silent on the issue of who pays for the assessment, the requirement in s. 8(3) of the *Education Act* that special education services and programs will be made available without payment of fees, makes clear that the school board will be responsible to pay for any health or psychological assessments required by and provided to the IPRC. However, the school board would not be responsible to pay the costs of any assessments obtained by a parent for submission to the IPRC, in the absence of any request by the IPRC at the school.

[50] S.O. 1996, c. 2, Sch. A.

[51] O. Reg. 181/98, s. 4.

Consent to the disclosure of the assessment to the IPRC may be assumed where the parent agrees to co-operate in obtaining the assessment in the first instance, although the doctor/psychologist may require written consent of the parent (or adult student) prior to providing the assessment directly to the school board.

Where the student is under 16 years of age and the parents consent, the IPRC may interview the student. Parents have the right to be present during the interview. A student who is 16 years of age or older is entitled to attend and participate in IPRC meetings and, accordingly, the Regulation does not extend any "authority" to the IPRC to "interview" a student who is 16 years of age or older. Presumably, where a student aged 16 or over does attend an IPRC meeting, the IPRC may engage the student in discussion sufficient to obtain the information which the IPRC would obtain in an interview. The IPRC probably does not have the power to compel the student to attend, even if the student is 16 years of age or older. As a result, if the student refuses to attend, the IPRC would be obliged to forego this potentially valuable source of information.[52]

In a review case, any individual education plans ("IEPs") (see Chapter 7) which have been previously prepared for the student would seem an obvious and relevant source of information. However, the IPRC may consider the student's progress with reference to the student's IEP *only* with the written permission of a parent or the student, if the student is 16 years of age or older.[53] Where parents (or the student) withhold permission, the IPRC would still be able to consider student progress based on the reports of teachers, the principal and/or consultants.

The Ontario Student Record ("OSR") may also contain information relevant to the IPRC's deliberations, including report cards, testing results or, in the case of a student who is being referred in the anticipation of an identification of a "behavioural" exceptionality, records detailing conduct by the student which bear on the identification. The *Education Act* specifically limits access to information contained in the OSR to supervisory officers, the principal and teachers of the school attended by the student, and to the parents of a student under the age of 18 years, or the student, if 18 years or older, except where a parent or pupil who is of an age to control his or her own documents, consents to the disclosure.[54]

---

[52]   *Ibid.*, ss. 5 and 15(4) and (5).

[53]   *Ibid.*, s. 23(2).

[54]   *Education Act*, s. 266. This section, which provides that the right of the student to control his or her own information does not arise until the student is no longer a minor — *i.e.*, has reached age 18 (as per the *Age of Majority and Accountability Act*, R.S.O. 1990, c. A.7) — is not consistent with O. Reg. 181/98 and with the *Municipal Freedom of Information and Protection of Privacy Act* ("MFIPPA"). O. Reg. 181/98 accords students aged 16 the right to participate in the special education process. The MFIPPA designates 16 years as the age at which persons may exercise rights in respect of their personal information, which includes the contents of the OSR; this includes the right to consent to the disclosure of the information. Since s. 53 of the MFIPPA provides that the Act overrides the confidentiality provisions of any other Act, and s. 52 makes the Act applicable to every document in the custody of a school board, including the OSR, it is at least arguable that, where students aged 16 and 17 consent, OSR documents can be disclosed. However, the matter is not entirely clear since s. 266(2) of the *Education Act*

Accordingly, members of the IPRC who are supervisory officers, or the principal or teachers at the school attended by the student may have access to the documents in the OSR, but the provisions of the *Education Act* appear to preclude access by any other members of the IPRC, even if they are school board employees, unless written consent is given by a parent, or the pupil, if of an age to control his or her own OSR documents. Normally such consent will be readily forthcoming from parents and no issue will arise.

When an issue does arise with respect to the disclosure of OSR documents, it would appear that the MFIPPA provides a solution which permits the disclosure of documents to all IPRC members who are school board employees even if they are not teachers or the principal of the school attended by the student, or supervisory officers of the school board. The MFIPPA permits the disclosure of documents containing "personal information" (which includes OSR records) to employees of the school board who need the information in the performance of their duties where the disclosure of the information is "necessary and proper in the discharge of the [school board's] functions".[55] In permitting disclosure in these circumstances, the Act specifically overrides any statutory confidentiality provisions which otherwise apply to documents containing personal information.[56] As a consequence, it has been suggested that to the extent that the IPRC considers any OSR record to be relevant to its deliberations (excepting only the IEP which, as noted previously, cannot be considered by the IPRC without parental consent), all members of the IPRC who are employees of the school board may be able to access information from the OSR without requiring the consent of a parent/pupil.[57]

---

imposes a strict prohibition on the disclosure of OSR documents and specifically defines the limited circumstances in which OSR documents may be disclosed (see footnote 57, *infra*); those circumstances do not include the consent of a student aged 16 or 17 years. Accordingly, it is also arguable that parental consent is still a prerequisite to disclosure of any OSR documents of a 16 or 17-year-old student to persons other than the student's principal, teachers and supervisory officers. Indeed, it may be necessary to obtain the consent of both the parent and the student, if aged 16 or 17 years, to disclosure of OSR documents in such a case.

[55] MFIPPA, s. 32(d). The identification and placement of exceptional pupils falls within the "necessary and proper discharge" of a school board's functions.

[56] Section 52 of the MFIPPA makes the Act applicable to any record in the custody of a school board and s. 53 provides that the Act prevails over the "confidentiality" provisions in any other Act (a "confidentiality override"), unless that Act specifically provides otherwise. Since the *Education Act* does *not* provide otherwise, the confidentiality provisions of s. 266 of the *Education Act* in respect of the OSR are overridden and must be read subject to the MFIPPA.

[57] A countervailing argument might be made that the "confidentiality override" provisions of the MFIPPA do not override s. 266(2) of the *Education Act*. This section stipulates that OSR documents are "privileged" and that, without parental permission, OSR documents may only be used by supervisory officers and the principal or teachers of the school which the student attends, and are not admissible in any legal proceeding. The thrust of the argument is that s. 266(2) is not a "confidentiality" provision. However, this argument has been rejected by several arbitration boards which decided that the

In the event that any member of the IPRC is not an employee of the school board, written permission of the parent[58] (or student, if aged 18 years or older) must be obtained before this IPRC member may review an OSR record. Normally consent to disclosure will be readily provided so that no issue about OSR documents arises. However, if written consent is not forthcoming, the IPRC must decide whether the record must be considered in order to make its decision. If it is determined that the OSR record is necessary, the non-employee member of the IPRC will be obliged to refrain from participating for the remainder of the case. Similarly, it should also be noted that where a non-employee is attending the IPRC meeting — for example, a child care worker who has worked with the student — consent to disclosure of OSR documents or information from the documents should be obtained if such documents and/or information are to be discussed while these non-employees are present at the meeting. In the absence of consent, the non-employee should be asked to leave the meeting while information from OSR documents is being discussed.

Where the IPRC does obtain or receive information relating to the student, the chair of the IPRC must provide the information to the parent of the pupil and, if the student is 16 years of age or older, to the student "as soon as possible after the chair ... obtains [the] information".[59] This includes any information about the student provided to an individual member of the IPRC. (For example, a former teacher of the student may provide information about his or her experiences with the pupil to the chair of the IPRC.)

Before any steps are taken by the IPRC, or any school board employee on behalf of the IPRC, to collect information about the student, the requirements of the MFIPPA should be considered. This Act operates to limit the collection of information about a student to the following circumstances: where express authority has been given by the student's parent or by the student if aged 16 or older, where the collection has been expressly authorized by a statute, or where the collection is "necessary to the proper administration of a lawfully authorized activity".[60] Collection of information by the IPRC pursuant to s. 15 of O. Reg. 181/98[61] constitutes a collection under the authority of a statute. Beyond this, any information which the IPRC actively solicits outside an IPRC meeting from

---

"confidentiality override" provision of the MFIPPA does apply to the "privilege" provisions of s. 266 of the *Education Act* with the result that, where permitted by the MFIPPA, information and documents can be disclosed: *Hastings and Prince Edward District School Board and O.S.S.T.F., District 29 (Willock) (Re)* (2000), 62 C.L.A.S. 193 (P. Knopf); *Windsor Board of Education and O.S.S.T.F., District 1 (Re)* (unreported, June 12, 1995) (J.W. Samuels). (These arbitrations concerned teacher discipline grievances where production of OSR documents was sought.) The matter has not yet been considered by the courts.

[58]   *Education Act*, s. 266(2).

[59]   O. Reg. 181/98, s. 15(8) and (9).

[60]   MFIPPA, s. 28(2).

[61]   This section requires the IPRC to collect an educational assessment, and a health assessment or psychological assessment where in the judgment of the IPRC the assessment is necessary to make a determination on identification or placement.

persons not employed by the school board (*e.g.*, former teachers or professionals no longer employed by the school board who previously worked with the student), may be properly collected so long as the information is relevant to the identification or placement of the student and is necessary for the purpose of determining identification or placement.[62] Where the IPRC does collect information about the individual from sources outside the school board without the consent of the parent, or student if aged 16 or older, the MFIPPA requires the school board to send to the parent, or to the student if aged 16 or older, a written notice of the collection; this written notice must set out the legal authority for the collection,[63] the principal purpose for which the information will be used (*i.e.*, for the determination or review of identification and/or placement), and the title, business address and telephone number of the "employee of the institution" who can answer questions about the collection of the information.[64]

Record of the Proceedings

It is important for the IPRC to maintain a record of its proceedings. Should the parents appeal the IPRC's decision, it will be necessary to forward the record, together with a statement of its decision, to a Special Education Appeal Board ("SEAB").[65]

A record of the IPRC's proceedings will include any written documents generated by the IPRC. This will include the notice of the hearing, the agenda, any letter requesting a health or psychological assessment and the written statement of decision, together with copies of all documents which the IPRC has received. The notes of individual committee members do not form part of the record unless the member is charged with making the notes on behalf of the IPRC. Should the IPRC ask a secretary to attend and make notes for the committee, these notes would form part of the record.

The record will include any report, assessment or other document which is presented by any party or which the IPRC might request or obtain in the course of its deliberations with respect to a particular student. This includes any document which has been obtained from the OSR. It should be noted that while an SEAB will not be able to require that OSR records be produced without parental permission, or the permission of a student aged 18 years or older,[66] the SEAB will be entitled to receive copies of all documents which form part of the IPRC's record, including records and assessments from the OSR. It will be important, therefore, that school board staff ensure that all relevant documents from the OSR are produced to the

---

[62] The authority for collection in this case is O. Reg. 181/98, s. 10 (which requires school boards to establish IPRCs to make determinations on identification and placement of exceptional pupils).

[63] In the case of an IPRC's collection of information (see O. Reg. 181/98, s. 15) and in the case of a review committee (see s. 22).

[64] MFIPPA, s. 29(2). In the case of collection of information by the IPRC, this person would be the chair of the IPRC.

[65] O. Reg. 181/98, s. 27(6).

[66] See footnote 54.

IPRC before it reaches its decision so that a complete record has been compiled in the event of an appeal to a SEAB. If parents do not consent to the production of OSR documents before the IPRC, and OSR documents are not produced,[67] then the IPRC should, in its decision, carefully set out all information supplied by the teachers and principal which may include information from OSR documents.

A form such as that suggested under the heading "Procedures" can be used to keep track of the proceedings in each case. The easiest way to keep track of documents is to number them consecutively as they are received by the IPRC and to maintain a list of the documents, setting out a brief description of each document by its assigned number.

Electronic Recording of Meetings

Since no formal written record (such as a court transcript) of IPRC meetings is created, an issue which can arise in conducting an IPRC meeting is whether the meeting may be taped by any participant. While people like recordings as a way to ensure clarity as to what was said, some people view the issue of electronic recording as a violation of their privacy rights. To others, a request to electronically record a meeting suggests a degree of mistrust of the process. Many people prefer not to be electronically recorded and, as a result, the taping of the proceedings can inhibit full and frank discussion either because of natural reticence or because of a fear that taped comments might subsequently be played out of context or, worse, electronically altered.

The issue of whether IPRC meetings may be electronically recorded may be dealt with in a policy of the school board dealing with IPRC procedures. For example, the policy might permit the electronic recording of IPRC proceedings subject to defined conditions. Conditions might include the following: that all participants must first agree to be electronically recorded; that the process of electronically recording the meeting will not interfere with or interrupt the meeting; that the person who seeks to electronically record the meeting will be responsible for the cost of recording the meeting and will provide a copy of the electronic record to the IPRC (in which case the electronic record becomes part of the IPRC's record). If the school board decides that, generally, meetings should not be electronically recorded, it should make exceptions for certain circumstances. For example, where a parent has a disability which precludes him or her from making notes of the meeting, the parent might be permitted to audiotape the proceeding. Conditions similar to those set out above may be imposed in these circumstances, if appropriate.

Where the issue of electronically recording an IPRC meeting has not been dealt with in a school board policy, the matter is left to be determined by each IPRC on a case-by-case basis. In this situation, the IPRC has the authority to determine whether it will permit the electronic recording to occur or not. Each case will be different and the decision whether to permit the electronic recording should be

---

[67]   See under the heading "Information to be Considered", *supra*, for a discussion of the disclosure of OSR documents where parents do not consent.

made based on the circumstances of each individual case. Where the members of the IPRC themselves are not opposed to being electronically recorded, the IPRC may canvass the other participants to obtain their views on being electronically recorded. This input, while not required,[68] will allow the IPRC to consider, before it makes a decision on the issue, whether permitting the electronic recording of the meeting might generate a discomfort level for some participants which would inhibit their participation in the meeting and therefore undermine the IPRC process. Where the IPRC does permit a participant to electronically record the meeting, the IPRC may impose conditions, including a requirement that the IPRC be provided with a copy of the electronic recording or that the making of the recording must not disrupt the IPRC process.

As noted previously, there will be unusual circumstances where the IPRC should permit an electronic recording to be made of the meeting. Again, conditions may be imposed on the granting of the request to electronically record the meeting, even where unusual circumstances justify the request. One condition which should always be imposed is that the IPRC be given a copy of the electronic recording.

The IPRC's Decision

Parents and the student (if aged 16 or older) and their representatives are entitled to be present when the IPRC makes its decisions on identification and placement.[69] This right exists whether the IPRC is dealing with a student who has not been identified as exceptional; a student who is being transferred from a demonstration school; or with a review of a student's identification and/or placement.

The Supreme Court of Canada has made clear that the IPRC must ensure that its determinations are made "from a subjective, child-centred perspective, one which attempts to make equality meaningful from the child's point of view as opposed to that of the adults in his or her life".[70] In addition, an IPRC's decision must be consistent with the school board's Special Education Plan.[71]

---

[68] Ministry of Education, "Identification, Placement and Review Committees", *Special Education Monograph No. 2* (October, 1985), suggests that there is a legal risk to a chairperson to allow a person to tape record an IPRC meeting unless every person present gives written permission. It is the writers' view that this statement is not accurate since the IPRC does have authority over its own processes and there are no individual common law or statutory privacy rights which would override the IPRC's right to permit or even direct a meeting to be electronically recorded.

[69] O. Reg. 181/98, s. 5(1)(b).

[70] *Eaton v. Brant County Board of Education*, [1997] 1 S.C.R. 241 at p. 278, 142 D.L.R. (4th) 385, 31 O.R. (3d) 574n, 97 O.A.C. 161, 41 C.R.R. (2d) 240, 207 N.R. 171. The Special Education Appeal Board, the school board and the Special Education Tribunal are equally bound by this direction of the Supreme Court of Canada.

[71] O. Reg. 181/98, s. 12(2).

Identification and Placement

In the case of a student who has not been identified as exceptional, the IPRC's mandate is to decide, first, whether the student should be identified as exceptional. If the IPRC decides that the student is exceptional, it must then determine which category or definition of exceptionality as defined by the Minister of Education applies to the student.[72]

Once the student is identified as exceptional, the IPRC must determine what the placement of the student should be. In making this determination, the IPRC must first consider whether a placement in a regular class with appropriate special education services would "meet the pupil's needs" and be "consistent with parental preferences" before it considers the option of placement in a special education class.[73]

The IPRC *must* decide in favour of a regular class placement for the student if, after considering all the relevant information it has obtained, it is satisfied that placement in a regular class "would meet the pupil's needs and is consistent with parental preferences". This does not mean that the IPRC must decide in favour of special class placement if it is satisfied that a regular class placement would meet the student's needs but the student's parents prefer a special class placement. Nor is the IPRC bound to decide in favour of a regular class placement if it concludes that the student's needs could *not* be met there with appropriate special education services, while parental preference is for the regular class placement. However, an IPRC decision which does not reflect parental preferences should be made carefully, recognizing that the outcome of a decision which is not reflective of parental preferences may be appealed by the parents.

It is often difficult to separate placement from the special education services and programs which a student may require. The IPRC is permitted to discuss proposals for special education services and programs for the student and *must* discuss proposals for special education services and programs if the parent/student (aged 16 years or older) requests it to do so. However, while the IPRC may discuss special education services or programs, it may not make decisions about the services and programs to be provided; rather, it is limited to making recommendations which it will set out in its "statement of decision".[74]

Once the IPRC has reached its decision, the chair of the committee is obliged, "as soon as possible" to send a written statement of the decision to the parents of the student and to the student, if 16 years of age or older; to the principal who made the referral, if the referral was made by a principal; and to the director of education of the school board which established the IPRC.[75]

The IPRC's written statement of decision must indicate whether the student has been identified as an exceptional pupil and, if so, must include the following:

---

[72] *Ibid.*, s. 18. See Chapter 4, "Identification and Exceptionality".
[73] *Ibid.*, s. 17(1).
[74] *Ibid.*, s. 16.
[75] *Ibid.*, s. 18.

- a description of the student's strengths and needs as assessed by the committee;
- the categories and definitions of any exceptionalities identified by the committee, based on the categories and definitions established by the Minister of Education;
- the IPRC's decision on placement;
- the IPRC's recommendations, if any, on the special education services and programs which it would be appropriate to provide to the student;
- if the recommended placement includes placement in a special education class, the reasons for that decision.[76]

While not required, where the IPRC's decision does not accord with parental preferences, it may be wise for the IPRC to record the reasons for its disagreement with the parents' wishes. This will provide parents with written insight on the IPRC's reasoning and will also make clear that consideration has been given to the parents' views.

Student Transferred from a Demonstration School

Where the IPRC is considering a student who is being transferred from a demonstration school, there will be no need to make a determination that the student is exceptional in the first instance, since the student will already have been identified. The IPRC is still obliged to consider the categories and definitions of exceptionality which apply to the pupil. However, the main focus of the IPRC's deliberations will be on placement.

As in the case of a student who has not been previously identified, when considering placement for a student transferred from a demonstration school, the IPRC must first consider the option of placement in a regular class with appropriate special education services. Again, only where the IPRC concludes that such a placement would not meet the student's needs, or where the parents would prefer a special education class placement, may the IPRC consider a placement other than the regular class.[77]

When the IPRC has reached its decision, the chair of the committee is obliged, "as soon as possible" to send a written statement of the decision to the parents of the student and to the student, if 16 years of age or older, and to the director of education of the school board which established the IPRC.[78]

The written statement must include the same points listed under the heading "Identification and Placement", above, which the IPRC must address where the student is already enrolled with the school board.[79]

---

[76] *Ibid.*
[77] *Ibid.*, s. 17.
[78] *Ibid.*, s. 18.
[79] *Ibid.*

Review of an Identified Student's Identification and Placement

Where the IPRC is charged with reviewing the identification or placement of an identified exceptional pupil, the committee must decide whether it is satisfied with the identification and placement of the student or whether either or both should be changed.[80]

When reviewing placement, if the student is in a regular class placement and the IPRC wishes to consider the option of special class placement, it must first determine that the regular class placement, with appropriate special education services support, is *not* meeting the student's needs and must also consider the parents' views on the student's placement.[81]

Where the IPRC determines, upon review, that it is satisfied with the identification and placement, it is required "as soon as possible" to send a written statement of confirmation of the student's identification and placement to a parent of the student and to the student, if aged 16 or older; to the principal of the school where the pupil's special education program is being provided; to the director of education of the school board which is providing the special education program; and, in the case where the special education program is being purchased by another board, to the director of education of the purchasing board.[82]

Where the IPRC decides that identification or placement or both should be changed, it is required, "as soon as possible", to provide written notification to the same individuals listed above. In this case, however, the written statement must also set out the following:

- whether the committee considers that the student should continue to be identified as an exceptional pupil and if not, the reasons for this determination;
- if the committee considers that the student should continue to be identified as exceptional, the written statement must set out the following:
  - the committee's description of the student's strengths and needs;
  - the categories and definitions of any exceptionalities identified by the committee, and, if these are changed from the prior identification, the reasons for the changed determination;
  - the committee's decision on placement and, if this represents a change from the prior placement, the reasons for the changed placement;
  - if the placement includes a special class placement, the reasons for this placement, whether or not this represents a change of placement.[83]

---

[80]   *Ibid.*, s. 23.
[81]   *Ibid.*, s. 23(6).
[82]   *Ibid.*, s. 23(3).
[83]   *Ibid.*, s. 23(4) and (5).

Recommendation that a Student Aged 21 Years or Older Remain in School

A "resident pupil" is entitled to attend an elementary school without payment of fees until the student reaches 21 years of age[84] and, where the student has completed elementary school, the student may attend secondary school without payment of fees for seven or more years.[85] Section 49.2 of the *Education Act* permits a school board to direct a student in certain circumstances to enrol in a continuing education course or class operated by the school board. Students who are subject to this direction are those who have attended one or more secondary schools for seven or more years, or who have not attended school for four or more years after the end of the calendar year in which they turned 16, or who are going to reach the age of 21 years of age by December 31st in the school year.[86] This provision will not apply to an "exceptional pupil" where an IPRC recommends to a school board that an "exceptional pupil" who is 21 years of age or older remain in a secondary day program.[87] Such students are exempted from the application of s. 49.2. Should the IPRC decline to make such a recommendation, there is no right of appeal.

PARENTAL REQUEST TO DISCUSS THE IPRC'S DECISION

Once the IPRC has rendered its decision and advised the parents of the decision in writing, the parents may request a meeting with the IPRC to discuss the decision. This request must be in writing and must be delivered to the principal (or the director of education if the student is coming from a demonstration school) within 15 days of the day on which the parent receives the IPRC's statement of decision, or confirmation of identification and placement, in the case of a review.[88] If the fifteenth day is a school holiday as defined in Regulation 304, *School Year Calendar*, then the time limit will be extended on a day-by-day basis to the next day which is not a school holiday. If the statement of decision or confirmation is sent by ordinary mail to the parent, the parent is deemed to have received the statement on the fifth day following the date of mailing (or, if the fifth day is a school holiday, the next day which is not a school holiday) and the 15 days starts to run from that date.[89] Otherwise, the time frame for the parent's request starts to run on the actual date of delivery of the statement of decision or confirmation. It is important, therefore, that a record be kept of the manner of delivery of the

---

[84] *Education Act*, ss. 32 and 33.

[85] *Ibid.*, s. 38.

[86] *Ibid.*, s. 49.2(1) and (2) and *Student Focused Funding — Legislative Grants for the 2000/2001 School Board Fiscal Year*, O. Reg. 170/00, s. 3(3).

[87] O. Reg. 181/98, s. 16(3).

[88] *Ibid.*, ss. 19 and 24.

[89] *Ibid.*, s. 3.

statement of decision or confirmation and the date it is either mailed or actually delivered.

In the case of a referral of a student to the IPRC by a principal, the parent's request must be delivered to the principal. In the case of the transfer of a student from a demonstration school, the request must be forwarded to the director of education of the school board to which the student is being transferred.[90] In the case of a review of identification and/or placement, the parent's request to discuss the IPRC's decision must be sent to the principal of the school at which the student's special education program is provided.[91]

While an IPRC may refuse to deal with a request to discuss a statement of decision or confirmation which is received after the time limit has expired, an IPRC is not precluded from meeting with the parents to discuss a statement of decision or confirmation where the request to do so is received out of time. Indeed, doing so might assist in avoiding an appeal by the parents. However, if an IPRC or a school board decides that the IPRC will accept late requests to discuss statements of decision or confirmation, guidelines should be established to determine the circumstances in which this will occur in order to ensure consistency in dealing with parents. For example, a late request might be accepted where the parent is able to establish to the satisfaction of the school board that the post office delivered the statement more than five days after it was mailed, or where an exceptional circumstance precluded the parent from forwarding the request in a timely manner (*e.g.*, this might include a death or serious illness in the family or absence of the family due to vacation). Where the IPRC does decide that it will meet with parents who have made a request outside the statutory time lines, the IPRC should set out in writing that it is agreeing to meet with the parents "without prejudice" to the fact that the parents did not request the meeting within the required time lines. This will make clear that the IPRC is not waiving the statutory time lines should the parents subsequently attempt to appeal, relying on the fact that the IPRC did meet with them despite the late request.

Upon receipt of the request, the principal or director of education, as the case may be, must arrange for the IPRC to meet "as soon as possible" with the parent. If the student, aged 16 or older, wishes to attend then the student must be included in the meeting. The principal or director of education should also be included in the meeting.[92]

Following the meeting between the IPRC and the parent (and the student if aged 16 or older), the chair of the IPRC must, "as soon as possible", send a written notice to each of the individuals who were originally entitled to receive a copy of the statement of decision or confirmation. The notice must state whether the IPRC has made any changes to its decision as a result of the meeting. If the IPRC has decided to make changes, it must reissue the statement of decision or confirmation

---

[90]   *Ibid.*, s. 19.
[91]   *Ibid.*, s. 24.
[92]   *Ibid.*, ss. 19 and 24.

and set out written reasons for the changes. The reissued statement and written reasons must be sent out with the notice of changes.[93]

TRANSITION

Where a student who is not in a special education placement has been referred to an IPRC for a determination on identification, the pupil must be provided with a program which is appropriate to the pupil's apparent strengths and needs, together with appropriate special education services, pending the IPRC's decision. Unless the student's needs cannot be met in the regular class with appropriate special education services, the program must be provided in the regular class.[94] Similarly, a student transferring from another school board who was identified while enrolled with the other school board, must be provided with an appropriate program and appropriate special education services pending a meeting with an IPRC of the new school board. Again, where appropriate special education services would permit the student's needs to be met in a regular class, this interim placement will be appropriate and should be provided where regular class is the parent's preferred placement.

IMPLEMENTATION OF THE DECISION

Where an IPRC has made a placement decision, the school board may not implement the placement unless the parent of the student consents in writing to the placement or the time period for the filing of a notice of appeal to an SEAB has expired without a notice of appeal being filed. However, upon parental consent being given or the time limit for appeal expiring without any notice of appeal being filed, the placement must be implemented "as soon as possible".[95]

Where the school board implements a placement decision of an IPRC without written consent of the parents (*i.e.*, after the expiry of the time period for filing an appeal), the school board must give written notice of the implementation to a parent of the pupil.[96]

The prohibition on changing a student's placement, except where the parent has consented or the time to appeal the IPRC's decision has elapsed, can prove to be troublesome for the party — whether the parent or the school board — who holds a strong belief that the existing placement is not in the student's best interests. The placement in place at the point an appeal is launched is effectively "stayed" pending completion of the appeal process — that is, it cannot be changed pending the completion of the appeal without the consent of the parent, unless the appeal is

---

[93]   *Ibid.*
[94]   *Ibid.*, s. 9.
[95]   *Ibid.*, ss. 20(1) and (2); 25(1) and (2).
[96]   *Ibid.*, ss. 20(3) and 25(3).

abandoned. An additional problem can arise where the stay is still in place at the point the student is eligible to be promoted from Grade 8 to Grade 9. Secondary schools are very different places from elementary schools and often the same special programs are offered in a very different manner in secondary schools than in elementary schools. It should be noted, first, that the stay of placement does not prevent promotion of the student from one grade to another. This may mean that, of necessity, the placement will have to be changed in some respects, but the school board is obliged to attempt to ensure that the placement in the new grade will be as close as possible to the "stayed" placement.

Where an appeal is launched which results in a stay of placement, the best solution will be for the school board and the parent to attempt to reach agreement on a temporary interim placement pending the completion of the appeal. Such agreement might be "without prejudice" to the position taken by either party in the appeal.

7

The Individual Education Plan

INTRODUCTION

An Individual Education Plan ("IEP") is a written plan setting out the educational goals and expectations, the special education programs and services to be provided to a student who has been identified as exceptional, and the methods by which the student's progress will be assessed.[1]

Prior to 1998, there was no specific legislative stipulation of what an IEP must contain, beyond the reference to such a plan in the definition of "special education programs":

> "special education program" means, in respect of an exceptional pupil, an educational program that is based on and modified by the results of continuous assessment and evaluation *and that includes a plan containing specific objectives and an outline of educational services that meets the needs of the exceptional pupil*".[2]

In 1998, further requirements for the IEP were spelled out in s. 6(3) of O. Reg. 181/98:

> The individual education plan must include,
> - (a) specific educational expectations for the pupil;
> - (b) an outline of the special education program and services to be received by the pupil; and
> - (c) a statement of the methods by which the pupil's progress will be reviewed.

The regulation also requires that for exceptional students aged 14 years or older (excepting gifted students), that the IEP include "a plan for transition to appropriate post-secondary school activities, such as work, further education and community living".[3]

In addition, the Ministry of Education has now developed several special education resource documents for the IEP which school boards are required to comply with in developing IEPs. In 1998, the Ministry released its *Individual Education Plan Resource Guide* which is, as the name implies, intended as a guide

---

[1] *Identification and Placement of Exceptional Pupils*, O. Reg. 181/98, s. 6(3).

[2] *Education Act*, R.S.O. 1990, c. E.2 (as amended), s. 1(1) (emphasis added).

[3] O. Reg. 181/98, s. 6(4).

only. In 2000, the Ministry released its *Individual Education Plans: Standards for Development, Program Planning, and Implementation* (the "*IEP Standards*") which sets out the Ministry's current policy on IEPs which the Ministry apparently intends school boards to comply with (at the time of writing, however, there was no regulatory authority enforcing such compliance).[4] The requirements which the *IEP Standards* impose in the creation of IEPs are quite detailed and, therefore, in this chapter we will include only a brief summary of the most important requirements. Educators who are charged with the responsibility of developing IEPs should have reference to both these Ministry documents.

The Ministry has indicated that it will conduct a review of IEPs from randomly selected school boards to assess compliance with the articulated standards.[5] School boards whose IEPs do not comply with the provincial standards will be required to amend their practices.[6]

This chapter will review the requirements of IEPs imposed by the regulations and Ministry policies.

MANDATORY INDIVIDUAL EDUCATION PLANS

An IEP must be developed for a student who has been identified as exceptional when the placement decision is implemented. This is so whether the placement decision is that of an Identification, Placement and Review Committee (IPRC) (either in the first instance or upon a review of placement), or of the school board following a recommendation from a Special Education Appeal Board or of a decision of the Special Education Tribunal.

In any of these cases, the school board is required to "promptly" notify the principal of the school where the student's special education program is to be provided of the need to develop an IEP for the student. The principal is charged with the responsibility of ensuring that the IEP is developed and that it is done in consultation with the parent and, where the student is aged 16 years or older, with the student.[7]

There are circumstances, which will be discussed under the heading "Optional Individual Education Plans", in which an IEP may be developed for a student who has not been identified as exceptional. However, where a school board wishes to claim extra funding in the form of an Intensive Support Amount ("ISA" funding), relating to the needs of a student who has not been identified but who is receiving

---

[4] Both of these documents are available on the Ministry's website: www.edu.gov.on.ca.

[5] At the time of writing, it was anticipated that the reviews would begin in the Spring of 2001 and would be repeated annually.

[6] *IEP Standards*, at pp. 1-2. A copy of the Board's IEP form must be included in the Board's special education plan and the Minister is authorized to require a board to amend its special education plan as the Minister determines necessary. (Ministry of Education, *Standards for School Board's Special Education Plans, 2000*; *Special Education Programs and Services*, R.R.O. 1990, Reg. 306, s. 2(5).)

[7] O. Reg. 181/98, s. 6(2).

special education programs and services, an IEP must be developed for the student.[8]

OPTIONAL INDIVIDUAL EDUCATION PLANS

IEPs can also be developed for students who are receiving special education programs or services, but who have not been formally identified and for whom no additional funding is sought. In fact, many school boards in Ontario develop IEPs to guide the special education programs and services for large numbers of students who have special needs, but who have never undergone a formal IPRC process.

DEVELOPMENT PROCESS

Legal Responsibility

The development of the IEP and its compliance with provincial standards are the principal's responsibility, just as it is the principal's responsibility to establish and maintain all student records.[9] Therefore, the principal has the authority to decide what should be included in the IEP; however, this is subject to the requirements set out in the legislation and Ministry policy.

A principal may designate a vice-principal or teacher to act on his or her behalf in coordinating and overseeing the development of the IEP. However, the ultimate responsibility for the IEP will remain with the principal. As a result, the principal is required to provide his or her assurance that the IEP is appropriate to the student's strengths and needs and meets the requirements of the *IEP Standards* by signing the IEP.[10]

Development Team

The "team" which will develop an IEP will be designated by the principal and, in addition to the principal (or vice-principal) may include the student's teachers, special education consultants and other professionals who work with the student.

---

[8] Ministry of Education, *2000-2001 Resource Manual for the Special Education Grant Intensive Support Amount (ISA): Guidelines for School Boards*, p. 26 (the page reference is from the online version); *Student Focussed Funding — Legislative Grants, 2000-2001*, O. Reg. 170/00. ISA funding is based on claims submitted for individual pupils. Claims may be for the purchase of specialized equipment for the student's needs. Claims may also be made for a "special incidence portion" (*e.g.*, payment for the assistance of an educational assistant as additional staff support in the classroom in which the student is placed). Although ISA grants are applied for based on individual student claims, the ISA amounts are paid to the school board as part of its total "special education allocation": see O. Reg. 170/00, s. 14.

[9] *IEP Standards*, pp. 19-20 and *Education Act*, s. 265(d).

[10] *Ibid.*, p. 19.

All school board team members who are involved in the development of the IEP must be identified in it. Collectively, they must have knowledge of the Ontario curriculum, of the student and, where possible, experience teaching the student, have knowledge of the special education strategies and resources available in the school board, and be qualified to provide or supervise the provision of special education programs and services to meet the needs of the student.[11]

Information

The *IEP Standards* impose on the principal an obligation to ensure that information from a variety of sources is considered in developing a student's IEP. This will include information in the OSR (including report cards and past IEPs), classroom observation, current work of the student, information from the student, the parent, school and board staff who have worked with the student and, where the parent consents (or freedom of information legislation permits) from outside professionals and paraprofessionals who have done assessments, performed diagnostic tests or otherwise worked with the student. The IEP must include a list of the information sources used in its development and updating.[12]

Consultation

In developing the IEP, the principal is required to consult with the parent and with the student (in the case of a student who is 16 years of age or older). In the case of a student for whom a transition plan is required,[13] the principal must also consult with such community agencies and post-secondary institutions as the principal considers appropriate in the process of completing the transition plan portion of the IEP.[14]

Parent and Student

In the case of the identification of the student in the first instance or in the case of a review situation where there is likely to be a disagreement over placement, the principal's consultation with the parent (and student, if aged 16 or older) will normally take place following the IPRC process. Where the placement is a continuing one and there is ongoing agreement on the student's special education program and the special education services to be provided to the student, the consultation process is likely to be much more informal and may even be part of the "pre-IPRC" process of discussion between the school and the parents.

Since the principal has a legal duty to consult when developing a student's IEP, the principal should, during the process of developing the plan, seek input from parents and students (over the age of 16 years) and give fair consideration to any

---

[11] *Ibid.*, pp. 18 to 19.

[12] *Ibid.*, pp. 13 and 20.

[13] A transition plan is required for any student who is 14 years of age or older, except in the case of a student who is identified solely as gifted.

[14] O. Reg. 181/98, s. 6(7).

suggestions made by the parent/student. While consultation is not defined, the presentation to a parent of an IEP for approval, in what appears to be a full and final form, might not be perceived by the parent to be consultation, particularly if the principal declines to make any changes to the IEP after the parent/student has reviewed the form. This does not mean that the principal is obliged to accept every suggestion which the parent/student provides. Indeed, the principal may decide to incorporate none of the parent/student suggestions into the IEP. However, in doing so, the principal must give due consideration to what the parent/student has had to say during the consultation process and the principal should have a legitimate reason for dismissing all parental/student suggestions which are not used. In this case it is prudent for the principal to ensure that his or her reasons have been clearly communicated to the parents/student. An open discussion and exchange of ideas will provide at least an opportunity for parents/students to feel that they have been consulted, even if the principal does not agree with all of their ideas.

Transition Plans

For exceptional students who are 14 years of age or older, other than those students identified as exceptional solely on the basis of giftedness, the IEP must include a plan for the transition of the student to "appropriate post-secondary school activities, such as work, further education or community living". The principal is required to "consult with such community agencies and post-secondary educational institutions as he or she considers appropriate".[15]

Documentation of Consultations

The IEP must include a form documenting the date and the outcome of each consultation.[16] The parent and student (if aged 16 or older) must be asked to sign the form and to indicate whether they were consulted in the development of the IEP, whether they declined the opportunity to be consulted and whether they received a copy of the IEP. Any comments they provide must be noted on the form.[17]

IPRC and Special Education Tribunal Recommendations

In developing the IEP, the principal is required to take into consideration any recommendations of the IPRC or Special Education Tribunal regarding special education programs or services.[18]

---

[15] *Ibid.*, s. 6(4), (5) and (7).
[16] *IEP Standards*, at p. 17.
[17] *Ibid.*
[18] *Ibid.*, pp. 11 and 19.

CONTENTS OF THE IEP

The contents of the IEP are dictated generally by s. 6(3) of O. Reg. 181/98 and in detail by the *IEP Standards.*

Generally, the IEP must include:

(a) a statement of the specific educational expectations for the pupil;

(b) an outline of the special education program and services to be received by the pupil; and

(c) a statement of the methods by which the pupil's progress will be reviewed.

As noted previously, the regulation also requires that where the student is 14 years of age or older, except in the case of a student who is identified solely as gifted, the IEP "must include a plan for transition to appropriate post-secondary school activities, such as work, further education and community living".[19] There is much additional information that must be included in order to meet the provincial standards,[20] which we have summarized below. [21]

1. **Reason for developing an IEP:** The IEP must state the reason it is being created (*e.g.,* because the student was identified as exceptional, or to support an ISA funding claim, or because the unidentified student requires special education programs or services).

2. **Student Profile:** The student's basic profile will include the student's full name, gender, date of birth, student identification number, current school year, name of the school and principal, date of the student's most recent IPRC and the student's exceptionalities.

3. **The Student's Strengths and Needs**: The IEP must include a description of the strengths and needs of the student. Where the student has been identified by the IPRC, this description must be based on the description of strengths and needs provided by the IPRC. Where the student has not been identified, the description of strengths and needs must be based on appropriate educational, psychological and/or health assessments, as well as by observing the student.

4. **The Special Education Program:** Where a student is working on unmodified provincial curriculum expectations at the regular grade level, the IEP need not set out the student's learning expectations. In this case, the IEP will indicate that fact and will set out the student's current level of achievement. In other cases, a student's program will include three components: an assessment of the

---

[19] O. Reg. 181/98, s. 6(4) and (5).

[20] See the *IEP Standards* at p. 5 for a full outline of the information which must be included.

[21] The summary is taken from the *IEP Standards.* The list which follows is not intended to be exhaustive. Other IEP requirements arising from the *IEP Standards* are mentioned elsewhere in this chapter. Please see the *IEP Standards* for the full list of requirements.

student's current level of achievement; annual goals for the student; and the learning expectations that meet the unique educational needs of the student.

If the student is working on learning expectations which are alternative to the provincial curriculum, the student's level of achievement will be based on a description of progress towards those learning expectations. If the student's learning expectations are based on modifications to the provincial curriculum, the student's level of achievement will be based on the letter grade or mark as reported on the student's Provincial Report Card.

Where the student's learning expectations are modified from the provincial curriculum in any respect or are alternative expectations, the IEP must set out annual goals for the student based on what the student can reasonably be expected to achieve by school year end. Similarly, where the student is working on modified expectations or alternative expectations, the IEP must set out learning expectations that describe the specific knowledge and skills the student will be expected to demonstrate during the school year in order to progress from the student's current level of achievement to achieve the annual goals.

5. **Special Education Strategies, Accommodations and Resources:** The IEP must set out the individualized teaching strategies, individualized accommodations and resources which will be provided to facilitate the student's learning. This includes an identification of teaching staff and non-teaching staff (including professional and paraprofessional special education support staff) who will be working with the student, the services which will be provided and the frequency of contact with the student. Individualized equipment to be used with the student must also be set out in the IEP.

6. **Assessment, Evaluation and Reporting**: The IEP must describe the methods that will be used to measure the student's achievement, including any accommodations made to regular classroom assessment procedures for the student (*e.g.,* administering tests individually or providing additional time to complete assignments.) Since the progress of exceptional students must be reported to parents with the same frequency as other students, the IEP must indicate the dates on which evaluations will be completed (at least once every reporting period) and the format to be used to report student progress to parents.

7. **Provincial Assessments:** The IEP must set out the testing accommodations which the student will be provided with to facilitate the student's participation in provincial assessments of student achievement. However, any such accommodations cannot impact the level or content of the assessment, performance criteria of the assessment or the reliability or validity of the assessment. Moreover, accommodations must comply with policies of the Education Quality and Accountability Office ("EQAO") and the Ministry of Education. In those rare cases where it is determined that a provincial assessment is not appropriate for the student, the IEP must include a statement

explaining the reasons for this and identify the applicable Ministry or EQAO policy under which the exemption arises.

8. **Transition Plan:** As has been noted, for identified students (other than those students identified solely as gifted) aged 14 years or older, the IEP must include a transition plan which identifies the student's transition from school into post-secondary activities that are appropriate for the student. Such activities include "work, further education and community living". The plan must set out goals for the transition which are specific, realistic and build on the student's identified strengths, needs and interests. Persons involved in providing assistance in the transition process must be identified and timelines must be included.

TIMELINES FOR COMPLETION OF THE IEP

The IEP must be completed within 30 days of the student's placement in a special education program.[22] The *IEP Standards* say that for this purpose, "placement" means "one of the following":

- the first day of attendance in a new special education program (whether specified in an IPRC decision or provided by the school board without formal identification);
- the first day of a new school year or semester in which the student continues in a placement confirmed by an IPRC review;
- the first day of enrolment in a special education program resulting from a change of placement.[23]

The *IEP Standards* do not address timelines for an IEP required because of a change of identification, although if the change of identification involves a new placement, then an IEP will be required.

Both the date on which the student begins the placement and the date on which the IEP is completed must be recorded in the IEP. A copy must be sent to the parent of the student and to the student (if aged 16 years or older).[24]

REVIEW

The IEP must be reviewed by the principal in order to determine whether it should be updated each time there is a change in placement and each time an existing placement is confirmed through the regular review process or through an appeal.[25] However, the *IEP Standards* impose a much more detailed process of

---

[22] O. Reg. 181/98, ss. 6(8) and 7(7).
[23] *IEP Standards*, see section 12, "Date of Completion of the IEP, at pp. 20-21".
[24] O. Reg. 181/98, ss. 6(8) and 7(7).
[25] *Ibid.*, s. 7(1) and (2).

monitoring which requires the assigned staff member to develop and implement the IEP in carrying out certain coordination activities. This includes establishing a plan for evaluating and monitoring the progress made by the student in achieving the learning expectations set out in the IEP.[26]

Where, through the process of regular evaluation and monitoring, it is identified that adjustments are needed in the student's special education program, either because the student is not progressing towards his or her goals or is exceeding the learning expectations identified in the IEP, the IEP must be adjusted. Where these adjustments require significant changes to the learning expectations set out in the IEP, the parent and student, if aged 16 years or older, must be consulted prior to the changes being made.[27]

ONTARIO STUDENT RECORD

The IEP is to be kept in the Ontario Student Record unless the parent of the student has objected in writing.

---

[26] *IEP Standards*, p. 22.
[27] *Ibid.*, p. 23.

8
Mediation

Mediation is assuming an increasingly central role in the special education appeal process. In this chapter, we have discussed some advantages of mediation — both in general and, more specifically, in the special education context.

SOME ADVANTAGES OF MEDIATION

It is now widely recognized that the litigation process is fundamentally ill-suited for achieving a lasting and mutually satisfactory resolution of many kinds of disputes.

Because of its adversarial nature, litigation can cause or exacerbate animosity between the parties. This can be very harmful where the parties need to maintain an ongoing relationship.

Litigation also focuses almost exclusively on the enforcement of legal rights. Some types of disputes, although framed in terms of competing legal rights, have more to do with emotional reactions, personal interests, relationship issues, value judgments, broader policy considerations and other factors. Although litigation provides a forum for the parties to determine their respective legal rights, it often results in "winner takes all" outcomes which do not address these deeper concerns. Accordingly, litigation can sometimes result in "lose-lose" situations where even the party who "wins" will not be truly satisfied with the outcome of the proceedings.

Moreover, litigation is a time-consuming and expensive process. Parties who expend considerable time and resources seeking a determination of their legal rights, only to find that the end result does not really address the interests which led them to commence the litigation, often feel that they have "lost" more than they have "won" through the litigation process.

Mediation is a process whereby the parties to a dispute enlist an experienced third party to assist them to resolve outstanding issues without the necessity for litigation. Through mediation, the parties are encouraged and assisted to focus less on the enforcement of legal rights, and more on identifying and addressing the interests underlying the dispute. From the perspective of the parties, the goal of the process is to find a "win-win" resolution which (where necessary or desirable) will preserve their relationship.

Mediation is a very low-risk method of dispute resolution. The process is entirely voluntary and consensual.[1] The mediator cannot make decisions that are binding on the parties.[2] In the vast majority of cases, the parties and the mediator will enter into an agreement protecting matters discussed in the mediation from disclosure in the event the matter proceeds to litigation. Mediation gives the parties the opportunity to work together, with the mediator, to reach a resolution of the dispute themselves — an opportunity which may not be available if formal litigation ensues. As a result, participants usually have very little to lose, and a great deal to gain, by agreeing to mediation.

Mediation is also an extremely flexible method of dispute resolution. Mediation provides the parties with an opportunity to be creative in finding a resolution to their dispute. The parameters of the resolution are not limited by the possible outcomes of litigation but only by the imagination of the parties. Mediation can take place at any time — before proceedings are commenced, after proceedings are commenced but before a hearing begins, or at any time up to the release of the final decision by the decision-maker.[3]

Finally, mediation is usually less time-consuming and less expensive than formal litigation. In most contexts, the cost of the mediation is split equally between the parties. In contrast, in special education mediations, school boards usually pay 100% of the fees of the mediator. If the mediation is lengthy, these costs can be significant. However, the time and expense associated with mediation will usually still be less than the time and expense associated with formal litigation — and, if the mediation results in a settlement, the results will usually be more palatable to all concerned.

MEDIATION AND SPECIAL EDUCATION

Special education disputes involve both ongoing relationships and a wide range of "non-legal" issues. As a result, these disputes are often very difficult to resolve "successfully" through formal litigation.

---

[1] It is widely recognized that mediation is unlikely to be successful unless the parties agree to mediation and accept the involvement and assistance of the mediator. Accordingly, mediation is generally only attempted where all the parties to a dispute agree to participate.

[2] The parties may decide to give the mediator the power to make binding decisions. In such a case, the mediation is usually called "mediation-arbitration" (commonly referred to as "med-arb") and the mediator is more properly referred to as a "mediator-arbitrator".

[3] Notably, a school board's decision in response to a recommendation by the Special Education Appeal Board (SEAB) is not considered a "final" decision because it can be appealed to the Special Education Tribunal. As a result, mediation can usefully occur after this decision has been made.

The home-school/parent-teacher relationship is fundamental to the special education process. A positive and co-operative relationship between the student, his or her parents, school board personnel and school staff is an essential component of a successful educational experience for a student with special needs. Both school boards and parents should give careful consideration to the impact which litigation may have on this relationship — and on the educational and emotional well-being of the student.

Special education disputes also cannot and should not be viewed merely as contests between competing legal rights. Rather, these disputes usually occur when the parents and school officials have conflicting views about the educational approach which will best serve the student's special needs. Differing medical diagnoses, pedagogical theories, religious or social values and perceptions of events often underlie disputes between parents and school officials about the appropriateness of identification and/or placement decisions. The kind of "all or nothing" outcomes generated by litigation will usually do little to resolve these differing views. As a result, even where one party "wins" the litigation, ongoing disputes may occur about the implementation of the decision.

In light of these considerations, it is not surprising that mediation of special education disputes is becoming increasingly popular with parents and school boards alike. Mediation can occur at any point in the special education decision-making process. It can take place even before the parents have appealed to the Special Education Tribunal, on the understanding that the parents can still appeal if mediation is not successful. However, to date, it has been more common for the parties to wait until an appeal has been filed with the Tribunal before exploring the prospect of mediation. While an appeal to the Tribunal is pending, the school board retains the right to change its decision on identification and/or placement in accordance with an agreement with the parents.[4] This gives the parties an incentive to engage in ongoing efforts to resolve their differences and thereby avoid the need for a hearing before the Tribunal. Mediation is widely perceived as a very valuable tool to assist the parties in achieving this end.

Mediation is also encouraged in appropriate cases by the Special Education Tribunal. When an appeal is filed with the secretary of the Special Education Tribunal, the secretary will inquire whether the parties are interested in mediation before scheduling a hearing date. Although the secretary will make this inquiry, the parties are under no obligation to agree to mediation. The process is entirely voluntary. If the parties do wish to attempt mediation, the secretary of the Tribunal may be able to assist them in identifying an appropriate mediator. However, in the final analysis, the choice of a mediator will also be left to the parties.[5]

---

[4] *Identification and Placement of Exceptional Pupils*, O. Reg. 181/98, s. 31(2). See also the discussion in Chapter 9, "The First Stage of Appeal".

[5] Ministry of Education, excerpts from the draft *Special Education Information Handbook* (2000), at pp. 2-3.

One unique characteristic of mediation in the special education context is that the mediator's fees and expenses are usually paid entirely by the school board.[6] In other contexts, the usual practice is to split the mediator's fees and expenses equally between the parties. However, in the special education context, the disparity in financial means between the parties and the importance of the underlying issues have led to a practice whereby school boards generally absorb the full cost of mediation. While this practice increases the costs of mediation for the school board, the benefits to be achieved will usually still outweigh the costs of mediation.

Given the potential benefits of mediation, both parents and school board officials should at least consider mediation when an appeal has been filed with the Tribunal. A private resolution which addresses the parties' underlying interests and concerns will almost invariably do more to preserve and strengthen the home-school relationship and thereby ensure that the student's educational best interests are served than any litigated outcome. Moreover, even if a resolution is not achieved, mediation can assist in clarifying the issues between the parties and/or reducing the number of issues to be litigated.

THE MEDIATION AGREEMENT

Where the school board and the parents agree to submit the issues between them to mediation, it is a very good idea to enter into a mediation agreement which sets out the terms of the mediation. The mediator, the school board and the parents should all be parties to this agreement.

The mediation agreement should always address confidentiality issues. In particular, the agreement should address what information will be available to the mediator and what limits exist on the disclosure of that information. The agreement may also address what will be done with any information exchanged during the course of the mediation (*i.e.*, whether mediation notes will be kept or destroyed and, if the former, how they will be stored).

In addition, if the parties agree to apply some novel or special terms to their mediation, those terms should be set out in the mediation agreement.

---

[6]   *Ibid.*, at p. 5.

APPENDIX
SAMPLE MEDIATION AGREEMENT

IN THE MATTER OF A MEDIATION

B E T W E E N :

("Parent(s)")

- and -

("School Board")

MEDIATION AGREEMENT

1. The Parent(s) and the School Board agree to submit the disagreement between them concerning the identification and/or placement of the student, _____, to mediation.

2. The Parent(s) and the School Board agree that _____ ("the Mediator") will act as mediator and the Parent(s) agree that, for the purposes of the mediation, information concerning the student, including information contained in the Ontario Student Record, may be disclosed to the Mediator. The Mediator shall hold this information in confidence.

3. The Parent(s), together with any person accompanying or representing the Parent(s), and the School Board, including any employee of the School Board or person representing the School Board, understand and agree that everything said by any person involved in the mediation during the mediation, including any statements, disclosures or offers to settle, are made without prejudice and shall not be disclosed by either party in any subsequent proceeding, excepting only if the parties reach a settlement, in writing, of the issues between them.

Dated at _____, Ontario on _____.

_____   _____
Parent(s)   Mediator

_____
School Board

9

The First Stage of Appeal

INTRODUCTION

A two-stage appeal process is provided under Ontario's special education scheme for parents who disagree with decisions on identification or placement. (Neither the student[1] nor the principal[2] is given the right to appeal the Identification, Placement and Review Committee's decision.) The final stage of appeal, to a Special Education Tribunal, involves a formal hearing under the *Statutory Powers Procedure Act*,[3] and is enshrined in the *Education* Act.[4] The first stage of appeal, a much more informal process, is set out in a regulation[5] under the *Education Act*.

This first stage of appeal is actually a two-step process. The first step involves an *ad hoc* committee called a Special Education Appeal Board ("SEAB") which is established when the school board receives a written notice of appeal from the parent.[6] The SEAB proceeds in the manner of a consultation, holding a "meeting" rather than a hearing. The SEAB's process results in recommendations. These recommendations are forwarded to the school board which, in the second step of the process, decides the outcome of the appeal.

---

[1] The failure of the regulation to give a right of appeal to the student may not meet the common law rules of standing. It is arguable at common law that students do have a common law right to appeal decisions that so directly affect them.

[2] See Chapter 10 under the heading "Initiating the Appeal" for further discussion of this issue.

[3] R.S.O. 1990, c. S.22.

[4] R.S.O. 1990, c. E.2 (as amended), s. 57. See Chapter 10, "The Final Appeal".

[5] *Identification and Placement of Exceptional Pupils*, O. Reg. 181/98. The Minister of Education is required, under s. 8(3) of the *Education Act*, to "provide for the parents or guardians to appeal the appropriateness of the special education placement". For this purpose, s. 11(1), para. 5 of the Act empowers the Minister to make regulations, subject to the approval of the Lieutenant Governor, which govern "procedures with respect to parents or guardians for appeals in respect of identification and placement of exceptional pupils in special education programs" (s. 11(1), para. 6).

[6] Parent should be read in this chapter to mean a parent with custody rights and to include a legal guardian of a student.

GROUNDS AND SCOPE OF APPEAL

Ontario Regulation 181/98 provides that a parent may appeal to an SEAB the following decisions of the IPRC:

> (a) [an IPRC] decision . . . that the pupil is an exceptional pupil;
>
> (b) [an IPRC] decision . . . that the pupil is not an exceptional pupil; or
>
> (c) [an IPRC] decision . . . on placement of the pupil.[7]

While the IPRC does have the power to make recommendations on special education programs and services, such recommendations cannot be challenged as part of an appeal to an SEAB. However, as will be discussed below, the distinction between placement, on the one hand, and programs and services, on the other hand, is not always clear-cut.

The ground on which a parent may appeal is that the parent disagrees with one or more of the decisions of the IPRC.[8] There are no limitations on the reasons for disagreement that a parent may assert in an appeal.

Exceptionality Appeals

The provision of the *Education Act* which requires the Minister to establish a process for parents to appeal "the appropriateness of the special education placement" does not actually make any mention of a process to appeal "exceptionality" or "identification".[9] However, the *Education Act* does contemplate that the decision on the identification or placement of the pupil as an exceptional pupil may be appealed by a parent to the Special Education Tribunal after "all rights of appeal under the regulations in respect of the identification or placement of the pupil as an exceptional pupil" have been exhausted.[10]

As noted under the heading "Grounds and Scope of Appeal", parents are given a right to appeal a finding that their child is or is not exceptional. The language of the regulation, however, does not specifically indicate that the right of a parent to appeal a decision that a student is exceptional includes the right to challenge the categories and definitions of the exceptionality determined by the IPRC.

As a practical matter, it must be noted that Special Education Tribunals have dealt with appeals where the category or definition of the exceptionality was appealed by the parents.[11]

---

[7]   O. Reg. 181/98, s. 26(1).

[8]   *Ibid.*, s. 26(4).

[9]   *Education Act*, s. 8(3). It is this provision which directs the Minister to establish the appeal process in O. Reg. 181/98.

[10]   *Ibid.*, s. 57(3).

[11]   See Chapter 10 under the heading "The Scope of the Appeal".

Placement Appeals

Placement appeals normally relate to the type of classroom setting in which the student has been placed. For example, the parents of an exceptional student who has been placed in a regular class with modifications to the curriculum may feel that the student should be placed in a special class placement or vice versa. As noted in Chapter 5, a determination of placement will usually involve a consideration of the special education programs and services which will be delivered in the placement. However, O. Reg. 181/98 defines the right of parental appeal in a manner which makes clear that special education programs and special education services cannot be the subject of an appeal. It does so by specifically prohibiting the IPRC from making decisions on special education programs and services, and limiting the IPRC's authority to making only "recommendations" on special education programs and services. It further provides specifically that these IPRC recommendations are not "decisions" which can be appealed to the SEAB.[12] Therefore an appeal on the special education programs or services to be provided to the student is not permitted.

There are limits to what can be considered to be "placement" and, therefore, appealable. Technically, placement does not specify the school at which the placement will take place. Placement does not include a specifically named teacher or aide.[13] Placement does not include a decision as to whether particular activities will occur on Tuesday or Wednesday.

On occasion, however, a placement may be so intricately linked with the special education programs or services which are to be delivered in the placement that it may be difficult to distinguish whether it is the placement or the program which is being appealed. In such cases, the matter might be considered to be an appeal of placement.

TIMING OF THE APPEAL

A parent who wishes to appeal the IPRC's decision on identification and/or placement resulting from an initial IPRC or a review IPRC must do so by providing written notice to the secretary of the school board (usually, the director of education). This notice of appeal must be received by the secretary within a

---

[12] O. Reg. 181/98, s. 16(4) and (6). These provisions state, in part: "(4) . . . the committee shall not make decisions about special education services or special education programs" and "(6) A recommendation [by an IPRC about special education services or special education programs] . . . is not a decision for the purposes of section 26(1)". Section 26(1) permits an appeal of an IPRC "decision on placement".

[13] In *Ormerod v. Wentworth County Board of Education* (unreported, June 5, 1987) (Houghton), the parents sought to have their deaf student's program delivered by a teacher fluent in cueing rather than by a special education teacher with the assistance of an educational assistant fluent in cueing, as the board proposed to do. The Tribunal, in dismissing the parents' appeal, actually directed a placement for the pupil different to the one recommended by the IPRC.

fixed time frame.[14] The particular time frame applicable in any case depends on whether or not the parent has requested a follow-up meeting with the IPRC to discuss its decision.

If no follow-up meeting with the IPRC is requested by the parent to discuss the IPRC's decision, the parent must file the notice of appeal within 30 days of receiving the statement of decision of the IPRC.[15]

If a follow-up meeting is requested by the parent to discuss the IPRC's decision, the parent must file the notice of appeal within 15 days of receiving the IPRC's statement as to whether it has made any changes to its original decision as a result of the meeting.[16]

In either case, if the day on which the appeal must be received by the secretary of the school board falls on a day which is a "school holiday", then the time limit is deemed to be extended to the next day which is not a school holiday.[17] School holidays are defined to include the following: every Saturday and Sunday, Canada Day if the school is open during July, Labour Day, Thanksgiving Day, the 14 consecutive days over Christmas during which the school is closed, the five days of March break week, Good Friday, Easter Monday and Victoria Day.[18] Summer holidays are not defined as school holidays with the result that days in July (with the exception of Canada Day) and August do count[19] for the purposes filing a notice of appeal.[20]

If the parent sends the notice of appeal by mail, the notice is deemed to be received on the fifth day after it has been mailed unless the fifth day is a school holiday. In that event, it is deemed to have been received on the next following day which is not a school holiday.[21]

A school board is not obliged to consider an appeal which has not been filed by a parent in a timely fashion. On the other hand, the parent's source of information about the time limit is likely to be the school board's own parent guide or the documents provided by the IPRC. If there has not been clear communication to the parent of the time lines, it may appear to be unduly technical for the school board to rely on the time limits to deny an appeal, particularly if the parent is late only by a

---

[14] O. Reg. 181/98, s. 26.

[15] *Ibid.*, s. 26(2)(a) and (3)(a).

[16] *Ibid.*, s. 26(2)(b) and (3)(b).

[17] *Ibid.*, s. 2.

[18] *School Year Calendar*, R.R.O. 1990, Reg. 304, s. 2(4).

[19] It should be noted that the Ministry of Education takes the view that July and August are not part of the school year and so are not designated as school holidays and do not count for deadline purposes. This interpretation, however, does appear to be at odds with Regulation 304 and the wording of s. 2 of O. Reg. 181/98.

[20] Since many schools are closed during July and August, and since many parents rely on schools to forward their communications to the main administration building, it may be prudent to ensure that mail addressed to the school is picked up and opened in the summer and that a notice be placed on the main entrance to the school advising parents how to get in touch with school board administration during the summer months in which the school is closed.

[21] O. Reg. 181/98, s. 3.

day or two. Accordingly, some school boards include a statement advising parents of their appeal rights — including the applicable time lines — in the IPRC's Statement of Decision, or in a covering letter to the Statement of Decision.

Where there has been clear communication of time lines to the parents and the parents fail to send the notice of appeal in a timely fashion, a school board may decide, nevertheless, to waive the time limits in any particular case. A school board is under no obligation to waive time limits and should recognize that, if it does waive time limits, it is establishing a precedent for future cases. Accordingly, a school board should carefully consider, before waiving the time limits, whether there are legitimate circumstances which led to the delay in filing the notice of appeal, which the school board feels would justify an exercise of its discretion to waive the time limits in the particular case. In such a case, careful note of the circumstances should be made so that they are available for future reference.[22] In addition, it would be prudent for the school board to state in a written communication to the parents that the waiver of time limits is on a "without prejudice" basis.

THE NOTICE OF APPEAL

The parents' notice of appeal must set out the issue being appealed (*i.e.*, identification, placement, or both) and must include a statement setting out the nature of the disagreement.[23] This should include an explanation of why the parents disagree with the decision.

The parents' notice of appeal cannot be rejected by a SEAB for deficiency, simply because the notice of appeal fails to indicate which of the decisions (*i.e.*, identification or placement) the appeal deals with or because it fails to set out the nature of the disagreement. Similarly, the SEAB may not refuse to deal with an appeal for the reason that the parents have not accurately set out the subject of disagreement in the notice of appeal.[24] The purpose behind this is to ensure that the parents' appeal is dealt with on the merits, rather than on technical deficiencies in the manner in which the notice of appeal has been drafted. On the other hand, it is important that both the SEAB and the school board understand the precise nature

---

[22]   As a practical matter, it should be noted that parents who have missed the time lines but are determined to appeal may do so after the passage of three months by exercising the parents' right to refer the matter back to the IPRC after the placement has been in effect for three months and appealing the IPRC's decision at that point (O. Reg. 181/98, s. 21(2)). However, should the decision of the IPRC which the parents failed to appeal in a timely manner involve a new placement, the school board would be able to put the new placement into effect (O. Reg. 181/98, s. 25(1)). Accordingly, where the school board does agree to a late appeal proceeding, it may wish to make clear that it will do so on the understanding that the placement directed by the IPRC will be put into effect in the interim.

[23]   O. Reg. 181/98, s. 26(4).

[24]   *Ibid.*, s. 26(5).

of the parents' disagreement. This will permit the SEAB to conduct the appeal in a focused manner and will allow the school board to address directly the parents' disagreement. Should the deficiency in the parents' statement of the nature of the disagreement become a problem for either the SEAB or the school board, the SEAB may direct the parents to provide a further and more clear statement of the issue being appealed and the nature of the disagreement. Alternatively, the SEAB may, through questions of the parents, clarify the parents' position.

Where the parents' notice of appeal indicates that the appeal relates solely to special education programs or services rather than identification or placement, the appeal will fall outside the SEAB's jurisdiction and the school board is not required to set up an SEAB. However, unless the school board is entirely certain that the parents are not intending to raise identification or placement issues, the prudent course would be to set up the SEAB and obtain the SEAB's recommendations on the matter. This will ensure that if the parents' appeal does relate to the IPRC's decision on identification or placement, issues over which the SEAB *does* have jurisdiction, but the appeal notice has been improperly written as an appeal on programs or services, the real issues will be dealt with.

PARTIES TO THE APPEAL

Generally, the "parties" in an appeal are referred to as the "appellant" (the party initiating the appeal) and the "respondent" (the party responding to the appeal). Although the "appeal" to an SEAB is much less legalistic than most appeals, the notion of "appellants" and "respondents" still applies.

In the case of a special education appeal, the appellant will be the parents or guardian of the student whose identification and/or placement is the subject-matter of the appeal except where the student is an adult. The right to appeal IPRC decisions on identification and/or placement is not extended to students (although they may certainly participate at SEAB meetings). However, a school board may wish to be very cautious before refusing to proceed with an appeal filed by a 16 or 17-year-old student living independently.

Generally, the principal of the school in which the pupil is placed will be a respondent. In most cases, it was the principal who referred the pupil to the IPRC in the first instance. The "designated representative" of the school board in which the pupil is placed is also a respondent to the appeal. As was described in Chapter 6, the "designated representative" of a board is defined to be the director of education or, if there is no director of education, the secretary of the board.[25] The director of education will normally delegate this responsibility to a supervisory officer of the board — usually a superintendent or administrator with responsibility for special education.

---

[25] O. Reg. 181/98, s. 1(1).

Where the student is enrolled with another school board which is purchasing the special education programs and services from the school board which the student attends, the designated representative of the school board that is purchasing the special education program also has a right to participate in the appeal.[26] The role of the purchasing school board is not, strictly speaking, that of either respondent or appellant, although the purchasing school board does have an interest in the proceeding, given that it is purchasing services for the student who is the subject of the appeal.

SETTING UP THE SPECIAL EDUCATION APPEAL BOARD

The SEAB is comprised of three members, including a member appointed by the school board, a member appointed by the parents and a chair, usually appointed by the other two members.[27]

The school board in which the student is placed must appoint its member to the SEAB within 15 days of the day[28] the secretary of the board receives the parents' notice of appeal. This appointee cannot be an employee of the school board making the appointment (or, where the placement arises by way of a purchase of services, an employee of the school board purchasing the services) or of the Ministry of Education. However, there is no prohibition against appointing an employee of another school board. It will be important that the SEAB have a member who understands the perspective of the school board and, accordingly, the school board's appointee to the SEAB often will be a supervisory officer of another school board or a retired supervisory officer of the school board making the appointment.

The school board may not appoint a person who has had any prior involvement in the matter. This would include an outside consultant, such as a psychologist, who assessed the student for the school board.

The parents must appoint a member to the SEAB within 15 days of receipt of the notice of appeal by the secretary of the school board. As with the school board appointee, the parents' appointee cannot be an employee of the school board (or of the purchasing board, where applicable) or an employee of the Ministry of Education. Nor can the parents appoint a person who has had any prior involvement in the matter. A person who has had prior involvement would include either parent or a representative of a support or advocacy group who provided support or advice to the parents through the IPRC process.

The chair is selected jointly by the school board and parents' appointees to the SEAB. Normally the appointees will each consult with the party who appointed

---

[26] *Ibid.*, s. 28(5).

[27] *Ibid.*, s. 27.

[28] *Ibid.*, s. 27(2). Where the final day for doing anything under O. Reg. 181/98 falls on a school holiday within s. 2(4) of Regulation 304, the time is extended to the next day that is not a school holiday: O. Reg. 181/98, s. 2.

her or him in making this selection. As with the other SEAB members, the chair may not be an employee of the school board (or the purchasing board) or of the Ministry of Education, or have had any prior involvement in the matter. The chair must be appointed within 15 days of the later of the date of the appointment by the school board of its appointee and the date of appointment by the parents of their appointee. If the two appointees are unable to agree on a chair, then the local district manager of the Ministry of Education is charged with appointing the chair.

ADMINISTRATIVE SUPPORT FOR AND EXPENSES OF SEAB MEMBERS

Administrative support for the SEAB in the form of secretarial and administrative services is to be provided by the school board.[29] This includes typing services and any other administrative assistance which the SEAB may require, such as coordinating meetings, arranging locations and sending out notices for the chair.

The travel expenses incurred by SEAB members to attend meetings with the parties or meetings amongst the SEAB members themselves, are to be reimbursed in accordance with the policies established by the school board for reimbursing trustees for travel expenses.[30] Depending on the particular school board's policy, this might be based on actual out-of-pocket expenses or on a per kilometre allowance between the SEAB member's residence and the place of the meeting.

If the school board has established a policy which reimburses trustees for other out-of-pocket expenses reasonably incurred in carrying out their duties, SEAB members may claim similar reimbursement.[31]

---

[29] *Ibid.*, s. 27(7).

[30] *Ibid.*

[31] It is noteworthy that the legislation and regulations are silent on the issue of whether the chair and nominees may be paid and, if so, by whom. Under the "arbitration model" where the parties to the arbitration each appoint a nominee and the nominees choose a chair, each party is responsible to pay the fees of his or her nominee and each party is responsible to pay half the fees of the chair. In the case of an SEAB, normally the parents will be able to secure an appointee through a local association who will not charge a fee. The school board will be responsible for fees, if any, charged by its appointee. (Where the school board appoints a supervisory officer from another school board, fees are not likely to be an issue.) The issue of fees is, however, more likely to arise in the case of a chair. In such a case, it is appropriate that the school board pay these costs — indeed, this may be necessary to secure the appointment of a chair in whom both parties have confidence. Where the appointment of a chair is contingent on the payment of a fee to the chair, an understanding should be reached between the school board and the parents on who will pay the fee *before* the SEAB meets.

THE SEAB MEETING

The SEAB does not proceed by way of a "hearing" but rather holds a meeting to which all persons who, in the opinion of the SEAB chair, might have something relevant to contribute are invited. This meeting must be conducted in an informal manner.[32] The SEAB has no power to compel attendance of witnesses, nor does it have the power to administer oaths or affirmations to witnesses. Like the IPRC, the SEAB must comply with basic elements of procedural fairness; however, the SEAB is not subject to the *Statutory Powers Procedure Act* or the more stringent elements of fairness applicable to a statutory adjudicator.[33] Required elements of fairness may include the following:

- the parents and appropriate representatives of the school board must receive notice of the meeting in accordance with the regulation;[34]
- although it is unlikely that the SEAB will receive information in the absence of either party, should this occur, the SEAB should ensure that any such information is shared with the parents and with the representatives of the school board in order to provide each party with the opportunity to rebut any information which that party disagrees with;
- the SEAB must be "unbiased" in carrying out its duties. In this respect, the Regulation sets out limitations, referred to above, on who is qualified to sit as a member of the SEAB; however, all properly qualified members of the SEAB must also conduct themselves in a way which is free from actual bias or a reasonable apprehension of bias.

Location and Timing of the SEAB Meeting

Responsibility for arranging the SEAB meeting rests with the chair of the SEAB. This responsibility can be carried out with the assistance of administrative staff provided by the school board.[35] The meeting must be held within 30 days[36] following the day on which the chair of the SEAB was "selected". However, with the written consent of the parents and the "designated representative" of the school board (see discussion under the heading "The Notice of Appeal", *supra*), the meeting may be scheduled for a date beyond the 30-day period.[37] Since appeals often occur at the end of the school year, it may be difficult or impossible to hold the meeting without impinging on the vacation of an SEAB member or a necessary party. It is not uncommon, therefore, that the SEAB meeting be deferred where all parties agree to do so. However, if either the parents or the school board insist, the meeting must be held within the time frame stipulated by the Regulation. It is

---

[32] O. Reg. 181/98, s. 28(2).
[33] These requirements are discussed further in Chapter 10, "The Final Appeal".
[34] O. Reg. 181/98, s. 28(1).
[35] *Ibid.*, ss. 27(7) and 28(1).
[36] *Ibid.*, s. 28(2).
[37] *Ibid.*, s. 28(2) and (3).

important that appointees to the SEAB understand this requirement before accepting the appointment.

Given the nature of the proceeding, it is assumed that an effort will be made to find a date for the meeting which is mutually convenient for all parties. However, if this proves to be impossible and agreement to postpone the meeting beyond the 30 days cannot be reached, the chair of the SEAB may be left with no alternative but to select a date within the 30 days which conveniences the greatest number of participants, including the other two members of the SEAB.

The location of the meeting must be at a convenient place for all parties.[38] The meeting might be held in a school or the school board's offices. However, particularly where there is some tension between school board staff and the parents, it may be wise to consider a more "neutral" location such as a meeting room in an outside facility. The school board would be responsible to pay the costs of such outside meeting facilities.

Notice of the Meeting

The chair of the SEAB is responsible to provide notice of the hearing to the parents and, if the student is 16 years of age or older, to the student as well. No notice is required to be given to the school board under the Regulation, although the dictates of fairness may require that the school board be given notice. Moreover, providing notice to the school board reduces the appearance, which might otherwise arise, that the chair is communicating "informally" with the school board "behind the scenes".

The notice must be received by the parents and, where entitled, the student, at least 10 days in advance of the meeting.[39]

Participants in the Meeting

Participants at the SEAB's meeting will include the parties: the parents, the student if aged 16 or older and the staff designated by the school board to represent the school board at the SEAB meeting. In addition, the chair of the SEAB must invite any person whom he or she believes may be able to contribute information with respect to the matters under appeal. This includes any persons whom the chair concludes may be able to contribute information or whom the chair is persuaded, either by one of the other appointees or by a party, may be able to contribute in some other way to the meeting. It is to be noted, however, that the chair is not obliged to invite a person to attend unless the chair personally believes that the person will be able to contribute information which, presumably, is relevant to the issues before the SEAB.[40]

The Regulation does not speak to the right of parties to bring along "witnesses" to provide information to the SEAB, but so long as the information which these

---

[38]   *Ibid.*, s. 28(2).
[39]   *Ibid.*, s. 5(5). See Chapter 6 for a discussion on the requirements of giving notice.
[40]   *Ibid.*, s. 28(4).

witnesses may provide is helpful or relevant to the SEAB, there is no doubt their participation will be welcomed. The SEAB does have an inherent power to control its own process which means that the SEAB may limit the number of witnesses, or the amount of time which each takes to provide information. Moreover, if a witness is not providing relevant information, that witness's participation may be limited.

A measure which the SEAB may take to better order its process is to request the parties to provide to the SEAB and exchange with each other, a list of the "witnesses" they intend to bring to the SEAB meeting, including a brief indication of the information which each witness will provide. This will better enable the parties to prepare, which should result in a more efficient and effective SEAB process.

The fact that the Regulation which governs the SEAB requires that its meeting is to be "informal"[41] may suggest that it is not anticipated that any party to the SEAB will be represented by counsel or another representative at the meeting. Whether a party will be permitted to bring counsel or a representative will be a matter to be determined by the SEAB in each case. It is noted, however, that parents do have the right to bring a representative to the IPRC and, accordingly, it seems likely that an SEAB would permit a parent to bring counsel or a representative to a meeting, although the SEAB may reserve the right to limit the involvement of the counsel or representative in the meeting.

IPRC Record

The SEAB must be provided, prior to the commencement of its meeting, with a copy of the IPRC decision being appealed together with the "record" of the IPRC proceeding. This record will include not only a statement of the decision reached by the IPRC but, as well, any reports, assessments or other documents received by the IPRC.[42] This would appear to include documents from the Ontario Student Record ("OSR") if they were considered by the IPRC and such documents arguably must be provided to the SEAB members whether or not the parents or student, if aged 18 or older, has provided written permission to the disclosure of the records.[43]

---

[41] *Ibid.*, s. 28(2).

[42] *Ibid.*, s. 27(6). See also Chapter 6, under the heading "Information to be Considered".

[43] It is a basic rule of statutory interpretation that a regulation cannot overrule a statute. Section 266 of the *Education Act* prohibits the OSR from being produced, without parental permission, in proceedings other than as specifically permitted by the section. It might be argued, therefore, that O. Reg. 181/98, s. 27(6), which requires any document received by the IPRC to be forwarded to the SEAB, applies only to non-OSR documents unless a parent consents in writing to the production. However, it may also be argued that s. 266(7) of the *Education Act* permits the Minister to override the necessity for parental written permission in respect of the compilation and delivery of information contained in the OSR. This, combined with the power of the Minister to promulgate regulations, arguably permits the Minister to direct that OSR records be disclosed to the SEAB if those documents form part of the record of the IPRC in reaching its decision. In

Conduct of the Meeting

Normally, an SEAB meeting will commence with an introduction, by the chair, of the members of the SEAB and a request that the parents and school board representatives introduce themselves. (SEAB meetings at a Roman Catholic school board may open with a prayer.)

As noted, the SEAB's meeting is to be conducted in an informal manner. The process envisioned by the Regulation resembles the "inquisitorial" model of adjudicative decision-making, as opposed to the "adversarial" model. Under the adversarial model, the adjudicator does not determine what witnesses will be called and is not responsible for eliciting evidence from the witnesses who are called. Rather, the adjudicator listens while the parties present the information they think is important. Under the inquisitorial (or "inquiry") model, the adjudicator plays a much more active role in determining what witnesses will be called and what evidence will be elicited. Since the SEAB operates on the latter model, it is to be expected that, led by the chair, there will be questions and discussion between the SEAB and the parties or other persons contributing information to the meeting.

It is traditional in an appeal that the appealing party submits that the decision which is the subject of the appeal is wrong and the responding party submits that the decision is right. In the case of an appeal from an IPRC's decision, the parents will be submitting that the IPRC's decision is wrong and, in most cases, the school board representatives will be supporting the decision of the IPRC. (On occasion, the principal may also disagree with the IPRC's decision on identification and/or placement, in which case the principal is not bound to support the IPRC's decision, but may put forward his or her own views on the decision.) Accordingly, the meeting should normally commence with the parents (or the parents' counsel or representative) explaining why the parents believe that the IPRC's decision is wrong. In support of this position, the parents may bring along any persons who the parents feel will be able to provide information relevant to the matters under appeal. So long as the chair is of the opinion that these persons may contribute relevant information to the meeting, they will be permitted to participate. The parents may also submit any new documentary information not already presented to the IPRC, which the parents feel supports their position. (Documents presented to the IPRC will form part of the IPRC's record which is forwarded to the SEAB before the meeting.)

Following the parents' presentation, the school board's staff will present its position to the SEAB. This presentation may involve an explanation by the IPRC

---

addition, it may be argued that once documents become part of the IPRC's record, they are part of a separate record to which the terms of s. 266 do not apply. It should be noted that while s. 266 of the *Education Act* stipulates 18 years as the age at which a student gains control over his or her OSR, the *Municipal Freedom of Information and Protection of Privacy Act*, R.S.O. 1990, c. M.56, s. 54(c) sets 16 years as the age at which students gain the right to control their personal documents, which would include OSR documents.

chair or another representative (*e.g.*, a superintendent) of the IPRC's proposed placement, together with the information which formed the basis for the IPRC's decision. This will likely include the observations of teachers or consultants who have been involved with the student. In addition, the school board's staff may wish to bring others to the SEAB who might contribute to the discussion, including psychologists, social workers or other professionals. Should there be any additional documents which do not form part of the IPRC's record which might assist the SEAB in its deliberations, these documents may be introduced by the school board. However, this will not include copies of the student's IEPs or OSR documents to the SEAB where there is no written consent of the parent (or student if aged 18 or over).[44]

After the school board has presented its case, the parents should be given an opportunity to respond. At that point, any other persons whom the chair of the SEAB feels might contribute information should be questioned or invited to speak.

Should either the parents or the school board introduce new information at the meeting which takes the other side by surprise, it may be necessary for the party caught by surprise to request an adjournment in order to have an opportunity to deal with and respond to the new information. The SEAB may grant the adjournment if it is of the view that the adjournment is necessary in order to permit the information to be properly dealt with.

The meeting of the SEAB will continue until the SEAB is "satisfied that the opinions, views and information that bear on the appeal have been sufficiently presented to it".[45] While the Regulation governing the procedure of the SEAB appears to contemplate that the meeting will be completed in one day, this may not be possible where the chair determines that other persons, not present, may have relevant information to contribute. If it is necessary that the meeting continue on another day, every effort should be made to ensure that the continuation be scheduled at a mutually convenient time for the parties and the SEAB during the 30-day period following the selection of the chair, unless there is agreement to schedule the continuation date beyond the 30-day period. In this case, the agreement should be confirmed in writing. The date for continuation of the meeting should be determined prior to the adjournment of the meeting so that

---

[44] Section 266(2) of the *Education Act*, precludes the introduction of OSR documents in any proceeding (including, presumably, an SEAB meeting) and s. 266(10) imposes a requirement to preserve secrecy in respect of the contents of the OSR, *except* where the disclosure of information contained in OSR documents is required in the performance of an employee's duties. It will be difficult for school board staff to justify their views as to identification or the appropriate placement for a student without reference to information contained in the OSR. However, it is arguable that the verbal disclosure to the SEAB of information which might be contained in OSR documents falls within the exception in s. 266(10) which permits disclosure of information in the performance of an employee's duties, even though the documents, themselves, cannot be put before the SEAB.

[45] O. Reg. 181/98, s. 28(6).

everyone leaves the meeting with knowledge of the continuation date. Notice of a continuation date should be sent to the parents, with a copy to school board officials — if possible, at least 10 days in advance of the continuation date.

DECISION OF THE SEAB

At the end of the meeting process, the SEAB has only two options. The SEAB may agree with the IPRC, in which case the SEAB will recommend that the IPRC decision be implemented. Alternatively, the SEAB may disagree with the IPRC and make a recommendation to the school board about the student's identification and/or placement.[46] While the IPRC is specifically given the power to make "recommendations regarding special education programs and special education services",[47] the same power is not extended to the SEAB.

The three members of the SEAB have only three days following the end of the meeting to decide whether they agree or disagree with the IPRC. If they disagree, they must also decide within the three-day period about the recommendations they will make to the school board on identification and/or placement.[48] While it is to be expected that the three members will attempt to find unanimity, this may not be possible. Two of the members may agree with one dissenting. In this case, the dissenting member will issue his or her own conclusion and reasons for reaching this conclusion. This dissenting or minority view will be forwarded to the school board along with the majority view. It is possible that the three members of the SEAB will be able to reach agreement on the final decision but not on the recommendations regarding identification or placement, resulting in two or even three sets of recommendations, all of which will be forwarded to the school board. There is no provision in the Regulation that requires the chair's view to prevail.

As noted, the three members of the SEAB must reach their decision within three days (or such longer period as the parents and board may agree to) following the end of the SEAB meeting. A written statement of the SEAB's recommendation (or recommendations, if multiple recommendations are reached)[49] must be sent to:

---

[46]   *Ibid.*

[47]   *Ibid.*, s. 16(2).

[48]   *Ibid.*, s. 28(6).

[49]   While the SEAB must reach its decision within three days as provided by s. 28(6) of O. Reg. 181/98, the requirement to send out a "written statement of its recommendations" is found in s. 29 which does not contain a time limit and makes no reference to s. 28(6). A question arises whether the three-day limit in s. 28(6) also requires the SEAB to send out its recommendations and reasons in writing within that very short time frame. The Ministry takes the position that since the manner in which the SEAB shows that it has reached its decision within the three-day limit is by sending out its written statement of recommendations, it is an implicit requirement that the SEAB's written statement be sent out within the three-day time frame. Because the time frame is such a short one, it may be difficult for an SEAB to provide meaningful reasons within this short time frame and, accordingly, the parties should be prepared to agree to extend this time frame if additional time is required.

- a parent of the student;
- the student, if aged 16 or older;
- the chair of the IPRC;
- the principal of the school in which the student is placed;
- the director of the board in which the pupil is placed; and
- where the student's special education program is being purchased by one school board from another, the designated representative of the board that is purchasing the special education program.[50]

The written statement must include written reasons for the SEAB's recommendations. As noted, if the SEAB has not reached unanimity in its decision, then a separate written statement will normally be prepared by any member who does not agree with the chair, subject to the same time frame as the majority decision.

THE SCHOOL BOARD'S DECISION

Once the SEAB has released its written statement, the matter must be put to the school board's trustees to determine what action will be taken by the school board with respect to the recommendations.

Within 30 days after receiving the SEAB's written statement, the school board must consider the SEAB's recommendations and decide what action to take with respect to the student.[51]

Although there is no statutory or regulatory requirement that the school board provide an opportunity for parents to be "heard" before it makes its decision, common law requirements of fairness dictate that an individual whose rights are to be determined by a statutory decision-maker, has a right to be heard by the decision-maker before the decision is made. Since school board staff will likely present their views to the school board on whether the SEAB's recommendations should be adopted or not, fairness would require that the parents also be given an opportunity to put forward their position on the SEAB's recommendations and on the position of school board staff on the recommendations. This may be accomplished by providing the parents with a written outline of the position of school board staff on the recommendations and extending to parents the opportunity to make either an oral presentation or a written submission before the school board makes its decision on the SEAB's recommendations.

Whether the parents are to be given an opportunity to make an oral submission or a written submission, they should be given reasonable notice (*i.e.,* sufficient notice to permit them to respond) of the date of the school board's meeting and of the opportunity to make a written or oral submission. If the opportunity being provided is to make a written submission, a date by which the written submission

---

[50] O. Reg. 181/98, s. 29.

[51] *Ibid.*, s. 30(1).

must be in the hands of the secretary of the board for distribution to trustees should be stated in the notice.

The school board, in making its decision, may adjourn to "the committee of the whole board", and then to a closed session to consider the SEAB's decision.[52] However, for the final decision of the school board to be effective, the school board must, in open session, adopt the resolution of "the committee of the whole board" with respect to the student.

It is important to note that the school board is not obliged to adopt the recommendations of the SEAB, even where there is unanimity in the SEAB. Nor is the school board bound by the limitations imposed on the SEAB to agree or disagree with the IPRC on the issues of identification or placement. The school board may go beyond the issue of placement and identification and may make a decision which involves special education programs and services.[53] This flexibility will often enable school boards and parents to reach an agreement in order to resolve the issues between them and avoid further litigation.

Once the school board reaches its decision, that decision must be communicated in writing to each of the persons who received notice of the SEAB's decision. The notice to the parents of the school board's decision must include an explanation of the parent's right to appeal the board's decision to a Special Education Tribunal pursuant to s. 57 of the *Education Act*. A paragraph such as the following would achieve this:

> If you disagree with this decision of the Board on the identification or placement of your child, you have the right, under s. 57 of the *Education Act*, to appeal to a Special Education Tribunal for a hearing in respect of the identification or placement of your child. You may initiate the appeal by forwarding to the Secretary of the Special Education Tribunal a written notice that you wish to appeal the Board's decision on identification and/or placement, together with a statement of the grounds on which you are appealing the decision. This notice may be sent to the Secretary at the following address:

The address, telephone number and fax number of the Secretary, Special Education Tribunal should be set out in the letter.[54]

---

[52]   A board of trustees constituted as the board must always sit in open session. A committee of the board may sit in closed session in limited circumstances which include the disclosure of personal information about a student of the board: *Education Act*, s. 207.

[53]   O. Reg. 181/98, s. 30(2).

[54]   At the date of writing, it is expected that the Special Education Branch will be moved shortly. It is wise, prior to sending out this letter to parents, to verify the address of the Branch since moves can take place at any time.

IMPLEMENTATION OF THE BOARD'S DECISION

The school board may implement the decision it has reached on the SEAB's recommendation only upon the occurrence of one of the following events:[55]

- a parent of the pupil consents in writing to the school board's decision;
- 30 days have elapsed from the day the parent receives (or is deemed to have received) notice of the board's decision *and* no appeal to the Special Education Tribunal has been commenced by the parent within this 30-day period;[56] or
- an appeal to the Special Education Tribunal is dismissed or abandoned.

Neither the Regulation nor the *Education Act* define when an appeal to the Special Education Tribunal is deemed to be abandoned and, accordingly, this will be determined by the Secretary of the Special Education Tribunal (or the chair of the Tribunal if the Tribunal has been constituted), on a case-by-case basis. One would expect a finding of abandonment to be made where the parent has failed to respond to the Secretary of the Tribunal even after a warning has been given that continued failure to respond will result in a finding that the appeal has been abandoned.

The school board has the discretion, in accordance with an agreement with the parents, to change any decision it has reached following its consideration of the SEAB's recommendations, but may only do so within the 30-day period following the parents' receipt of the school board's decision in the first instance or while an appeal to the Special Education Tribunal is pending.[57] This will permit continuing dialogue between school board staff and parents in an effort to resolve the differences between them. Where an appeal is pending to the Special Education Tribunal, the fact that the school board can change its decision will facilitate the mediation of the dispute between parents and the school board by an outside third party who may be able to assist the parents and the school board in finding a resolution which both are prepared to live with. Mediation at this stage is becoming more common across the province and is discussed further in Chapter 8, "Mediation".

If the school board does change its decision, notice of the new decision must be given in writing to each of the persons who received notice of the school board's first decision on the matter. The notice to the parents of the new decision must include the explanation of the parents' right to appeal the new decision to the Special Education Tribunal.[58]

---

[55] O. Reg. 181/98, s. 30.

[56] *Ibid.*, s. 31(2). Note: if the notice is sent by mail, it will be deemed to be received on the fifth day after the notice was sent.

[57] *Ibid.*

[58] *Ibid.*, s. 30(3).

10

The Final Appeal

INTRODUCTION

In some cases, the student's parents or guardian still may be dissatisfied with the identification or placement decision made by the school board after the appeal to the Special Education Appeal Board ("SEAB"). If so, there is an additional avenue of appeal available to the parents. The *Education Act*[1] provides for a further appeal of identification and/or placement decisions to the Special Education Tribunal (the "Tribunal").

The basic right of appeal to the Tribunal is set out in s. 57(3) of the *Education Act*, which provides:

> Where a parent or guardian of a pupil has exhausted all rights of appeal under the regulations in respect of the identification or placement of the pupil as an exceptional pupil and is dissatisfied with the decision in respect of the identification or placement, the parent or guardian may appeal to a Special Education Tribunal for a hearing in respect of the identification or placement.

This chapter focusses on the practical and strategic considerations involved in initiating an appeal to the Tribunal and on the procedures followed by the Tribunal once the appeal has been filed.

THE SPECIAL EDUCATION TRIBUNAL

The *Education Act* authorizes the Lieutenant Governor in Council to establish one or more Special Education Tribunals.[2] Pursuant to this power, the Lieutenant Governor in Council has established a Special Education Tribunal (English) and a Special Education Tribunal (French).

Each Tribunal consists of a chair (who is so designated in the Order-in-Council appointing him or her) and a roster of additional panel members. All of the members of the Tribunal are appointed by the Lieutenant Governor in Council on a fixed-term basis.

---

[1] R.S.O. 1990, c. E.2 (as amended), s. 57.
[2] *Ibid.*, s. 57(1).

The Tribunal sits in three-person panels. Each panel consists of the chair and two additional members selected on a case-by-case basis.

The composition of the Tribunal varies from time to time, as existing appointments are terminated and new appointments are made in their place. Traditionally, the members of the Tribunal have been drawn from a wide variety of backgrounds — including the legal profession, the clergy, educators, psychologists, members of special education associations and special education specialists — and therefore have brought a wide range of viewpoints and expertise to the special education decision-making process.

Appeals to the Special Education Tribunal must be filed with the Secretary of the Tribunal. The Secretary's address changes from time to time; current contact information can be obtained from the Ministry of Education.

The Tribunal usually holds its hearings at a location (usually a meeting room in a local hotel or government office) within the jurisdiction of the school board involved in the appeal. The reason for this practice is that it is considered more convenient, efficient and economical to conduct the proceedings at the place where the majority of the parties and the witnesses are located.

INITIATING THE APPEAL

Under s. 57(3) of the *Education Act*, only a parent or guardian may initiate an appeal to the Tribunal.

At first blush, it may appear inequitable that the school board is not granted appeal rights. However, this apparent difference in treatment makes sense when considered in the context of the broader legislative scheme. Under O. Reg. 181/98, the school board is given a very broad discretion to accept or reject the SEAB's recommendations and to take virtually any action it deems appropriate in response to those recommendations.[3] Given this broad discretion, it is clear that appeal rights are of primary importance to the parents or guardian.

Of greater concern is the absence of any appeal rights for the students themselves.[4] Usually, the student's parents will be in the best position to determine whether it is in the student's best interests to appeal the school board's decision and to take the steps necessary to do so. However, the Supreme Court of Canada has recognized in the special education context that children have rights and interests which are separate and distinct from those of their parents and therefore the parents' views of what is in the student's best interests will not always be

---

[3]   *Identification and Placement of Exceptional Pupils*, O. Reg. 181/98, s. 30.
[4]   Section 1(2) of the *Education Act* provides that the rights accorded to parents under the Act may be exercised by the pupil, if the pupil is an adult. The Act does not define when a pupil becomes an adult. The Ministry of Education uses age 18 — the age specified under the *Age of Majority and Accountability Act*, R.S.O. 1990, c. A.7 — as the age at which a pupil will be deemed to be an adult. However, except as specifically stated in the statute and regulations, the rights of students under age 18 are exercised by their parents or guardian.

dispositive of the question.[5] Accordingly, it is possible that, in an appropriate case, a student — particularly a student over 16 who has withdrawn from parental control — could successfully persuade the Tribunal to allow him or her to proceed with an appeal to the Tribunal in the absence of his or her parents.

An appeal to the Tribunal is initiated by making a request for a hearing, in writing, to the Secretary of the Tribunal. This request need not follow a particular form; a letter will suffice. However, the letter should include the name of the parents or guardian; the name and age of the student; the student's school board; the student's current grade level or placement; and a brief description of the nature of the appeal (*i.e.*, whether the appeal is of identification or placement or both). The written request may also name a lawyer or agent who is representing the parents or guardian, in order to notify the Secretary to communicate with the lawyer or agent. The request should provide full contact information (including full name, title if any, mailing address, telephone number(s) and (if available) facsimile number and/or e-mail address) for the parents or guardian, or their representative, as the case may be. Finally, the written request should always be signed by the parents or guardian initiating the appeal.[6]

THE SCOPE OF THE APPEAL

Section 57(3) of the *Education Act* contemplates an appeal to a Special Education Tribunal of either or both of: (a) the identification of the pupil as an "exceptional pupil"; and (b) the placement decision of the school board.

There has been some debate concerning whether an appeal of identification can extend beyond the question of whether or not the student is exceptional. This issue does not seem to have been fully canvassed by the Tribunal. However, in several cases, the Tribunal has dealt with appeals involving the particular category or definition of exceptionality applicable to a student.[7]

Another question which arises from time to time is whether issues concerning the special education programs or special education services offered by the school board may be addressed by the Tribunal.[8] Under the old Regulation 305, the right of appeal to the SEAB was limited to identification and placement decisions.[9] The language of s. 57(3) similarly limited the right of appeal to the Tribunal to

---

[5] *Eaton v. Brant County Board of Education*, [1997] 1 S.C.R. 241 at pp. 277-9, 142 D.L.R. (4th) 385, 31 O.R. (3d) 574*n*, 97 O.A.C. 161, 41 C.R.R. (2d) 240, 207 N.R. 171.

[6] Ministry of Education, excerpts from the draft *Special Education Information Handbook*, 2000 ("Draft *Handbook*"), at p. 9.

[7] See, for example, *Labute v. Windsor Board of Education* (unreported, 1988) (Houghton); *Fripp v. Nipissing Board of Education* (unreported, July 18, 1986) (Duchesneau-McLachlan).

[8] This issue is discussed further in Chapter 5, "Placement" and Chapter 9, "The First Stage of Appeal".

[9] *Special Education Identification Placement and Review Committees and Appeals*, R.R.O. 1990, Reg. 305, ss. 4 and 9 (repealed by O. Reg. 181/98).

identification and placement decisions. Nevertheless, soon after the special education scheme was introduced, it was recognized that the issue of appropriate programs and services is often intimately intertwined with the issue of placement[10] and, on occasion, the Tribunal has addressed special education programs and services in the course of deciding placement appeals.[11]

This issue was addressed in O. Reg. 181/98, which replaced Regulation 305 effective September 1, 1998. Under O. Reg. 181/98, the right of appeal is still limited to identification and placement; there is no right to appeal concerning the special education programs or special education services provided by the school board.[12] However, under the Regulation, the Identification, Placement and Review Committee ("IPRC") is authorized to discuss and make recommendations — although not final decisions — about special education programs and special education services.[13] Ontario Regulation 181/98 also contemplates that the Special Education Tribunal may make recommendations concerning these issues in the context of hearing placement appeals. The Tribunal's recommendations are not binding on the school board, but they must be considered by the school principal in developing or reviewing the pupil's individual education plan ("IEP").[14]

Thus, O. Reg. 181/98 now expressly authorizes the Special Education Tribunal to give some consideration to special education programs and services when considering an appeal of placement. However, the Tribunal is only empowered to make recommendations concerning these matters; all final decisions regarding special education programs and services must be left to the school board.

THE TIMING OF THE APPEAL

Section 57(3) of the *Education Act* specifically requires that the parents or guardian must have exhausted all other rights of appeal under the Regulations before pursuing an appeal to the Special Education Tribunal. In other words, the parents or guardian must have exhausted all avenues of appeal before the IPRC[15]

---

[10]   In one of the first cases dealing with the special education scheme, the Ontario Divisional Court recognized that consideration of the nature and content of the programs and services offered in the placement was an essential component of determining whether the placement directed was appropriate. See *Dolmage v. Muskoka Board of Education* (1985), 49 O.R. (2d) 546 at p. 555, 15 D.L.R. (4th) 741, 6 O.A.C. 389 (Div. Ct.). See Chapter 5, "Placement".

[11]   See, for example, *Ormerod v. Wentworth County Board of Education* (unreported, June 5, 1987) (Houghton); *Fripp, supra,* footnote 7; *Barger v. Board of Education for the City of North York* (unreported, September 13, 1985) (Houghton); and *Hukowich v. Timmins Board of Education* (unreported, June 27, 1984) (Houghton).

[12]   *Education Act,* s. 57(3).

[13]   O. Reg. 181/98, ss. 16 and 23.

[14]   *Ibid.,* ss. 6(6)(b) and 7(3)(b).

[15]   The parents'/guardian's ongoing right of review of the IPRC's decision as often as once every three months is not considered a right of appeal which must be exhausted before the parents can appeal to the Tribunal: O. Reg. 181/98, s. 21(2).

and must also have exhausted their right of appeal to the SEAB before initiating an appeal to the Tribunal.

The requirement that appeal rights must be "exhausted" before an appeal can be filed with the Tribunal will likely be interpreted in a flexible manner which takes into account the particular facts of individual cases. Where, for example, the parents have attempted to appeal to the SEAB but that appeal did not proceed for some reason (*i.e.*, because the appeal was filed outside the time limits contemplated by O. Reg. 181/98), the parents may be able to argue that they have "exhausted" their rights to appeal to the SEAB. It would, of course, be up to the Tribunal to determine whether it was prepared to proceed with the appeal in these circumstances.

PROCEDURAL RULES GOVERNING THE HEARING

Where a parent or guardian appeals an identification or placement decision, the Tribunal must hold a hearing into the identification or placement in question.[16]

The Tribunal's Procedures

Section 57(2) of the *Education Act* allows the Lieutenant Governor in Council to make regulations concerning, among other things, the practices and procedures to be followed by the Special Education Tribunal in holding a hearing. However, no such regulations have ever been made. This does not mean that there are no procedural rules which govern hearings before the Tribunal. Rather, the Tribunal's procedures are governed by both the *Statutory Powers Procedure Act*[17] and by the general rules of "natural justice" and "procedural fairness" applicable to administrative tribunals.

The SPPA sets out the minimum procedural rules which must be followed by a wide range of administrative tribunals in Ontario, including the Special Education Tribunal. These procedural rules are designed to ensure that uniform, minimum standards of procedural fairness are maintained, unless they are expressly waived by the parties.[18]

In addition to the procedural rules set out in the SPPA, the Tribunal is also governed by general rules of natural justice or procedural fairness established by

---

[16] *Education Act*, s. 57(3).

[17] R.S.O. 1990, c. S.22 (as amended to 1999, c. 12, Sch. B) ("SPPA"). By virtue of s. 3(1), the SPPA applies "to a proceeding by a tribunal in the exercise of a statutory power of decision conferred by or under an Act of the Legislature, where the tribunal is required by or under such Act or otherwise to hold or to afford to the parties to the proceeding an opportunity for a hearing before making a decision". Section 57(3) of the *Education Act* provides for an appeal of an identification or placement to the Special Education Tribunal, and specifically states that the Tribunal must hold a hearing in respect of the identification or placement. Thus, the Tribunal is covered by the SPPA.

[18] SPPA, s. 4(1). Section 4(1) allows the parties and the tribunal to consent to waive any procedural requirement set out in the SPPA or any other statute or regulation.

the courts. The SPPA was intended in part to codify some of these judge-made rules and, as a result, there is considerable overlap between the procedural rules established by the courts and the procedural rules set out in the statute. However, the overlap is not complete and there are some rules of natural justice or procedural fairness with which the Tribunal must comply which exist outside the SPPA.

In the discussion which follows, we will identify both the statutory and the judge-made rules with which the Tribunal must comply in carrying out a hearing.

The Parties to the Hearing

Section 5 of the SPPA provides that the parties to a proceeding "shall be the persons specified as parties by or under the statute under which the proceeding arises or, if not so specified, persons entitled by law to be parties to the proceeding".

The *Education Act* does not specify all of the persons who are entitled to be parties to a proceeding before the Tribunal. Obviously, the parents or guardian who initiated the appeal will be parties. The school board whose decision is under review will also be a party to the appeal. Where the student is being transferred from a demonstration school or the student's special education program is purchased from another school board, the demonstration school or the purchasing school board may also be a party. Usually, the parents/guardian and school board(s) in question will be the only parties to the appeal.[19]

An interesting question, which remains unresolved, is whether the student is "entitled by law" to participate as a party to the appeal. The Supreme Court of Canada has recognized that the student's rights and interests in special education proceedings are separate and distinct from the rights and interests of his or her parents.[20] Identification and placement may be of direct interest to any student who is able to understand these concepts. Moreover, the student who is the subject of the proceedings can be adversely affected by the outcome. These factors suggest that, at least where there is a divergence in views between the student and his or her parents, or where the student is capable of expressing the desire to be a party, the student may be entitled to independent party status.

Notice of the Hearing

Section 6(1) of the SPPA requires that the parties to a proceeding must be given "reasonable notice" of the time and place of the hearing by the Tribunal. The period of notice which is "reasonable" will depend on the particular circumstances of the case.

The SPPA allows a tribunal to hold written, oral or electronic hearings, depending on the circumstances. It also specifies what information must be

---

[19] Section 5 of the SPPA provides an avenue for others who believe they are "entitled by law" to participate in the proceedings to seek party status in appropriate cases.

[20] *Eaton v. Brant County Board of Education*, [1997] 1 S.C.R. 241 at pp. 278-9, 142 D.L.R. (4th) 385, 31 O.R. (3d) 574n, 97 O.A.C. 161, 41 C.R.R. (2d) 240, 207 N.R. 171.

included in the notice of hearing. The content of the notice which is required depends on whether the hearing will be a written, oral or electronic.[21]

In some cases, the parties to a proceeding before the Special Education Tribunal may elect to deal with preliminary matters by way of a written or electronic hearing. However, the Tribunal virtually always holds an oral hearing to deal with the merits of the appeal.

Sections 6(2) and (3) of the SPPA require that notice of an oral hearing must include the following:

- a reference to the statutory authority for holding the hearing (*i.e.*, s. 57 of the *Education Act*);
- a statement of the time, place and purpose of the hearing; and
- a statement that, if a party notified does not attend at the hearing, the Tribunal may proceed in that party's absence, and the party will not be entitled to any further notice in the proceeding.

In special education appeals, the parties are normally consulted by the Secretary of the Special Education Tribunal when hearing dates are set in order to ensure that the hearing is held at a time which is convenient to all parties and the members of the Tribunal. In such a case, sending out the notice tends to be a matter of form.

Typically, the Tribunal Secretary will schedule the hearing at least one month after the receipt of the parents' request in order to ensure that the parties have enough time to prepare for the hearing. If either party requires a longer period of time to prepare, the Secretary will usually accommodate them within reason. If the parties have agreed to participate in mediation, the Secretary will postpone the scheduling of the hearing pending the outcome of mediation. This may further extend the period between filing the request for an appeal and the commencement of the hearing.[22]

The place of the hearing will usually be a location within the geographic jurisdiction of the school board. Usually, a meeting room will be arranged in a local hotel or government office to provide a venue for the hearing.

The Format of the Hearing

In the previous section, we have noted that, if the parties agree, the Tribunal may hold written or electronic hearings to deal with preliminary matters. However, the Tribunal virtually always holds an oral hearing to deal with the merits of the appeal.

The hearing before the Tribunal is a formal, adversarial[23] proceeding. The parties to the hearing have a right to be represented by legal counsel or an

---

[21] SPPA, s. 6.

[22] Draft *Handbook*, *op cit.*, footnote 6, at p. 10.

[23] Hearings before courts and administrative tribunals in common law jurisdictions, such as Canada, proceed on the "adversarial model". That is, the parties are responsible to put before the decision-maker any evidence which is relevant to the decision. This is to be

agent,[24] if they so choose. The hearing will typically involve full examination and cross-examination of witnesses, including expert witnesses, and the parties will usually make legal argument concerning the decision which the Tribunal should reach. The details of how the hearing is conducted are described further under the heading "Proceedings Before the Special Education Tribunal", *infra*.

It is important to understand that the hearing before the Tribunal is a hearing *de novo*. That is, the Tribunal does not merely review the decisions of the IPRC and the SEAB to determine whether errors have been committed and correct those errors. Rather, the Tribunal hears all of the evidence presented by the parties and comes to its own conclusion on identification and/or placement. This approach ensures that the Tribunal can take into account any changes in the pupil's circumstances between the time the SEAB decision is released and the time the hearing before the Tribunal begins.

Open vs. Closed Hearings

In Ontario, the general rule is that tribunal hearings must be open to the public. However, the SPPA contemplates an exception to this general rule where,

> . . . intimate financial or personal matters or other matters may be disclosed at the hearing of such a nature, having regard to the circumstances, that the desirability of avoiding disclosure thereof in the interests of any person affected or in the public interest outweighs the desirability of adhering to the principle that hearings be open to the public.[25]

The usual practice of the Special Education Tribunal is to hold public hearings. However, if the circumstances described above exist in a particular case, the Tribunal may be asked to hold a closed hearing. Alternatively, if the testimony of only one or a small number of witnesses is expected to be sensitive, a request may be made to close the hearing only while particular witnesses testify.

If a party wishes to request a closed or partially closed hearing, the appropriate course of action is to raise the issue as a preliminary matter. The issue should be raised at the outset of the hearing, before the Tribunal begins to hear evidence or argument on the merits of the appeal. Each side will be given the opportunity to present their arguments on the issue to one another and to the Tribunal. The Tribunal will then issue a decision on the matter and the hearing will proceed in accordance with the Tribunal's decision.

The Right to Legal Counsel

Section 10 of the SPPA guarantees every party to a proceeding covered by the statute the right to be represented by legal counsel or an agent during the proceeding, if they so choose. In most cases, the parties to an appeal to the Special

---

contrasted with the "inquisitorial model", where the adjudicator seeks out or participates in the calling of evidence.

[24]   SPPA, s. 10.

[25]   *Ibid.*, s. 9(1)(b).

Education Tribunal will be represented by legal counsel. However, particularly where cost is an issue, one of the parties (typically the parents) may be represented by counsel or someone from an association involved in advocating for the rights of parents, children or persons with disabilities, or they may represent themselves.

PRE-HEARING DISCLOSURE

The parties to an appeal to the Special Education Tribunal should provide certain basic information to one another prior to the hearing in order to clarify the issues in dispute and streamline the hearing process. However, they are not required to disclose evidence to the other party before the hearing commences.

Basic Information

Under the SPPA, a tribunal is required to give notice of the hearing, which must include notice of (among other things) the time, place and purpose of the hearing.[26] However, there is no express statutory requirement that the parties provide any further information to one another prior to the hearing. Although the SPPA is silent on these issues, the exchange of some basic information prior to the hearing is necessary to ensure that the parties are treated fairly and that the hearing can be conducted in an efficient and effective manner.[27]

To this end, once the hearing dates have been set, the Secretary of the Special Education Tribunal will direct the parents or guardian or their representative to provide the following information in writing within a specified time period:

1. A statement of the grounds for the appeal (*i.e.*, what aspects of the school board's decision do the parents or guardian disagree with?).
2. A statement of the remedy sought (*i.e.*, what do the parents or guardian want the Tribunal to order the school board to do?).
3. A statement of whether the parents or guardian intend to call any witnesses and, if so, how many witnesses will be called.
4. An estimate of how long it will take to present the parents'/guardian's case.
5. A statement of any preliminary issues the parents/guardian intend to raise at the outset of the hearing (*i.e.*, do they want the hearing to be closed or partially closed to the public?).[28]

Once the Secretary has received this information from the parents or guardian or their representative, it will be provided to the school board and the members of the Tribunal. The school board will then be directed to provide the following information in response, again within a specified time period:

---

[26] *Ibid.*, s. 6.
[27] Draft *Handbook*, *op cit.*, footnote 6, at pp. 10-11.
[28] *Ibid.*

1. A response to the parents'/guardian's statement of the grounds for appeal.
2. A response to the remedy requested by the parents/guardian and a statement of the remedy proposed by the school board.
3. A statement of whether the school board intends to call any witnesses and, if so, how many witnesses will be called.
4. An estimate of how long it will take to present the school board's case.
5. A statement of any preliminary issues the school board intends to raise at the outset of the hearing (*i.e.*, the school board may wish to seek clarification of the parents'/guardian's position).[29]

The school board's response will be provided to the members of the Tribunal and the parents or guardian or their representative in advance of the commencement of the hearing.[30]

Disclosure of this basic information is essential to ensure that both parties understand the case to be met, which is a basic requirement of procedural fairness. It also assists in clarifying the issues in dispute so that the hearing can proceed more expeditiously and the most efficient use can be made of the Tribunal's time and resources.

Depending on the circumstances, it may be possible to arrange a conference call with the Tribunal in advance of the hearing to deal with any preliminary issues identified by either party. If this is not possible, the issues can be addressed on the first scheduled day of hearing. An adjournment of the hearing may be requested by either party if necessary to prepare a response to any issues raised by the other party that were not anticipated. It will be up to the Tribunal to decide, after hearing argument from both sides, whether to grant an adjournment.

Disclosure of Evidence

The parties to an appeal to the Special Education Tribunal do not have a right to any pre-hearing disclosure of the evidence on which the other party intends to rely.

The SPPA allows a tribunal to make rules governing its procedures, including rules authorizing itself to make orders requiring pre-hearing disclosure.[31] However, no such rules have ever been made by the Special Education Tribunal. Accordingly, at present, there is no general right to pre-hearing disclosure of evidence in a proceeding before the Tribunal. The sole exception (as outlined in the previous section) is that the Tribunal will request each party to disclose the number and names of witnesses to be called and will disclose that information to the other party.

Although there is no general right to pre-hearing disclosure of evidence, there are measures available to the parties to obtain disclosure at the hearing itself. One of these measures is to serve a summons on a person believed to have relevant evidence. An alternate measure is to request the Tribunal to order disclosure at the hearing.

---

[29] *Ibid.*
[30] *Ibid.*
[31] SPPA, s. 5.4.

The Special Education Tribunal has the authority to issue a summons upon the request of one of the parties before it. A summons is a legal document which requires the recipient to attend at the hearing to give evidence and to bring with him or her any documents or things specified in the summons. The summons may cover any documents or things which are arguably relevant to the proceedings and admissible in evidence. Failure to comply with a properly issued summons without lawful excuse can be grounds for arrest and for the initiation of proceedings for contempt of the Tribunal.[32]

Although the Special Education Tribunal has the authority to issue a summons, that authority tends to be used somewhat sparingly. The summons is not used frequently as a device to obtain documentary disclosure. More often, one of the parties will simply make a request at the hearing that the Tribunal order any further disclosure which is necessary in order to enable that party to prepare its case and/or respond to the issues raised on appeal. In considering this issue, the Tribunal will hear argument from both parties and will decide whether fairness dictates that further disclosure will be provided.

There are also measures available to counteract the effect of "surprise" evidence which arises for the first time at the Tribunal's hearing. If an opponent's witness gives oral testimony at the hearing which catches a party by surprise, that party may request an adjournment of the proceedings before cross-examining the witness. The Tribunal will hear argument from both sides and will decide whether the adjournment will be granted.

Because surprise evidence may lead to adjournment of the proceedings, the parties will often conclude that it is in their mutual best interest to exchange any documents upon which they intend to rely in advance of the hearing. This co-operative approach minimizes unnecessary delays in the proceeding, and is viewed favourably by many administrative tribunals. Co-operation is certainly highly desirable in special education proceedings, in which the tactical advantages of non-disclosure should be outweighed by the importance for all parties of ensuring that the best interests of the student are being served.

PROCEEDINGS BEFORE THE SPECIAL EDUCATION TRIBUNAL

Preliminary Matters

It is not uncommon for preliminary issues to arise which will need to be addressed before the hearing can commence. Examples might include questions concerning the scope of the Tribunal's jurisdiction, clarification of the grounds for

---

[32] *Ibid.*, ss. 12 and 13. What might constitute a lawful excuse for failure to comply with a summons is a complex question which may well warrant consultation with a lawyer. The question will be decided by the Tribunal, which may want to see the disputed documents and/or question the person who failed to comply before making its decision.

appeal or the remedy sought, determining whether the proceeding should be open or closed, disclosure issues and the like.

In some cases, it may be possible to deal with these preliminary issues by conference call prior to the first scheduled hearing day. This approach has the advantage that it avoids spending valuable hearing time on preliminary matters. However, if time does not permit the parties to schedule a conference call, or doing so is not feasible for some other reason,[33] preliminary matters may be addressed at the outset of the first hearing day.

Whether or not a conference call is feasible, both parties are encouraged to advise the Tribunal as early as possible of any preliminary issues they intend to raise. In notifying the Tribunal of any preliminary issues, a party may also request that the issue(s) be addressed prior to the actual hearing, if so desired.

Order of Proceedings at the Hearing

The Special Education Tribunal hearing will usually begin with introductory statements by the chair of the Tribunal. These introductory statements will include introduction of the members of the Tribunal, the Tribunal Secretary, the court reporter transcribing the proceedings;[34] introduction of the parties; and an overview of the procedures which will be followed. The chair will usually ask whether there are any preliminary matters to be addressed and the parties can then discuss with the Tribunal how the preliminary matters should be dealt with. Sometimes preliminary matters are addressed immediately after introductory statements from the chair; sometimes the parties will deliver their opening statements before preliminary matters are addressed.[35]

With respect to any preliminary issues, the party raising the issue will proceed first. The other party will then have an opportunity to respond. Often, preliminary matters can be resolved solely on the basis of the submissions of the parties. However, in some cases, it may be necessary for the Tribunal to hear evidence before making its decision on the preliminary matters. Once the parties have presented their evidence and/or made their submissions, the members of the Tribunal will typically confer — sometimes a recess will be necessary for this purpose — and then advise the parties of how they will proceed.[36]

In some cases, the Tribunal may request further written submissions before making their decision; in other cases, they may make their decision on the preliminary matter right away; still in other cases, they may reserve their decision on the preliminary matter and adjourn the hearing pending that decision; yet in

---

[33] For example, there may be cases in which evidence may have to be called in support of the preliminary issues. Obviously, a conference call would not be sufficient to deal with the underlying issues in such a case.

[34] Proceedings of the Special Education Tribunal are always transcribed verbatim by a court reporter, so that a transcript can be made available to the Tribunal members and the parties.

[35] Draft *Handbook*, *op cit.*, footnote 6, at pp. 14-15.

[36] *Ibid.*, at p. 14.

other cases, the Tribunal may reserve their decision on the preliminary matter, continue with the hearing and release their decision at a later date.

Before hearing the parties' evidence on the merits of the appeal, the chair will ask each party to give an opening statement. The purpose of opening statements is to summarize each party's position, clarify the issues in dispute and the result being sought, and thereby enable the Tribunal to place the parties' evidence in its proper context. The parents or guardian, or their legal counsel, will be asked to present their opening statement first, followed by the school board, or its legal counsel.

It is also common for there to be some discussion of documentation at the outset of the hearing. Documents may be submitted to the Tribunal in three ways. They may be introduced as evidence during the questioning of witnesses; they may be admitted by agreement at the outset of the hearing, subject to further proof; or, where both parties intend to refer to many of the same documents, the parties may agree on a joint book of documents which can be introduced at the beginning of the hearing. Where the parties intend to utilize one or both of the latter two methods, the documents will generally be submitted during or immediately after opening statements.

The next stage of the hearing is the presentation of evidence. The parents or guardian who initiated the appeal, or their legal counsel, will be expected to proceed first in calling and questioning witnesses to give evidence supporting their position. The questioning of witnesses may include the introduction of documents about which those witnesses have personal knowledge.

As noted above, the Tribunal has the power to issue summonses to witnesses.[37] Each summons must be signed by the chair of the Tribunal, who is entitled to ask the requesting party to justify either the number of summonses requested or the particular witnesses summoned. A summons is not required for every witness. In practice, they are usually used only for witnesses who require a summons in order to obtain a leave of absence from their place of employment or who are unwilling (or potentially unwilling) to testify for the party who had the summons issued.

As discussed previously, the Tribunal requires the parties to exchange witness lists in advance of the hearing. The parties should compare these witness lists to see if there are any witnesses they are both planning to call. If so, the number of summonses requested may be reduced.

Evidence which is given at a hearing of the Special Education Tribunal must be given under oath or affirmation. That is, before giving evidence, each witness will be asked to swear or affirm that he or she will tell the truth.[38]

The party who called the witness — or that party's legal counsel — will have the first opportunity to question the witness. These questions must be non-leading questions; that is, the question cannot suggest the answer. For example, a question

---

[37] SPPA, s. 12.
[38] Technically, to give an oath, a person must swear on the Bible that he or she will tell the truth. An affirmation is a secular form of oath, whereby a person promises to tell the truth after being advised of the penalties for perjury. Many administrative decision-makers now use affirmations instead of oaths, in recognition of the diverse religious beliefs of the persons coming before them.

such as, "Then did you tell the teacher you were dissatisfied?" is a leading question and cannot be asked at this stage of the proceeding. Non-leading questions usually take the form of "who/what/when/where/why" questions, which do not suggest to the witness how the question should be answered. For example, the examiner might ask the witness, "What did you say to the teacher?" to elicit the same information covered by the leading question set out above. A party's examination of a witness whom that party has called to testify is referred to as "direct examination" or "examination-in-chief".

Once direct examination is completed, the school board — or its legal counsel — will be entitled to cross-examine the witness. Cross-examination is designed to achieve four main purposes: to obtain additional helpful evidence; to qualify or limit any adverse evidence which has been given; to impeach, contradict or minimize adverse evidence that has been given; and to undermine the credibility of the witness. In contrast with direct examination, leading questions can and will be asked during cross-examination.

Following cross-examination, the party who called the witness — or his or her legal counsel — will have a limited opportunity to ask additional questions of the witness. This final stage of questioning is known as "re-direct examination". Re-direct examination is limited to clarification of matters which arose for the first time in cross-examination; it cannot be used as an opportunity to repeat evidence already given or question the witness on entirely new areas not covered in examination-in-chief. Again, questions asked during re-direct examination cannot be leading questions.

The members of the Tribunal can ask a witness questions at any time in order to clarify any matters raised during questioning by the parties or to ensure that the witness's answer was understood.[39] Sometimes the Tribunal will reserve its questions until the end of questioning by the parties. When this occurs, the parties will be given a further opportunity to question the witness on the evidence given in response to the Tribunal's questions.

Once each of the parents' or guardian's witnesses has been questioned in this manner, the school board — or its legal counsel — will have an opportunity to present its evidence. The school board's witnesses will be put through the same sequence of direct examination, cross-examination and re-direct examination described above and may also be subject to questioning by the Tribunal.

---

[39] Members of the Tribunal should exercise restraint in asking questions of witnesses. In the adversarial system, it is up to the parties to bring forward the evidence the Tribunal requires in order to reach its decision. In *Majcenic v. Natale* (1967), 66 D.L.R. (2d) 50 at p. 65, [1968] 1 O.R. 189, the Ontario Court of Appeal emphasized the risks associated with active intervention by the decision-maker:

When a Judge intervenes in the examination or cross-examination of witnesses, to such an extent that he projects himself into the arena, he of necessity, adopts a position which is inimical to the interests of one or other of the litigants. His action, whether conscious or unconscious, no matter how well intentioned or motivated, creates an atmosphere which violates the principle that "justice not only be done, but appear to be done".

Documents may also be introduced through the witnesses' testimony and they may be asked questions in relation to or about the documents.

Once the school board has called all its witnesses, the parents or guardian — or their legal counsel — will have an opportunity to present reply evidence. Like re-direct examination, reply evidence is limited in scope to any matters which arose for the first time during the school board's evidence. However, reply evidence may involve new witnesses and new documentation where necessary in order to respond to the other party's position.

Finally, once all the evidence is completed, each party will have an opportunity to make a closing statement (sometimes called a "summary statement").[40] Again, the parents or guardian or their legal counsel, proceed first, followed by the school board or its legal counsel. The closing statement allows each party to summarize the evidence, make legal argument (the applicable legal tests are discussed further under the heading "The Special Education Tribunal's Decision", *infra*) and generally try to persuade the Tribunal in favour of the outcome they are seeking.

Preventing Abuse of Process

The Special Education Tribunal has wide powers to control its proceedings in order to prevent abuse of process. Some examples of the Tribunal's powers include the following:

- The Tribunal has authority to exclude evidence or limit a witness's testimony, on the basis that it is "unduly repetitious".[41]
- The Tribunal can reasonably limit examination or cross-examination of witnesses if it is satisfied that the examination or cross-examination "has been sufficient to disclose fully and fairly all matters relevant to the issues in the proceeding".[42]
- The Tribunal has the authority to make whatever orders or give whatever directions it "considers proper to prevent abuse of its processes".[43]
- The Tribunal has authority to make any orders or give any directions it considers necessary to maintain order at the hearing, including the authority to call for the assistance of a peace officer if its orders or directions are disobeyed.[44]

THE EVIDENCE BEFORE THE TRIBUNAL

Elsewhere in this chapter, we have noted that the proceedings before the Special Education Tribunal are adversarial proceedings. That is, the Tribunal is

---

[40]   Draft *Handbook, op cit.*, footnote 6, at p. 15.
[41]   SPPA, s. 15(1).
[42]   *Ibid.*, s. 23(2).
[43]   *Ibid.*, s. 23(1).
[44]   *Ibid.*, s. 9(2).

not permitted to seek out evidence on its own.[45] Rather, it is the responsibility of the parties to ensure that all relevant evidence is presented to the Tribunal during the hearing.

The evidence presented to the Special Education Tribunal will normally take two forms. First, evidence may be presented through the *viva voce* (*i.e.*, in person, oral) testimony of witnesses. Second, evidence may be presented through documents introduced during testimony of the witnesses.

The Special Education Tribunal is not strictly bound by the rules of evidence applicable in a court of law.[46] Nevertheless, it is important to have an understanding of the rules of evidence in order to appreciate what limits there are on admissibility of evidence and how those limits will affect the presentation of a case to the Tribunal.

Competence

One issue which can arise in proceedings before the Special Education Tribunal is whether a particular witness is "competent" to give evidence — that is, capable of understanding the nature of the oath or affirmation, of understanding what it means to tell the truth and the importance of doing so, and/or of observing events, recalling those events and communicating them to the decision-maker. Competence is most likely to be an issue in proceedings before the Tribunal if the student is to be called as a witness.[47]

Under Canadian law, witnesses are presumed to be competent unless proven otherwise.[48] However, both age and disability may provide grounds for challenging a witness's competence. If the competence of a particular witness is challenged, the decision-maker (in this case the Special Education Tribunal) must inquire into the competence of the witness and rule on the issue before the witness can give his or her evidence.[49]

---

[45]   The adversarial nature of Special Education Tribunal proceedings was highlighted in the seminal *Eaton* case, in which the Ontario Court of Appeal criticized the Tribunal for conducting its own literature search and relying in part upon the results of that search in reaching its decision: *Eaton v. Brant County Board of Education* (1995), 123 D.L.R. (4th) 43 at pp. 51-2, 22 O.R. (3d) 1, 77 O.A.C. 368, 27 C.R.R. (2d) 53 (C.A.), revd on other grounds [1997] 1 S.C.R. 241, 142 D.L.R. (4th) 385, 31 O.R. (3d) 574*n*, 97 O.A.C. 161, 41 C.R.R. (2d) 240, 207 N.R. 171.

[46]   SPPA, s. 15.

[47]   There may be good reasons in some cases to avoid calling the student who is the subject of the appeal, if at all possible. Many younger children find the process of testifying before a tribunal very intimidating, particularly if they are being asked to contradict the views of authority figures such as parents, teachers and other school officials. Nevertheless, the Supreme Court of Canada's decision in *Eaton, supra*, footnote 45, suggests that the student has a right, independent of his or her parents, to express his or her views concerning the issues under appeal. Moreover, there may be cases in which calling the student as a witness is necessary in order to ensure that the Tribunal has all of the relevant facts before it in making its decision.

[48]   *Evidence Act*, R.S.O. 1990, c. E.23, s. 18(1) (as amended to 2000, c. 26, Sch. A).

[49]   *Ibid.*, s. 18(2) and (3).

Section 18.1 of the *Evidence Act* provides that, where the competence of a person under 14 years of age is challenged, a court may admit the evidence if the court is satisfied that the person is able to communicate the evidence and understand the nature of the oath or affirmation and that person testifies under oath or affirmation. If the person does not understand the nature of the oath or affirmation, the evidence may still be admitted if the person understands what it means to tell the truth and promises to do so. Further, even if the person does not understand what it means to tell the truth, the court can still admit the evidence if satisfied that the evidence is sufficiently reliable.[50]

Many children understand the importance of telling the truth at a reasonably young age and therefore may be competent to give evidence. The authors are aware of children as young as 8 years old who have been found to be competent to give sworn evidence. Certainly, most adolescent children will have sufficient understanding of the importance of truth-telling to be competent witnesses. Nevertheless, if an objection to competence is raised, the Tribunal will need to question the child in order to satisfy itself that the child has the necessary understanding to be a competent witness.

The *Evidence Act* also contemplates that persons under 18 may be permitted to give their evidence under special conditions if it will assist them to give complete and accurate testimony. Examples of such special conditions include testifying on videotape or behind a screen or similar device. Similarly, a witness under 18 may be accompanied by a support person while giving evidence. Limits may also be placed on cross-examination of a person under 18 where cross-examination would be likely to adversely affect the witness's ability to give evidence, or would otherwise be contrary to the best interests of the witness.[51]

Ontario Regulation 181/98 gives students aged 16 and over the right to be present at and participate in both IPRC and SEAB proceedings, thereby implicitly recognizing that students in this age group are competent to participate in special education proceedings.[52] However, if any person under the age of 18 is called as a witness and the other party objects, the Tribunal will need to hear arguments from both sides and make a determination of whether the witness is competent. It may be that setting conditions on the testimony or the circumstances in which it is given (*i.e.*, by closing the part of the hearing where the witness testifies or by allowing a support person to be present while the witness testifies) will be sufficient to address any concerns about the witness's competence. However, there may be significant questions concerning the weight that should be assigned to the witness's evidence, particularly where the witness testified under special conditions.

Disabilities which interfere with an individual's ability to understand the importance of telling the truth or his or her ability to observe, recall or

---

[50]   *Ibid.*, s. 18.1(1) to (3). Notably, s. 18.2 further provides that the evidence of a person under 14 need not be corroborated by other evidence in order to be relied upon.

[51]   *Ibid.*, ss. 18.3 to 18.6.

[52]   O. Reg. 181/98, s. 5.

communicate information, may also call into question the individual's competence to give evidence. Determining the competence of a disabled individual can be a complex task, sometimes requiring expert evidence concerning the individual's capabilities.

In special education proceedings, circumstances are likely to arise in which a potential witness is both disabled and a child. In these cases, complex questions may have to be resolved concerning what evidence the witness is competent to give and what weight should be assigned to their evidence. These questions will have to be determined by the Tribunal, following submissions from the parties, based on the particular facts of the case.

Admissibility

The Special Education Tribunal is given considerable latitude under the SPPA to determine what evidence will be admitted at the hearing.[53] Although the courts have developed a number of "rules" governing the admissibility of evidence, the Tribunal is not bound by the rules of evidence which apply in courts of law. As a result, the Tribunal may admit evidence which would not be admissible in court. However, like a court, the Tribunal will listen to arguments about the weight to be accorded to such evidence and will determine the appropriate weight when making its final decision.

Section 15(2) of the SPPA does place two restrictions on the scope of the evidence which may be admitted by the Tribunal. First, the Tribunal may not admit evidence which would be inadmissible in court because it is "privileged" (*i.e.*, protected from disclosure) under the laws of evidence. Second, the Tribunal may not admit evidence which is rendered inadmissible under the *Education Act* or any other statute. These restrictions will be discussed under the heading "Privileged Information", *infra*.

Relevance and Weight

The main factor which the Special Education Tribunal will consider in determining whether evidence should be admitted is whether the evidence is relevant to the issues before the Tribunal. Evidence is "relevant" if it tends to prove or disprove facts which are in dispute.

In considering relevance, the Tribunal will balance the value of the evidence in proving key matters in dispute (often referred to as its "probative value") against the prejudice or harm which could be caused to a party or other person if the evidence is admitted. Extremely prejudicial evidence which is of dubious or limited assistance to the Tribunal will often be excluded.

The question of whether evidence is relevant should be distinguished from the question of what weight should be given to it. The concept of "weight" describes the importance or significance accorded to a piece of evidence in reaching a

---

[53] SPPA, s. 15.

particular factual conclusion. A witness's evidence may be relevant yet may be given little weight, because of circumstances such as the witness's limited direct knowledge of or involvement in events, questions about the witness's competence or credibility, the existence of a preponderance of evidence to the contrary and many other factors.

It is not uncommon for tribunals such as the Special Education Tribunal to take a broad view of what is relevant. Often, the degree of relevance of a particular piece of evidence will not be clear until all of the evidence has been presented. Accordingly, the Tribunal may decide to admit the evidence and reserve its decision on the relevance of the evidence and the weight it should be given until the hearing has concluded.

Privileged Information

Section 15(2) of the SPPA prohibits the Tribunal from admitting evidence which is "privileged" (*i.e.*, protected from disclosure) under the laws of evidence or which is rendered inadmissible under the *Education Act* or any other statute.

Privilege under Evidence Law

The law of evidence recognizes a number of different categories of "privileged" communications which cannot be the subject of evidence in legal proceedings, unless the party for whose benefit the privilege is imposed agrees to waive it. The most common categories of privilege include solicitor-client privilege (which protects communications between a client and his or her lawyer), litigation privilege (which protects communications with third parties which were made for the dominant purpose of preparing for actual or anticipated litigation) and settlement privilege (which protects communications made in the course of good faith efforts to resolve a dispute where litigation has been commenced or is contemplated.)[54]

In addition to the categories of privilege discussed previously, the common law recognizes that privilege may extend to other communications which meet all four of the following criteria:

(i)   the communications must originate in a confidence that they will not be disclosed;

(ii)   this element of confidentiality must be essential to the full and satisfactory maintenance of the relationship between the parties;

(iii) the relationship must be one which in the opinion of the community ought to be sedulously fostered; and

---

[54] Notably, settlement privilege may protect mediation discussions from disclosure in litigation, provided that litigation has been commenced or was in contemplation at the time the mediation was held. However, parties to mediation are nevertheless well-advised to confirm any understanding about confidentiality in a written agreement.

(iv)   the injury that would be caused to the relationship by disclosure of the communication must be greater than the benefit thereby gained for the correct disposal of the litigation.[55]

This latter type of privilege is often referred to as "case-by-case" privilege, because the question of whether the above criteria are met, with the result that the communication is privileged, must be determined on a case-by-case basis.

Significantly, the fourth criterion listed above grants a court a wide discretion to override the confidentiality of the communication in the interests of the administration of justice. Accordingly, it is often quite difficult in practice to establish that a communication is "privileged" under this test.

Privilege under the Education Act

As noted above, s. 15(2) of the SPPA also prohibits the Tribunal from admitting any evidence that is rendered inadmissible under its governing statute, the *Education Act*. Section 266(2) of the *Education Act* creates a privilege for the contents of the Ontario Student Record ("OSR"):

> A record is privileged for the information and use of supervisory officers and the principal and teachers of the school for the improvement of instruction of the pupil, and such record,
> (a) subject to subsections (2.1), (3) and (5), is not available to any other person; and
> (b) except for the purposes of subsection (5), is not admissible in evidence for any purpose in any trial, inquest, inquiry, examination, hearing or other proceeding, except to prove the establishment, maintenance, retention or transfer of the record,
> without the written permission of the parent or guardian of the pupil or, where the pupil is an adult, the written permission of the pupil.

At first blush, the result of this provision appears to be that the documents in the student's OSR are not admissible in proceedings before the Special Education Tribunal without parental consent. However, this result is widely perceived as problematic because it would allow the parents/guardian unilaterally to control what OSR material is before the Tribunal, even if that material was before the IPRC when the original identification/placement decision was made.[56]

---

[55]   See *Wigmore on Evidence*, 3rd ed. (McNaughton rev.) (Boston: Little, Brown & Co., 1961), vol. 8, §2285 at p. 527, quoted in *Slavutych v. Baker*, [1976] 1 S.C.R. 254 at p. 260, 55 D.L.R. (3d) 224, [1975] 4 W.W.R. 620, 38 C.R.N.S. 306, 3 N.R. 587 *sub nom. Slavutch v. Board of Governors of University of Alberta*. See also *R. v. Gruenke*, [1991] 3 S.C.R. 263, [1991] 6 W.W.R. 673, 6 W.A.C. 112, 75 Man. R. (2d) 112, 67 C.C.C. (3d) 289, 7 C.R.R. (2d) 108 *sub nom. R. v. Fosty*, 8 C.R. (4th) 368, 130 N.R. 161; *M. (A). v. Ryan*, [1997] 1 S.C.R. 157, 143 D.L.R. (4th) 1, [1997] 4 W.W.R. 1, 138 W.A.C. 81, 29 B.C.L.R. (3d) 133, 34 C.C.L.T. (2d) 1, 8 C.P.C. (4th) 1, 4 C.R. (5th) 220, 42 C.R.R. (2d) 37, 207 N.R. 81.

[56]   The authors note that s. 266 was enacted before the special education scheme was introduced. Arguably, the provision is no longer responsive to the diverse array of administrative proceedings carried on under the *Education Act* and needs to be reviewed by the Legislature.

There are a number of arguments which can be made to counter the proposition that OSR documents are not admissible before the Tribunal without parental consent. One such argument is that, by appealing the school board's decision, the parents/guardian must be taken to have waived any privilege that might apply to the OSR documents, at least to the extent necessary to allow the school board to make a full and fair response to the appeal.[57]

Another argument flows from the fact that the very reason that many OSR documents relevant to the special education process are obtained or compiled is for use in that process. Section 32(c) of the *Municipal Freedom of Information and Protection of Privacy Act*[58] permits the disclosure of personal information "for the purpose for which it was obtained or compiled or for a consistent purpose". Section 53(1) then provides that the MFIPPA prevails over the confidentiality provisions of any other Act unless the other Act specifically says that it does not. Thus, the MFIPPA "trumps" s. 266 and any OSR documents to which this argument applies may be disclosed before the Tribunal.[59]

A similar argument can be made in support of the proposition that, quite apart from the admissibility of OSR documents, the teachers and school board personnel involved in obtaining, compiling, reviewing or using those documents, can give oral evidence about their contents before the Tribunal. Section 266(10) of the *Education Act* allows a person to disclose the contents of OSR documents "as may be required in the performance of his or her duties". A teacher or other school board representative who discloses such information in the context of testifying in support of the school board before the Tribunal is surely acting "as may be required in the performance of his or her duties".

Hearsay Evidence

"Hearsay evidence" is evidence given by a person who did not observe events first-hand, but rather is relying on an account of events provided by another person. For example, if a parent gave evidence of what he or she was told by the student about the student's experiences in the classroom or gave evidence about classroom observations reported by the teacher, the evidence would be hearsay evidence.

---

[57] Many tribunals and courts take the view that, where evidence which would otherwise be privileged relates to a matter placed in issue by the party protected by the privilege, the opposing party is entitled to sufficient disclosure of the evidence to ensure that it can make a full and fair response to the issue raised. However, in such cases, the decision-maker may place limits on disclosure to ensure that it does not go any further than is necessary in order to ensure fairness to the other party. Although the authors are not aware of a case in which this issue has arisen before the Tribunal, the same principles would seem to apply in such a case.

[58] R.S.O. 1990, c. M.56 (as amended to 2000, c. 26, Sch. J), s. 32(c) ("MFIPPA").

[59] The authors note that, thus far, this argument does not appear to have been tested before the Tribunal or the courts. However, it appears consistent with the approach arbitrators have taken to this issue, which is discussed further in Chapter 6, "The Identification, Placement and Review Committee".

Hearsay evidence is generally inadmissible in court for the purpose of proving the truth of the position being put forward. There are two main reasons for this. First, the courts generally require the parties to put forward the "best evidence" in support of their case. Hearsay evidence is not the best evidence of what transpired; evidence from witnesses with first-hand knowledge is far more persuasive. Second, hearsay evidence is viewed as unreliable because of the absence of any opportunity to cross-examine the person who provided the original account of events. Without the opportunity for cross-examination, it is not possible to draw any conclusions about the credibility of the person who provided the information.

Although hearsay evidence is generally inadmissible in court, there are a number of specific situations in which hearsay may be admitted.[60] In addition, the Supreme Court of Canada has held that, in some very limited circumstances, hearsay evidence may be admitted if the party putting forward the evidence can establish that the evidence is both reasonably necessary and reliable.[61]

The Supreme Court has also recognized that, because of the special challenges young children may face in giving evidence, hearsay evidence may also be admissible in some exceptional cases involving child witnesses.[62] However, even in these cases, hearsay evidence is very much the exception rather than the rule and direct evidence will always be preferable.

Despite the fact that hearsay evidence is generally not admissible in court, all tribunals covered by the SPPA, including the Special Education Tribunal, can admit hearsay evidence, subject to a later assessment of the weight it should be given. In this way, the Tribunal can ensure that it has the fullest possible evidentiary record before it when it makes its decision. If the hearsay evidence is not corroborated through other evidence or the truth of the evidence is in dispute, the Tribunal may decide to give little or no weight to the hearsay evidence in reaching its final decision. Accordingly, even though the Tribunal can admit hearsay evidence, it is generally preferable to rely on first-hand evidence rather than hearsay evidence.

Expert Evidence

As a general rule, witnesses are not permitted to give evidence in a court of law about their opinions — particularly their opinions concerning the disposition of the issues in dispute in the litigation. However, there is one significant exception to the prohibition on opinion evidence. The courts will permit a qualified expert to give opinion evidence concerning matters within his or her area of expertise,

---

[60] For example, under s. 35(2) of the *Evidence Act*, records made in the usual and ordinary course of business are exempted from the hearsay rule, provided that certain statutory preconditions are met.

[61] *R. v. Khan*, [1990] 2 S.C.R. 531, 41 O.A.C. 353, 59 C.C.C. (3d) 92, 79 C.R. (3d) 1, 113 N.R. 53; *R. v. Smith*, [1992] 2 S.C.R. 915, 94 D.L.R. (4th) 590, 55 O.A.C. 321, 75 C.C.C. (3d) 257, 15 C.R. (4th) 133, 139 N.R. 323.

[62] *R. v. F. (W.J.)*, [1999] 3 S.C.R. 569, 178 D.L.R. (4th) 53, [1999] 12 W.W.R. 587, 205 W.A.C. 161, 180 Sask. R. 161, 138 C.C.C. (3d) 1, 27 C.R. (5th) 169, 247 N.R. 62.

provided that the evidence is: (1) relevant to an issue in the case; (2) necessary to assist the decision-maker (in the sense that it concerns matters outside the experience of a lay person and the decision-maker cannot reach a decision without the benefit of the evidence); (3) otherwise admissible; and (4) given by a properly qualified expert.[63]

Proceedings before the Special Education Tribunal will often involve evidence from numerous experts. Physicians, psychiatrists, psychologists, audiologists, speech-language pathologists, speech-language therapists, physiotherapists, occupational therapists and educators specializing in education of children with special needs are but a few of the kinds of experts who may be called as witnesses by either party to give evidence about the appropriate identification and/or placement of the student.

In many cases, these experts will have prepared reports or assessments and these reports or assessments will have been relied upon by the IPRC and/or the SEAB to support a particular identification or placement. On appeal, the individuals who prepared these reports or assessments will often be called as witnesses to elaborate on or explain their conclusions.

In some cases, classroom teachers and others who deal with the student on a daily basis may also be able to provide expert evidence to the Tribunal. With respect to identification as an "exceptional pupil", the classroom teacher will not necessarily have the expertise to provide an opinion on whether the student has "behavioural, communicational, intellectual, physical or multiple exceptionalities", or what category of exceptionality applies. However, the teacher may be able to provide an expert opinion on whether the student appears to "need placement in a special education program".[64] A teacher may also be able to give evidence about proposed placements and what special education programs and services can be delivered in the various placements. Depending on the circumstances and the teacher's particular expertise, the teacher may even be able to provide an expert opinion concerning the student's learning style and progress (or lack of progress) in the regular class or in a particular placement.[65]

Although expert evidence is a legitimate and often a necessary part of an appeal to the Tribunal, both the school board and the parents should be cautious of being drawn into a contest of opposing experts. Each party should carefully consider the implications of the expert witnesses they call and the manner in which they handle the expert witnesses called by the other party. For example, it may be that teachers

---

[63] *R. v. Mohan*, [1994] 2 S.C.R. 9, 114 D.L.R. (4th) 419, 18 O.R. (3d) 160*n*, 71 O.A.C. 241, 89 C.C.C. (3d) 402, 29 C.R. (4th) 243, 166 N.R. 245.

[64] The definition of "exceptional pupil" is found in s. 1(1) of the *Education Act*.

[65] It may be appropriate to distinguish here between the student's classroom teacher, who knows the student and is able to observe the student in the classroom, and the student's special education teacher, who may not know the child well but will understand how the placements work. Each of these teachers may bring different expertise to the appeal process.

and other school board personnel who will be working with the student in the placement proposed by the school board have valuable expertise to share with the Tribunal. However, being examined and cross-examined in contentious legal proceedings can inject an adversarial note into the student-teacher relationship. Both parties must remember that the purpose of the special education appeal process is to ensure the student's educational needs and best interests are met and keep that objective uppermost in their minds when dealing with the expert evidence submitted to the Tribunal.

THE SPECIAL EDUCATION TRIBUNAL'S DECISION

Timing

At the conclusion of the hearing, a Special Education Tribunal will usually "reserve" its decision. This means that the Tribunal will not issue its decision right away, but will take some time to consider the matter and prepare a decision in writing. In contrast to IPRC and SEAB decisions, there is no time limit within which the Tribunal must issue its decision.

In some cases, particularly where there is some specific urgency with respect to the student's placement, the Tribunal may make its order verbally at the end of the hearing and then issue its written reasons at a later time.

Weighing the Evidence

As part of the decision-making process, the Tribunal will have the task of sorting through the evidence and making findings with respect to any material facts which are in dispute. This task will require the Tribunal to decide what weight should be assigned to various items of evidence and is often referred to as "weighing the evidence".

Where expert evidence has been presented, the Tribunal will often have to decide between conflicting expert opinions. In weighing the expert evidence, the Tribunal will consider factors such as the relative expertise of the various witnesses, whether they had an opportunity to observe or examine the student and, if so, the extent of those observations or examinations and the degree of the expert's objectivity.

The Legal Test

Once the Tribunal has weighed the evidence and made its findings of fact, the Tribunal must apply the appropriate legal test to those facts in order to reach its decision on identification and/or placement.

In dealing with identification, the question before the Tribunal is whether the expert evidence supports a finding that the student is an "exceptional pupil" because of "behavioural, communicational, intellectual, physical or multiple exceptionalities . . . such that he or she is considered to need placement in a special education program".[66]

The question before the Tribunal on a placement appeal is somewhat more complex. In the *Eaton* decision, the Supreme Court of Canada confirmed that the legal test to be applied by the Tribunal in reviewing placement is whether, from the student's perspective, the placement is in his or her best interests. In determining the student's best interests, some weight is to be given to parental preferences; however, parental preferences are not determinative. The Court said:

> We cannot forget, however, that for a child who is young or unable to communicate his or her needs or wishes, equality rights are being exercised on his or her behalf, usually by the child's parents. Moreover, the requirements for respecting these rights in this setting are decided by adults who have authority over this child. For this reason, the decision-making body must further ensure that its determination of the appropriate accommodation for an exceptional child be from a subjective, child-centred perspective, one which attempts to make equality meaningful from the child's point of view as opposed to that of the adults in his or her life. As a means of achieving this aim, it must also determine that the form of accommodation chosen is in the child's best interests. A decision-making body must determine whether the integrated setting can be adapted to meet the special needs of an exceptional child. Where this is not possible, that is, where aspects of the integrated setting which cannot reasonably be changed interfere with meeting the child's special needs, the principle of accommodation will require a special education placement outside of this setting. For older children and those who are able to communicate their wishes and needs, their own views will play an important role in the determination of best interests. For younger children, and those like Emily, who are either incapable of making a choice or have a very limited means of communicating their wishes, the decision-maker must make this determination on the basis of other evidence before it.[67]

Reasons

By virtue of s. 17(1) of the SPPA, a tribunal must give its decision and order and the underlying reasons in writing. Where the Tribunal has given a verbal decision at the end of the hearing, it will subsequently confirm its decision in writing and will provide its reasons at that time.

Once the Tribunal's written decision is completed, the Tribunal must give a copy of the decision, including the reasons, to each party who participated in the hearing.[68] Usually the Secretary of the Tribunal will forward the decision to the parties by regular mail or by courier.[69]

It is important to note that, particularly where there are unresolved preliminary issues, the Tribunal may issue a number of separate decisions in a single appeal. Depending on the circumstances, these decisions may either be issued separately

---

[66] *Education Act*, s. 1(1). This issue is discussed further in Chapter 4, "Identification and Exceptionality".

[67] *Eaton v. Brant County Board of Education*, [1997] 1 S.C.R. 241 at pp. 277-8, 142 D.L.R. (4th) 385, 31 O.R. (3d) 574*n*, 97 O.A.C. 161, 41 C.R.R. (2d) 240, 207 N.R. 171.

[68] Depending on the student's age, it may also be prudent for the Tribunal to give its decision to the affected student, whether or not the student was a party.

[69] SPPA, s. 18.1.

at different times during the litigation or consolidated into a single decision issued at the end of the litigation. Regardless of which of these courses of action is followed, the decisions will all be issued in accordance with the statutory rules described above.

REMEDIES AVAILABLE

The Special Education Tribunal is given broad remedial powers under s. 57(4) of the *Education Act*:

> The Special Education Tribunal shall hear the appeal and may,
> (a) dismiss the appeal; or
> (b) grant the appeal and make such order as it considers necessary with respect to the identification or placement.

In other words, the Tribunal may dismiss the appeal and confirm the identification and/or placement decision of the school board. Alternatively, the Tribunal may grant the appeal and set aside the identification or placement decision, or both. If the Tribunal grants the appeal, it may substitute its own identification and/or placement decision for that reached by the IPRC or the school board (following an appeal to the SEAB). It may also make any further or other order it considers necessary with respect to the identification and/or placement.

There have been cases in which the Tribunal has ordered a placement different from what was proposed by either the parents or the school board. For example, in *Lewis v. York Region Board of Education*,[70] the parents sought to have the student identified as "multi-handicapped" and placed in a regular Kindergarten or Grade 1 class in her neighbourhood school, with the assistance of a teacher's aide and other support staff as required. The school board argued that the IPRC's decision, identifying the student as "trainable retarded" (a category of exceptionality which has since been removed from the *Education Act*) and directing that she be placed in a special school for the trainable retarded, should be confirmed. The Tribunal accepted the parents' position that the student should be identified as "multi-handicapped" but rejected both the parents' proposed placement and the school board's proposed placement. Instead, the Tribunal directed that the student should be placed in another school which already offered a class for multi-handicapped students and had specialized services and staff available on a regular basis to assist such students.

Similarly, in *Ormerod v. Wentworth County Board of Education*,[71] the parents submitted that the student should be provided with "a teacher's aide fluent in cued speech in the regular classroom, a resource teacher fluent in cued speech and a speech pathologist, 'until it is demonstrated that [his] needs have significantly changed'". The school board submitted that "the provision of a non-cueing

---

[70] (unreported, September 10, 1985) (Houghton).
[71] (unreported, June 5, 1987) (Houghton), at p. 5.

resource withdrawal teacher, assisted by a teacher's aide who is fluent in cueing" was an appropriate placement.[72] However, the Tribunal observed that: "evidence called by both parties through several witnesses caused the Tribunal to examine [the student's] overall needs beyond the positions of the parties taken in their written submissions".[73] In the end result, the Tribunal ordered the following:

1. [the student] continue in a regular class for about 50 per cent of each school day with the assistance of a cueing teacher's aide/interpreter; and
2. the Board provide a teacher of the deaf for [the student] for approximately 50 per cent of each school day . . . [and]
3. the Board ensure that an effective mechanism be established to co-ordinate the various aspects of [the student's] program; and
4. that the Board establish an effective mechanism for the continuous assessment of [the student] and the evaluation of his program.[74]

The Tribunal's decision may also include recommendations concerning special education programs and special education services. These recommendations are not binding on the school board, but must be considered by the principal in developing and/or reviewing the pupil's IEP.[75]

In one case, *Blais v. Sudbury District Catholic School Board*,[76] the parents requested the Tribunal to make a number of specific orders with respect to the program to be provided to their child, who was autistic. The parents' request included:

*   clinical in-service training for the teachers and the educational assistant in the method of behaviour modification and education in the disorder of autism;
*   an educational assistant with training in modification and specific knowledge of PDD/autism assigned to the student for 100% of the school day; and
*   a speech pathologist with knowledge and experience in PDD/autism overseeing her program and the involvement of an occupational therapist also with knowledge and experience in PDD/autism.[77]

The school board responded that these were programming matters which were not properly the subject of an appeal. However, in its decision, the Tribunal recommended a number of specific programming outcomes:

---

[72] *Ibid.*

[73] *Ibid.*, at p. 35.

[74] *Ibid.* The Tribunal also specified in its decision that the special education class contemplated by item 2 must provide for "(i) language, speech and social skills development, auditory training and the development of independent work habits; (ii) resource support for [the student's] regular class placement; (iii) ongoing support from a speech pathologist". *Ibid.*, at p. 34.

[75] O. Reg. 181/98, ss. 6(6)(b) and 7(3)(b). As was discussed under the heading "The Scope of the Appeal", *supra*, the line between placement and program is not always clear.

[76] (unreported, September 21, 1999) (Tompkins).

[77] *Ibid.*, at p. 3.

- [the student] must receive daily instruction in language skills from a trained educational assistant;
- in the development of the IEP, benchmarks and appropriate activities and resources must be specified;
- in planning and implementing this special education program, and services including the necessary in-service staff, in particular the educational assistant, the Board should avail itself of the services and expertise of [a specified doctor];
- the selection of the teacher and the educational assistant who work with [the student] must be done with great care;
- the selection of materials and the training of staff must become a high priority of the Catholic Board to ensure that [the student] has a successful school experience;
- the placement for [the student] be in a life skills program with appropriate integration.[78]

Notably, even before O. Reg. 181/98 came into force, the Tribunal often considered and made orders concerning the special education programs and services available when reviewing placement decisions. For example, in *Ormerod*, the Tribunal found that it had jurisdiction to consider the parents' request for "a resource withdrawal teacher fluent in cued speech", even though the requirement of fluency in cued speech related to the special education programs and services available in the placement, rather than to the placement *per se*.[79] In *Razaqpur v. Carleton Roman Catholic Separate School Board*,[80] the Tribunal ordered the Board to purchase a special education program for the student, who was gifted, from the Ottawa Board of Education.

As the above examples illustrate, the Tribunal exercises broad remedial jurisdiction in dealing with identification and/or placement appeals. This broad discretion provides the Tribunal with the flexibility it requires in order to address the circumstances of individual cases.

LEGAL COSTS

Order in Council 1382/97, which establishes the Special Education Tribunal, also authorizes the Tribunal to order a party to pay certain costs associated with appeal proceedings. The Order in Council states as follows:

> Pursuant to s. 36(2)(b) of the *Education Act*, the Tribunals are hereby authorized to fix the maximum costs assessable against a party in respect of,
>
> (a)　the fees of expert witnesses subpoenaed to attend the hearing;
> (b)　the fees of witnesses subpoenaed to attend the hearing;
> (c)　counsel fees of counsel for the parties; and
> (d)　the travelling and living expenses of the parties, counsel for the parties and of any witnesses, that are incurred for the purpose of attending a hearing.

---

[78]　*Ibid.*, at pp. 32-3.
[79]　*Ormerod, supra*, footnote 71, at pp. 2-5.
[80]　(unreported, undated) (Houghton).

The said Tribunals are also authorized to assess such other costs of the hearing as they find appropriate, other than the remuneration and expenses of the members of the Tribunal, against one or other of both the parties, regardless of success at the hearing, and for such purpose the Tribunal may, but need not, require the parties to speak to the matter of costs prior to or at the conclusion of the hearing.[81]

The provisions of the Order in Council dealing with costs were based on the authority to fix costs set out in s. 36(2)(b) of the *Education Act*. This provision has since been repealed and replaced by s. 57(2)(c), which requires that costs issues be dealt with by regulation.[82] It is therefore questionable whether the provisions of the Order in Council authorizing the Tribunal to order costs are still valid.[83] Accordingly, as of the date of this writing, there is some doubt concerning the authority of the Tribunal to award costs.

EFFECT OF THE SPECIAL EDUCATION TRIBUNAL'S DECISION

Section 57(5) of the *Education Act* provides that the decision of a Special Education Tribunal is "final and binding on the parties to the decision". This provision has a number of important implications.

Section 57(5) states that the Tribunal's decision must be considered final. This means that, once it has released its decision, the Tribunal cannot reopen it. It cannot amend or revise its decision, except to correct a "typographical error, error of calculation or similar error".[84] Similarly, once the Tribunal has rendered its decision on a particular set of facts, the issues underlying the decision generally cannot be relitigated by the same parties before another Tribunal or in any other forum. Note, however, that this does not preclude parents from appealing a subsequent IPRC decision. Even though the issue may be the same, the underlying facts will have changed.

There is no direct appeal to the courts from the Special Education Tribunal's decisions. However, there is one set of circumstances in which the Special Education Tribunal's decision can be reviewed by the courts. Where a party is dissatisfied with the Tribunal's decision, that party can apply to the Divisional Court of the Ontario Superior Court of Justice for judicial review of the Tribunal's decision. However, in the event of judicial review proceedings, the statutory admonition in s. 57(5) that the Tribunal's decision is "final and binding on the parties to the decision" will be viewed as a signal that the Legislature intended the

---

[81]   OIC 1382/97, dated June 25, 1997.

[82]   No such regulations have ever been issued.

[83]   Notably, the fact that the costs provisions of the Order in Council may no longer be valid does not affect the validity of the Order in Council as a whole.

[84]   SPPA, s. 21.1. See also, *Chandler v. Alberta Assn. of Architects* (1989), 62 D.L.R. (4th) 577, [1989] 2 S.C.R. 848, [1989] 6 W.W.R. 521, 70 Alta. L.R. (2d) 193, 101 A.R. 321, 40 Admin. L.R. 128, 36 C.L.R. 1, 99 N.R. 277, the leading Canadian authority on the doctrine of *functus officio*.

courts to defer to the Tribunal's decision. As a result, judicial review will be available only on certain narrowly circumscribed grounds. Judicial review proceedings are discussed in greater detail in Chapter 11, "Review by the Courts".

Section 57(5) also states that a decision of the Tribunal is binding on the parties. In other words, the decision has the force of law and must be implemented by the parties.[85] By virtue of s. 19(1) of the SPPA, the Tribunal's decision can be filed in a court of law, with the result that it is enforceable as though it was an order of the court.[86] Accordingly, the Tribunal's decision must be implemented by the parties in accordance with its terms.

---

[85] It may be open to the parties to agree not to implement the Tribunal's decision, but rather to implement some other agreed upon course of action. However, such an agreement should be consistent with the educational best interests of the student.

[86] SPPA, s. 19(1).

11

Review by the Courts

INTRODUCTION

There are a limited range of circumstances in which a school board, parent or guardian, or any other party to proceedings before the Special Education Tribunal (the "Tribunal") who is dissatisfied with the procedure followed or the decision reached may apply to the courts for review of the Tribunal's decision.[1] Proceedings of this nature are referred to as judicial review proceedings.

In this chapter, we discuss both the procedures for initiating judicial review proceedings and the grounds for judicial review which are available.

REVIEW OF IPRC AND SEAB DECISIONS

In most cases, the courts will decline to review the decisions of an Identification, Placement and Review Committee ("IPRC") or a Special Education Appeal Board ("SEAB"). The *Education Act*[2] and O. Reg. 181/98[3] provide for broad rights of appeal from the IPRC to the SEAB and from the SEAB to the Tribunal. These broad appeal rights provide an opportunity for review and correction of any procedural or substantive errors which may have occurred at an earlier level. As a matter of general principle, the courts .will almost always conclude that judicial review proceedings are premature until the party seeking the review has exhausted any statutory appeal rights which are available.[4] Accordingly, judicial review proceedings usually cannot be commenced until the case has proceeded to the Special Education Tribunal and the Tribunal has issued its decision.

---

[1] See also Chapter 10, "The Final Appeal".

[2] R.S.O. 1990, c. E.2 (as amended).

[3] *Identification and Placement of Exceptional Pupils*, O. Reg. 181/98 ("O. Reg. 181/98" or "the Regulation").

[4] *Harelkin v. University of Regina*, [1979] 2 S.C.R. 560, 96 D.L.R. (3d) 14, [1979] 3 W.W.R. 676, 26 N.R. 364.

It is possible that a case could arise in which the errors occurring at the IPRC or SEAB level were so fundamental to the Tribunal's jurisdiction or of such a serious nature that appeal rights would not provide an adequate remedy. For example, if the IPRC refused to allow the parents to participate or the SEAB held a hearing without notice to the parents, or if there was a reasonable apprehension of bias at the IPRC or at the SEAB level, a court might be persuaded to deal with the judicial review without requiring the matter to proceed to the Tribunal. Nevertheless, such cases will be extremely rare and, more often, the parties will be required to exhaust their internal remedies before seeking the assistance of the courts.

THE PROCEDURE FOR JUDICIAL REVIEW

We have noted above that the courts usually will not intervene in the special education decision-making process until after a hearing has been held by the Special Education Tribunal and the Tribunal has issued its decision. At that point, if one of the parties believes that the Tribunal has committed a procedural or substantive error, that party may apply for judicial review of the Tribunal's decision.

Below, we discuss the procedural rules which apply to judicial review proceedings in Ontario. The grounds for judicial review are discussed later in this chapter.

Commencing an Application for Judicial Review

In Ontario, judicial review proceedings are generally dealt with by the Divisional Court of the Superior Court of Justice (the "Divisional Court").[5] The Divisional Court is a specialized "branch" of the Superior Court, which sits in panels comprised of three Superior Court judges.[6]

Judicial review proceedings are commenced by filing a legal document called a "Notice of Application for Judicial Review" with the Divisional Court.[7] After it has been filed, the Notice of Application must be served on any other parties to the judicial review proceedings.[8] Generally, the parties to the judicial review

---

[5] *Judicial Review Procedure Act*, R.S.O. 1990, c. J.1, s. 6(1) ("JRPA").

[6] *Courts of Justice Act*, R.S.O. 1990, c. C.43 (as amended to 2000, c. 26, Sch. A), s. 21(1) ("CJA"). Section 6(2) of the JRPA contemplates judicial review by a single judge of the Superior Court of Justice in cases involving a high degree of urgency. In order to bring an application under s. 6(2), the party seeking to do so must persuade the judge that "the case is one of urgency and that the delay required for an application to the Divisional Court is likely to involve a failure of justice". This is a very strict test, which is rigorously enforced by the judiciary, even where both parties have consented to a hearing before a single judge. As a result, judicial review proceedings before a single judge of the Superior Court are available only in very exceptional circumstances.

[7] JRPA, ss. 2 and 6(1); Rules of Civil Procedure, R.R.O. 1990, Reg. 194, rule 68.01.

[8] Rules of Civil Procedure, rule 38.06.

proceedings will be the same parties who participated in the proceedings before the Special Education Tribunal.[9]

The JRPA contemplates that, in certain cases, the tribunal under review may participate in judicial review proceedings.[10] However, the courts have placed strict limits on the role an administrative tribunal may play in judicial review proceedings challenging its own decisions,[11] and generally discourage tribunals from participating in such proceedings.[12]

Despite these restrictions, it is common practice to serve the Notice of Application on the tribunal as well as the parties. This ensures that the tribunal is aware of the proceedings and has an opportunity to assert any participatory rights it may be entitled to exercise. Thus, in cases involving judicial review of the Special Education Tribunal, the Notice of Application should usually be served upon the Tribunal as well as the parties.

---

[9] See Chapter 10, "The Final Appeal".

[10] JRPA, s. 9(2).

[11] The leading case concerning the extent of an administrative tribunal's role in judicial review proceedings challenging its own decisions is *Northwestern Utilities Ltd. v. Edmonton (City)*, [1979] 1 S.C.R. 684, 89 D.L.R. (3d) 161, 7 Alta. L.R. (2d) 370, 12 A.R. 449, 23 N.R. 565. In the *Northwestern Utilities* decision, the Supreme Court of Canada emphasized that an administrative tribunal should not participate as a party in a proceeding in which one of its own decisions is being challenged. Rather, the tribunal's role in such a proceeding should be limited to intervention as an *amicus curiae* ("friend of the court") and, even then, should be very narrowly circumscribed. This approach is designed to protect the real and perceived impartiality of the tribunal's decision making. Mr. Justice Estey stated (at pp. 709-10):

> . . . active and even aggressive participation [in judicial review proceedings] can have no other effect than to discredit the impartiality of an administrative tribunal either in the case where the matter is referred back to it, or in future proceedings involving similar interests and issues or the same parties. The Board is given a clear opportunity to make its point in its reasons for decision, and it abuses one's notion of propriety to countenance its participation as a full-fledged litigant in this Court, in complete adversarial confrontation with one of the principals in the contest before the Board itself in the first instance.
>
> It has been the policy in this Court to limit the role of an administrative tribunal whose decision is at issue before the Court, even where the right to appear is given by statute, to an explanatory role with reference to the record before the Board and to the making of representations relating to jurisdiction [citations omitted].
>
> . . . . .
>
> Where the parent or authorizing statute is silent as to the role or status of the tribunal in appeal or review proceedings, this Court has confined the tribunal strictly to the issue of its jurisdiction to make the order in question [citations omitted].

[12] For example, in *Great Atlantic & Pacific Co. of Canada Ltd. v. Ontario (Human Rights Commission)* (1993), 109 D.L.R. (4th) 214, 13 O.R. (3d) 824, 65 O.A.C. 227, 12 Admin. L.R. (2d) 267 *sub nom. Gale v. Miracle Food Mart*, 18 C.H.R.R. D/97, 93 C.L.L.C. ¶17,017 (Div. Ct.), the Court expressed its disquiet with the decision-maker's request to participate in the judicial review proceedings arising from her decision. Due to the exceptional circumstances of the case, which included allegations of personal bias against the decision-maker, the Court permitted her to participate. However, when the bias objection was ultimately upheld, the decision-maker was held jointly and severally liable for costs.

The party filing the Notice of Application for Judicial Review must also serve a copy of it on the Attorney General for Ontario.[13] The Attorney General has an institutional interest in overseeing administrative tribunals in the province, including the Special Education Tribunal. As such, the Attorney General has a right to intervene in any judicial review proceedings, if he chooses to do so. In practice, the Attorney General will rarely become involved unless the issues in dispute have a public aspect which transcends the purely private interests of the parties, such as an important issue of legislative policy or tribunal governance or a constitutional issue, such as an issue under the *Canadian Charter of Rights and Freedoms* (the "Charter").[14]

Any person (including the tribunal or the Attorney General) who is served with a Notice of Application for Judicial Review and wishes to defend against the application must file a legal document called a Notice of Appearance.[15] The Notice of Appearance informs the Divisional Court that the person filing it wishes to be notified of further steps in the proceeding and to participate in the hearing.

The Divisional Court charges a fee both for commencing and for defending against a Notice of Application for Judicial Review. These fees are subject to change from time to time. As of the date of this writing, the filing fee for a Notice of Application for Judicial Review was $157 and the filing fee for defending a Notice of Appearance was $89.[16]

Constitutional Issues

If the Notice of Application for Judicial Review raises a constitutional issue, such as an issue concerning the constitutional validity of legislation or an issue under the Charter,[17] the party raising the issue must serve a Notice of Constitutional Question on the other parties and on the Attorney General of Canada and the Attorney General of Ontario.[18] Both Attorneys General have a discretion as to whether to intervene in the proceeding. One or both Attorneys General are likely to intervene in any case involving an important constitutional issue.[19] Where they do intervene, they have full rights to adduce evidence and make submissions concerning the constitutional question.[20]

---

[13] JRPA, s. 9(4).

[14] For a further discussion of the Attorney General's role in Charter and other constitutional cases, see the discussion under the heading "Constitutional Issues", *infra*.

[15] Rules of Civil Procedure, rule 38.07.

[16] Rules of Civil Procedure, Schedules of Fees.

[17] *Canadian Charter of Rights and Freedoms*, being Part I of the *Constitution Act, 1982*, being Schedule B of the *Canada Act 1982* (U.K.), 1982, c. 11.

[18] CJA, s. 109.

[19] For example, the Attorney General for Ontario (as well as the Attorneys General for Quebec and British Columbia) intervened in the ground-breaking decision, *Eaton v. Brant County Board of Education,* [1997] 1 S.C.R. 241, 142 D.L.R. (4th) 385, 31 O.R. (3d) 574*n*, 97 O.A.C. 161, 41 C.R.R. (2d) 240, 207 N.R. 171, a case involving judicial review of the Special Education Tribunal, because of the important issues raised concerning the application of s. 15 of the Charter.

[20] CJA, s. 109(4).

The Material Before the Court

The starting point for the judicial review proceedings is the record of proceedings before the Special Education Tribunal. In most cases, the record will consist of the following:

- the notice of appeal to the Special Education Tribunal;
- the IPRC and SEAB decisions appealed to the Tribunal;
- any documentary evidence submitted to the Tribunal (which will usually include any documents that were part of the record before the IPRC and/or the SEAB);
- a transcript of the oral evidence before the Tribunal (if one has been prepared); and
- the written decision and reasons of the Tribunal.[21]

Sworn affidavit evidence will sometimes be put before the Divisional Court on an application for judicial review to identify and explain the record. Affidavit evidence may also be submitted to supplement the record in exceptional cases. Generally, supplementary affidavit evidence is only permissible to show a breach of procedural fairness (discussed further below) or to show that there was a complete absence of evidence on a point which was essential to the decision.[22]

The documentation on which each party wishes to rely in judicial review proceedings — including both the record of proceedings and any affidavit evidence — must be served on the other parties and filed with the Divisional Court well in advance of the hearing.[23]

Prior to the hearing, each party will also be required to prepare written legal argument, known as a factum. The factum must be served on all of the other parties and filed with the Divisional Court in advance of the hearing.[24]

The Hearing

The hearing before the Divisional Court will be conducted on the basis of the documentary material filed by the parties. This material will include any affidavits which have been filed. It is very rare for any oral evidence to be presented.

At the hearing, each party will be expected to present an oral argument setting out the basis for its position. The party seeking judicial review will present its oral argument first. The responding party(ies) will then present their oral argument. The party seeking judicial review will then have an opportunity to reply to any new matters raised for the first time during the argument by the responding party(ies).

---

21 See the *Statutory Powers Procedure Act*, R.S.O. 1990, c. S.22 (as amended to 1999, c. 12, Sch. B), s. 20 ("SPPA").

22 See, for example, *Keeprite Products Ltd. v. Keeprite Workers' Independent Union* (1980), 29 O.R. (2d) 513, 114 D.L.R. (3d) 162 (C.A.), leave to appeal to S.C.C. refused 35 N.R. 85n; *Securicor Investigation and Security Ltd. and Ontario (Labour Relations Board) (Re)* (1985), 50 O.R. (2d) 570, 18 D.L.R. (4th) 151 (Div. Ct.).

23 Rules of Civil Procedure, rule 68.04.

24 *Ibid.*

Judicial review proceedings are formal legal proceedings. The parties must follow the procedural steps required under the Rules of Civil Procedure. The legal principles involved are reasonably complex. As a result, the parties will usually find that it is very much in their interest to be represented by legal counsel familiar with administrative law principles.

The Court's Decision

In the vast majority of cases, the Divisional Court will decide the case on the day of the hearing and issue a brief decision called an "endorsement". An endorsement sets out the Court's "bottom-line" decision, but generally includes no reasons or only very brief reasons.

In some cases, the Divisional Court will "reserve" its decision — that is, it will not issue its decision immediately but will take time to prepare a full judgment with written reasons and will then provide the judgment to the parties. If the Divisional Court reserves its decision, it can take anywhere from a few days to many months before its judgment is released.

To date, there have been very few judicial review applications in special education matters which have reached the Divisional Court. However, one can expect that the Court would likely reserve its decisions in many of these cases, due to the complexity, sensitivity and importance of the issues involved.

Reimbursement for Legal Costs

The Divisional Court's usual practice is to award "costs" of the judicial review proceeding to the successful party. These "costs" usually will not constitute full compensation for the expenses associated with the litigation. Rather, the parties will usually agree upon, or the Court will fix, a lump sum award of costs. The size of the lump sum award will depend on a number of factors, including the length of the hearing and the complexity and novelty of the issues raised. Occasionally, the Court may also consider the relative ability of the parties to pay and whether or not it was reasonable for the applicant to seek judicial review.

Further Appeal Rights

A party who is dissatisfied with the Divisional Court's decision may seek leave (or permission) to appeal the decision to the Ontario Court of Appeal.[25] If the Court of Appeal grants leave and hears the case, a further level of appeal is available, again with leave, to the Supreme Court of Canada.[26]

---

[25] CJA, s. 6(1)(a); Rules of Civil Procedure, Rule 61.

[26] *Supreme Court Act*, R.S.C. 1985, c. S-26 (as amended to 2000, c. 9), s. 40(1).

THE GROUNDS FOR JUDICIAL REVIEW

There are two broad categories of grounds for judicial review of the Special Education Tribunal's decisions. First, the Tribunal's decision can be judicially reviewed on the grounds that the Tribunal committed a breach of procedural fairness. Second, a court may consider whether the Tribunal had the legal power or jurisdiction to make the decision in question and, if so, whether its reasoning or the conclusions it reached should be judicially reviewed.

Within each of these broad categories, a number of separate grounds of judicial review can be identified. It is to a discussion of these grounds of judicial review which we now turn.

Procedural Fairness

The first general category of judicial review which may be available is a challenge to the procedures or process followed by the Special Education Tribunal (or, in rare cases, an IPRC or SEAB) in the course of reaching its decision. That is, a party may seek judicial review of an interim or final decision of the Tribunal on the basis that the Tribunal did not comply with the rules of procedural fairness.

Standard of Review of Procedural Issues

When reviewing the procedures followed by an administrative tribunal such as the Special Education Tribunal, the courts will show very little deference to the tribunal. The courts will give some consideration to the tribunal's own choice of procedures when considering the extent of the procedural safeguards which are required in order to provide procedural fairness to the parties. However, once this question has been answered, the courts will show no deference to the tribunal in deciding whether a breach of procedural fairness occurred. Rather, the courts will be critical of any procedural errors and may overturn the tribunal's decision if, in the court's view, the parties were not treated fairly during the proceedings.

Procedural Fairness — General Principles

Every administrative tribunal in Ontario has a duty to treat the parties that come before it in a procedurally fair manner.[27] This is often referred to as the "duty of fairness".

The content of the duty of fairness varies from tribunal to tribunal, depending on the interplay between a number of factors. The relevant factors include the following:

- *The nature of the decision being made and the process followed in making it*: The more adversarial and formal the proceeding, and the closer the process resembles that of a court of law, the higher the standards of procedural fairness that will be applied.

---

[27] *Nicholson v. Haldimand-Norfolk (Region) Board of Police*, [1979] 1 S.C.R. 311, 88 D.L.R. (3d) 671, 78 C.L.L.C. ¶14,181, 23 N.R. 410.

- *The nature of the statutory scheme*: The statutory scheme will often contain provisions which signal the degree of deference intended by the Legislature. For example, a higher standard of procedural fairness may be imposed where the legislation states that the tribunal's decision is a final decision than where a full appeal is available under the statute.
- *The importance of the decision for the individuals involved*: The greater the impact of the decision on individual rights, the higher the standard of procedural fairness that will be required.
- *The legitimate expectations of the parties*: If the tribunal has published rules or guidelines establishing the procedures it will follow, or has otherwise undertaken to follow particular procedures, the parties will be entitled to expect that those procedures will be followed.
- *The choices of procedure made by the tribunal itself*: The tribunal will generally be accorded some leeway to establish its own procedures, in light of its expertise and institutional constraints.[28]

The Special Education Tribunal

Applying the above principles to the Special Education Tribunal, a high standard of procedural fairness will be required. The Tribunal holds full, adversarial, court-like hearings, involving examination and cross-examination of witnesses and legal argument. The *Education Act* provides that its decisions are "final and binding on the parties to the decision".[29] Proceedings before the Special Education Tribunal can have a considerable impact on the parties involved — particularly the student whose educational future and legal right to appropriate special education programs and services will be at stake. Accordingly, high standards of fairness will be imposed on the Special Education Tribunal.

The Statutory Powers Procedure Act

In the previous section, we noted that the content of the duty of fairness varies from tribunal to tribunal. In Ontario, the issue is simplified somewhat by the enactment of the *Statutory Powers Procedure Act*, which sets out a uniform code of minimum procedural rules which must be followed by tribunals covered by the statute. The Special Education Tribunal is covered by the SPPA.[30] Thus, at the very least, the Tribunal must comply with the procedural rules set out in the SPPA.

The requirements of the SPPA have already been discussed at length in Chapter 10, in describing the procedures to be followed before the Special Education

---

[28] The factors discussed above were set out in *Baker v. Canada (Minister of Citizenship and Immigration)*, [1999] 2 S.C.R. 817 at pp. 837-41, 174 D.L.R. (4th) 193, 14 Admin. L.R. (3d) 173, 1 Imm. L.R. (3d) 1, 243 N.R. 22.

[29] *Education Act*, s. 57(5).

[30] By virtue of s. 3(1), the SPPA, applies "to a proceeding by a tribunal in the exercise of a statutory power of decision conferred by or under an Act of the Legislature, where the tribunal is required by or under such Act or otherwise by law to hold or to afford to the parties to the proceeding an opportunity for a hearing before making a decision". Section 57(3) of the *Education Act*, provides for an appeal of an identification or placement to

Tribunal. For present purposes, we will merely note that the statute sets out important procedural requirements in a number of areas, including the following:

- who is entitled to be a party to the hearing;
- what type of hearing must be held;
- whether the hearing should be open or closed to the public;
- how much advance notice of the hearing must be given;
- who should receive the notice;
- what information should be included in the notice;
- the right to be represented by legal counsel;
- what rules govern the presentation and admissibility of evidence;
- what information must be included in the Tribunal's decision;
- whether reasons for decision must be given; and
- what powers the Tribunal has to control its processes and prevent abuse of process.

If the Special Education Tribunal has failed to comply with the procedural requirements set out in the SPPA, the Divisional Court may set aside the Tribunal's decision on judicial review. Although a matter of some debate in legal circles, the prevailing view seems to be that a tribunal's decision may be set aside on procedural grounds, even if there is no positive proof that the procedural irregularity caused actual prejudice to the party who commenced the judicial review proceedings.[31]

Common Law Rules of Procedural Fairness

In addition to the procedural rules set out in the SPPA, administrative tribunals such as the Special Education Tribunal are also subject to myriad "common law" — that is, court-made rules of procedural fairness. To some extent, these common law rules overlap with the procedural requirements set out in the SPPA. However, the common law rules may also cover procedural issues which are not specifically addressed in the statute.

A full discussion of the common law rules of procedural fairness is beyond the scope of this book. However, the rules can be divided into the following two broad categories:

- *The right to be heard*: A party affected by the decision of a tribunal is entitled to adequate notice of the case which must be met and a full-and-fair opportunity to respond. The SPPA covers certain aspects of this rule — such as the tribunal's obligation to give formal notice of the hearing and the nature of the hearing

---

the Special Education Tribunal and specifically states that the Tribunal must hold a hearing in respect of the identification or placement. Thus, the Tribunal is clearly covered by the SPPA.

[31] See, for example, *Kane v. University of British Columbia (Board of Governors)*, [1980] 1 S.C.R. 1105, 110 D.L.R. (3d) 311, [1980] 3 W.W.R. 125, 18 B.C.L.R. 124, 31 N.R. 214; *Milne v. Nipissing District Secondary School Athletic Assn.*, [1998] O.J. No. 4678 (QL), 115 O.A.C. 363, 15 Admin. L.R. (3d) 126 (Div. Ct.).

which will be held.[32] However, this rule can also have broader consequences than those addressed in the SPPA. It means, for example, that the tribunal must disclose to the parties any factual information which has come to its attention outside the hearing upon which it intends to rely and must provide the parties with a full opportunity to respond to that information.

• *The right to an impartial hearing before an independent tribunal*: The members of the tribunal must be free of actual bias. Examples of actual bias include a financial or business interest in the outcome of the case, or a personal or familial relationship with one of the parties. The members of the tribunal also must conduct themselves in a way which does not give rise to a reasonable apprehension of bias. In determining whether a reasonable apprehension of bias exists, the courts will apply the following test:

> . . . What would an informed person, viewing the matter realistically and practically — and having thought the matter through — conclude. Would he think that it is more likely than not that [the decision-maker] . . . whether consciously or unconsciously, would not decide fairly.[33]

A reasonable apprehension of bias may arise, for example, where an individual sitting on the Tribunal has been involved in the case at an earlier stage of the proceedings, is employed by one of the parties, runs a private school providing specific special education programs and services, has publicly expressed opinions favourable (or unfavourable) to one of the parties or their position in the proceeding, or has conducted himself or herself in such a way during the proceeding as to give rise to a reasonable belief that he or she has prejudged the outcome of the proceeding.

The Tribunal's Decision

In addition to reviewing the procedures followed by the Special Education Tribunal, the Divisional Court may also review the substance of the Tribunal's decisions. Substantive review may include consideration of whether the Tribunal had the legal authority or jurisdiction to make the decision in question, and review of both the reasoning employed by the Tribunal and the conclusions it reached. However, substantive review of the Tribunal's decision is available on a much more limited basis than the procedural review discussed in the preceding section.

Judicial Deference: The Fundamental Principle

The courts exercise a considerable degree of deference to administrative tribunals when reviewing the substance of their decisions. This deference is based on a recognition that the reason the Legislature establishes administrative tribunals and assigns certain decision-making functions to them is to take advantage of the

---

[32] SPPA, ss. 5.1, 5.2 and 6.

[33] *Committee for Justice and Liberty v. Canada (National Energy Board)* (1975), 65 D.L.R. (3d) 660, [1976] 2 F.C. 20, 9 N.R. 150 (C.A.), affd [1978] 1 S.C.R. 369, 68 D.L.R. (3d) 716, 9 N.R. 115; recently affirmed in *Baker, supra,* footnote 28, at pp. 849-50 S.C.R.

specialized expertise which they can bring to bear upon the decision-making process. The tribunal will usually have more expertise than the reviewing court with respect to the particular issues assigned to it under the statutory scheme. As a result, it only makes sense that, as a general rule, the courts should bear in mind the tribunal's expertise and defer to its decisions.

The recognition of administrative tribunals' expertise has led the courts to develop what is often referred to as a "spectrum" or "continuum" of deference. Under this approach, the degree of deference accorded will depend on the expertise of the tribunal, the language of the statutory scheme and the nature of the decision being made.[34]

At one end of the spectrum, where deference is at its highest, the tribunal's decision is reviewable on the standard of "patent unreasonableness". At the other end of the spectrum, where deference is at its lowest, the tribunal's decision is reviewable on the standard of "correctness".[35] The courts have also recognized an intermediate standard of review — simple "reasonableness" — which has now been applied in a number of cases found to fall towards the middle of the spectrum of deference.[36]

Expertise of the Special Education Tribunal

The Special Education Tribunal's core area of expertise is fact-finding and adjudication in the special education context. In particular, it has been recognized that the Tribunal's primary area of expertise is in identifying exceptional pupils and placing such pupils into educational settings where special education programs and services appropriate to meet their needs can best be delivered. The Divisional Court and the Ontario Court of Appeal have confirmed that, within this core area of expertise, the Special Education Tribunal is entitled to judicial deference.[37]

---

[34] *Pezim v. British Columbia (Superintendent of Brokers)*, [1994] 2 S.C.R. 557 at p. 590, 114 D.L.R. (4th) 385, [1994] 7 W.W.R. 1, 75 W.A.C. 1, 92 B.C.L.R. (2d) 145, 22 Admin. L.R. (2d) 1, 14 B.L.R. (2d) 217, 168 N.R. 321.

[35] *Pezim, supra*, at pp. 589-90; *Baker, supra*, footnote 28, at pp. 852-5.

[36] See, for example, *Canada (Director of Investigation and Research) v. Southam Inc.*, [1997] 1 S.C.R. 748, 144 D.L.R. (4th) 1, 50 Admin. L.R. (2d) 199, 71 C.P.R. (3d) 417, 209 N.R. 20; *Pushpanathan v. Canada (Minister of Citizenship and Immigration)*, [1998] 1 S.C.R. 982, 160 D.L.R. (4th) 193, 11 Admin. L.R. (3d) 1, 43 Imm. L.R. (2d) 117, 226 N.R. 201, supplementary reasons [1998] 1 S.C.R. 1222, 11 Admin. L.R. (3d) 130; *Baker, supra*, footnote 28.

[37] *Eaton v. Brant County Board of Education* (1994), 71 O.A.C. 69 at pp. 70-71 (Div. Ct.), revd 123 D.L.R. (4th) 43 at p. 50, 22 O.R. (3d) 1, 77 O.A.C. 368, 27 C.R.R. (2d) 53 (C.A.), revd [1997] 1 S.C.R. 241, 142 D.L.R. (4th) 385, 31 O.R. (3d) 574*n*, 97 O.A.C. 161, 41 C.R.R. (2d) 240, 207 N.R. 171. Although the Ontario Court of Appeal reversed the Divisional Court's decision, it agreed with the Divisional Court on this point. The degree of deference owed to the Tribunal was not an issue when the case reached the Supreme Court of Canada. However, the Supreme Court implicitly endorsed the principle of judicial deference to the Tribunal's decisions in upholding the original Tribunal decision.

The Statutory Scheme

Section 57(5) of the *Education Act* provides as follows: "The decision of the Special Education Tribunal is final and binding on the parties to the decision."

Provisions like s. 57(5) are often referred to by the courts as "finality" clauses. They are viewed as a signal that the Legislature intended that a degree of deference should be paid to decisions of the Tribunal within its core area of expertise.[38] The fact that the Legislature intended the Tribunal's decisions to be "final and binding" on the parties is another factor indicating that the courts should defer to those decisions.

The Nature of the Decision

The final factor to be considered in determining the degree of deference which should be accorded to a decision of the Special Education Tribunal is the nature of the decision confronting the Tribunal. In this regard, four distinguishable categories of decisions can be identified.

The Scope of the Tribunal's Jurisdiction

No deference will be paid to a decision by the Special Education Tribunal interpreting the scope of its own statutory jurisdiction. The Tribunal must be correct in interpreting any provisions limiting or defining its jurisdiction.[39] If the interpretation is not correct, it can be reversed.

The jurisdiction of the Special Education Tribunal is defined in broad terms in s. 57 of the *Education Act*. As a result, there will be relatively few circumstances in which the Tribunal will be called upon to interpret provisions which define or limit its jurisdiction. However, some examples of issues which could arise with respect to the scope of the Tribunal's jurisdiction include the following:

- issues concerning whether a particular child is a "resident pupil" to whom the identification, placement, review and appeal provisions of the *Education Act* and O. Reg. 181/98 apply;[40]

---

[38] *United Brotherhood of Carpenters and Joiners of America, Loc. 579 v. Bradco Construction Ltd.*, [1993] 2 S.C.R. 316 at p. 333, 102 D.L.R. (4th) 402, 106 Nfld. & P.E.I.R. 140, 12 Admin. L.R. (2d) 165, 93 C.L.L.C. ¶14,033, 153 N.R. 81.

[39] See, for example, *U.E.S., Loc. 298 v. Bibeault*, [1988] 2 S.C.R. 1048, 24 Q.A.C. 244, 35 Admin. L.R. 153, 89 C.L.L.C. ¶14,045, 95 N.R. 161, *sub nom. Syndicat National des Employes de la Commission Scolaire Regionale de L'Outaouais (CSN) v. Union des Employes de Service, Local 298* (FTQ); *Dayco (Canada) Ltd. v. C.A.W.-Canada*, [1993] 2 S.C.R. 230, 102 D.L.R. (4th) 609, 13 O.R. (3d) 164*n*, 63 O.A.C. 1, 14 Admin. L.R. (2d) 1, 93 C.L.L.C. ¶14,032, 152 N.R. 1.

[40] Section 57(3) of the *Education Act* permits a parent or guardian to appeal the identification or placement of a pupil as an exceptional pupil. "Exceptional pupil" is defined in s. 1 as "a pupil whose behavioural, communicational, intellectual, physical or multiple exceptionalities are such that he or she is considered to need placement in a special program" by an IPRC established (in most cases) by the board of which the pupil is a resident pupil. Resident pupil qualifications are outlined in ss. 32 to 36.

- issues concerning whether a particular individual who seeks to appeal qualifies as the pupil's parent or guardian;[41]
- issues concerning whether the parent or guardian has exhausted all rights of appeal under the Regulations;[42] or
- issues relating to the special education programs and services provided to the pupil, rather than to identification and/or placement.[43]

Decisions Outside of the Tribunal's Expertise

Similarly, little deference will be paid to decisions of the Special Education Tribunal which are outside the core area of its specialized expertise.[44] The Tribunal's core area of expertise is fact-finding and adjudication in the special education context. With respect to issues outside this area, the Tribunal's decisions must be correct.

Some examples of issues which fall outside the Special Education Tribunal's core area of expertise and with respect to which the Tribunal will be required to be correct, include the following:

- interpretation of the Charter;
- interpretation of external statutes, such as the Ontario *Human Rights Code*;[45]
- interpretation of common law principles from outside the Tribunal's core area of expertise, such as the interpretation of a contract or a common law concept such as "good faith".

---

[41] Section 57(3) provides that only a parent or guardian of a pupil may appeal to the Tribunal. The term "parent" is reasonably straightforward, but, where there is a custody order in place, it will mean the parent or parents with legal custody of the pupil. "Guardian" is defined in s. 1 of the *Education Act* as "a person who has lawful custody of a child, other than the parent of child".

[42] Section 57(3) of the *Education Act* also requires that a parent or guardian must have "exhausted all rights of appeal under the regulations" (*i.e.*, by appealing to the SEAB) before appealing to the Tribunal.

[43] Section 57(3) of the *Education Act* only provides a right to appeal identification and/or placement. An appeal which relates exclusively to special education programs or services falls outside the Tribunal's jurisdiction.

[44] See, for example, *Bradburn v. Wentworth Arms Hotel Ltd.*, [1979] 1 S.C.R. 846, 94 D.L.R. (3d) 161, 79 C.L.L.C. ¶14,189, 24 N.R. 417; *Douglas/Kwantlen Faculty Assn. v. Douglas College*, [1990] 3 S.C.R. 570, 77 D.L.R. (4th) 94, [1991] 1 W.W.R. 643, 52 B.C.L.R. (2d) 68, 50 Admin. L.R. 69, 13 C.H.R.R. D/403, 91 C.L.L.C. ¶17,002, 2 C.R.R. (2d) 157, 118 N.R. 340; *Cuddy Chicks Ltd. v. Ontario (Labour Relations Board)*, [1991] 2 S.C.R. 5, 81 D.L.R. (4th) 121, 3 O.R. (3d) 128*n*, 47 O.A.C. 271, 50 Admin. L.R. 44, 91 C.L.L.C. ¶14,024, 4 C.R.R. (2d) 1, [1991] O.L.R.B. Rep. 790, 122 N.R. 361; *Bradco, supra*, footnote 38 ; *Canadian Broadcasting Corp. v. Canada (Labour Relations Board)*, [1995] 1 S.C.R. 157, 121 D.L.R. (4th) 385, 27 Admin. L.R. (2d) 1 *sub nom. A.C.T.R.A. v. Canadian Broadcasting Corp.*, 95 C.L.L.C. ¶210-009, 177 N.R. 1; *Newfoundland (Green Bay Centre) v. N.A.P.E.*, [1996] 2 S.C.R. 3, 134 D.L.R. (4th) 1, 140 Nfld. & P.E.I.R. 63, 39 Admin. L.R. (2d) 1, 28 C.H.R.R. D/224, 96 C.L.L.C. ¶230-023, 196 N.R. 212; *Eaton v. Brant County Board of Education*, [1997] 1 S.C.R. 241, 142 D.L.R. (4th) 385, 31 O.R. (3d) 574*n*, 97 O.A.C. 161, 41 C.R.R. (2d) 240, 207 N.R. 171.

[45] R.S.O. 1990, c. H.19.

Issues Within the Tribunal's Core Area of Expertise

Where the Tribunal is involved in determining issues within its core area of expertise (*i.e.*, special education), the courts will usually exercise a high degree of deference.[46] The precise degree of deference will depend on the specific issue involved. Depending on the issue, the reviewing court will apply either the "patent unreasonableness" standard (the most deferential standard of review) or the simple "reasonableness" standard (which is slightly less deferential).

The Supreme Court of Canada has made clear that the "patently unreasonable" standard is an "extremely high standard", and a "strict" or "severe" test.[47] In order for a decision to be "patently unreasonable", it must be "clearly irrational".[48] The following passage illustrates the high standard which must be met to establish that a decision is "patently unreasonable":

> It is said that it is difficult to know what "patently unreasonable" means. What is patently unreasonable to one judge may be eminently reasonable to another. Yet any test can only be defined by words, the building blocks of all reasons. Obviously, the patently unreasonable test sets a high standard of review. In the Shorter Oxford English Dictionary, "patently", an adverb, is defined as "openly, evidently, clearly". "Unreasonable" is defined as "[n]ot having the faculty of reason; irrational . . . Not acting in accordance with reason or good sense". Thus, based on the dictionary definition of the words "patently unreasonable", it is apparent that if the decision the Board reached, acting within its jurisdiction, is not clearly irrational, that is to say evidently not in accordance with reason, then it cannot be said that there was a loss of jurisdiction. This is clearly a very strict test.[49]

In contrast, the standard of simple "reasonableness" is a somewhat less deferential standard of review. The Supreme Court of Canada has described this standard of review in the following terms:

> An unreasonable decision is one that, in the main, is not supported by any reasons that can stand up to a somewhat probing examination. Accordingly, a court reviewing a conclusion on the reasonableness standard must look to see whether any reasons support it. The defect, if there is one, could presumably be in the evidentiary foundation itself or in the logical process by which conclusions are sought to be drawn from it. An example of the former kind of defect would be an assumption that had no basis in the evidence, or that was contrary to the overwhelming weight of the evidence. An example of the latter kind of defect would be a contradiction in the premises or an invalid inference.

---

[46] *Bibeault, supra*, footnote 39; *Dayco, supra*, footnote 39; *Bradco, supra*, footnote 38.

[47] *Toronto (City) Board of Education v. O.S.S.T.F., District 15*, [1997] 1 S.C.R. 487 at p. 505, 144 D.L.R. (4th) 385, 98 O.A.C. 241 *sub nom. Board of Education of Toronto v. Ontario Secondary School Teachers' Federation District 15*, 44 Admin. L.R. (2d) 1, 25 C.C.E.L. (2d) 153, 97 C.L.L.C. ¶220-018, 208 N.R. 245; *Blanchard v. Control Data Canada Ltd.*, [1984] 2 S.C.R. 476 at p. 493, 14 D.L.R. (4th) 289, 14 Admin. L.R. 133, 84 C.L.L.C. ¶14,070, 55 N.R. 194; *Canada (Attorney General) v. Public Service Alliance of Canada*, [1993] 1 S.C.R. 941 at p. 963, 101 D.L.R. (4th) 673, 11 Admin. L.R. (2d) 59, 93 C.L.L.C. ¶14,022, 150 N.R. 161.

[48] *Public Service Alliance of Canada, supra*.

[49] *Ibid.*, at pp. 963-4.

The difference between "unreasonable" and "patently unreasonable" lies in the immediacy or obviousness of the defect. If the defect is apparent on the face of the tribunal's reasons, then the tribunal's decision is patently unreasonable. But if it takes some significant searching or testing to find the defect, then the decision is unreasonable but not patently unreasonable.[50]

Legally, the standard of review applicable to a particular case is often somewhat unclear. However, practically, the courts have often found ways to set aside decisions with which they disagree. Clearly, whatever standard of review is applied, a party who is seeking to persuade a court to set aside a decision by the Tribunal within its core area of expertise faces an uphill battle. This result is consistent with the view that the Tribunal should generally be accorded the "last word" with respect to special education matters and that resort to the courts should be discouraged in all but the most exceptional cases.

Factual Issues

The scope for judicial review is at its narrowest with respect to factual findings or credibility issues. It is generally recognized that decision-makers who actually hear and observe the witnesses as they testify are in the best position to judge their credibility and make factual findings. As a result, reviewing courts are extremely reluctant to intervene in the fact-finding process. Even if the reviewing court might have reached different factual conclusions based on the evidence presented, the court cannot overturn the tribunal's decision on that basis alone. Rather, an administrative tribunal's decision will only be overturned for an error of fact where a complete absence of evidence on a point which was essential to the tribunal's decision has been demonstrated.[51]

A large part of the function entrusted to the Special Education Tribunal under the *Education Act* is fact-finding in the special education context. Many Tribunal decisions will be highly dependent on the factual findings reached. Given the very narrow scope for judicial review of findings of fact, the scope for judicial review of Tribunal decisions will, in many cases, be quite limited.

REMEDIES AVAILABLE ON JUDICIAL REVIEW

If the party seeking judicial review successfully persuades the Divisional Court that legitimate grounds for judicial review are present, the Court will "quash" (*i.e.*,

---

[50]   *Canada (Director of Investigation and Research) v. Southam Inc.*, [1997] 1 S.C.R. 748 at pp. 776-7, 144 D.L.R. (4th) 1, 50 Admin. L.R. (2d) 199, 71 C.P.R. (3d) 417, 209 N.R. 20.

[51]   *Toronto (City) Board of Education, supra*, footnote 47, at pp. 507-8; *Lester (W.W.) (1978) Ltd. v. United Assn. of Journeymen and Apprentices of the Plumbing and Pipefitting Industry, Loc. 740*, [1990] 3 S.C.R. 644 at p. 669, 76 D.L.R. (4th) 389, 88 Nfld. & P.E.I.R. 15 *sub nom. Planet Development Corp. and Lester (W.W.) (1978) Ltd. v. United Assn. of Journeymen and Apprentices of Plumbing and Pipefitting Industry in the United States and Canada, Loc. 740*, 48 Admin. L.R. 1, 91 C.L.L.C. ¶14,002, 123 N.R. 241 *sub nom. Planet Development Corp. v. UA, Local 740*.

reverse, overturn or set aside) the Tribunal's decision. Usually, the Court will also send the decision back to the Tribunal — or, less commonly, to a differently constituted Tribunal or to the IPRC or SEAB — to allow the Tribunal to reconsider the matter in light of the Court's decision. In some rare cases — such as where there has been a very serious breach of procedural fairness by the Tribunal which calls its impartiality into question or where there has been a very long delay — the Court may simply quash the decision and declare the proceeding to be at an end.[52]

In addition, in an appropriate case, the Court may direct the school board to take specific action or the practical effect of its decision may be to require the school board to take specific action. For example, the Court may quash the school board's decision and order it to implement a particular placement. However, many panels of the Divisional Court will be reluctant to order that specific action be taken, as such an order is often seen as an undue incursion into the school board's special education decision-making.

IMPLEMENTATION OF THE JUDICIAL REVIEW DECISION

A decision of the Divisional Court is a binding legal decision and must be implemented in accordance with its terms. What those terms are will depend on the terms of the Court's order. As noted above, implementation may involve referring the matter back to the Tribunal or even to the IPRC or SEAB. Alternatively, the Court may direct the school board to take specific action — for example, to implement a specific placement — in which case that direction must be implemented by the school board.

The school board's implementation responsibilities may be suspended if leave to appeal is granted by the Ontario Court of Appeal. Generally, the fact that an appeal is filed does not relieve the parties from implementing the decision under appeal. However, in many cases, the parties will be able to reach an agreement that the Tribunal's decision need not be implemented pending the appeal. If no agreement can be reached, there are some rare circumstances in which a party may be able to obtain an order called a "stay of proceedings", which will preserve the status quo while the appeal is underway.[53]

The test to obtain a "stay of proceedings" is an onerous one. In order to obtain a stay, the party seeking it must show: (1) that there is a serious issue to be tried; (2)

---

[52] See, for example, *Commercial Union Assurance v. Ontario (Human Rights Commission)* (1988), 63 O.R. (2d) 112*n*, 47 D.L.R. (4th) 477, 26 O.A.C. 387, 20 C.C.E.L. 236, 9 C.H.R.R. D/5144 (C.A.), leave to appeal to S.C.C. refused 51 D.L.R. (4th) vii, 65 O.R. (2d) x, 31 O.A.C. 240*n*, 93 N.R. 168*n, sub nom. Commercial Union Assurance and Cormack v. Human Rights Commission (Ont.) and Prashad.*
[53] Rules of Civil Procedure, rule 63.02.

that it would suffer irreparable harm if the stay was not granted; and (3) that the balance of convenience favours granting the stay.[54] Thus, while a stay may be available in some cases involving Tribunal decisions, those cases will be the exception rather than the rule.

---

[54] *R.J.R.–Macdonald Inc. v. Canada (Attorney General)*, [1994] 1 S.C.R. 311, 54 C.P.R. (3d) 114, 111 D.L.R. (4th) 385, 60 Q.A.C. 241, 164 N.R. 1.

12

Preparation and Presentation of Your Case

INTRODUCTION

The manner in which information is presented, whether at the Identification Placement and Review Committee ("IPRC"), the Special Education Appeal Board ("SEAB") or the Special Education Tribunal (the "Tribunal"), will affect the conduct of the proceeding and may even influence the decision-makers. It can also either damage or sustain the relationship between school board staff and the parents of the student whose identification or placement is at issue. A presentation which, in a balanced and professional way, delivers complete information on the student, demonstrates that there has been a careful consideration of all the alternatives and provides a cogent explanation why that placement recommended by the school staff is most appropriate for the student, can impress both the parents and the decision-maker. Care also must be taken to ensure that the presentation is made in language which parents can understand.

It should always be remembered that "preparation" in any case begins long before any date is set for the IPRC. This chapter will suggest the steps which might be taken to prepare and present the school board's case at each step of the process.

"PREPARATION" BEGINS LONG BEFORE THE IPRC

It must always be remembered by school board staff that the actions which they take in relation to an exceptional pupil and, more particularly, that student's parents, could one day be subject to the scrutiny of the Tribunal or even a court. On occasion, parents, who have felt aggrieved by what they perceived to be unfair treatment from school board staff, have presented to special education committees, boards or tribunals before whom they were appearing details of the conduct by school board staff which they viewed as offensive or upsetting. While decisions on placement do not turn on the conduct of school board staff, in some cases, the Special Education Tribunal has recorded in decisions criticisms of the actions of school board staff[1] and have noted situations where both parties — parents and school board staff — have contributed to an acrimonious relationship.

School board staff should keep this in mind at all times and should take every reasonable step to ensure that the relationship between home and school is a good one. Where a courteous relationship has been established, any appeals are likely to run more smoothly.

Problems can arise between home and school as a result of misunderstandings. Clear communication, in advance, of what a parent can expect in any circumstance can assist in preventing misunderstandings in the first place. Where a parent has been told that something will happen at a particular time (*e.g.*, an assessment completed, a piece of equipment purchased, or a meeting held) and circumstances intervene to prevent it from happening, it is wise for the school to contact the parent as soon as the school becomes aware of the problem. Following this contact, it is wise for the school board to make every reasonable effort to ensure that the matter is rescheduled or completed or otherwise dealt with at the earliest opportunity and to keep the parent advised along the way.

Most parents appreciate the efforts of staff on behalf of their children. However, on occasion, the relationship between school and home may become strained. Some parents may make demands which might seem unreasonable or may even display anger towards staff. It is important, if the relationship does become troubled, for both parents and school staff to try to stand back and attempt to see things through the eyes of the other. At any point, the teacher can involve the principal who might deal with the matter or involve the special education coordinator or appropriate supervisory officer in an effort to facilitate a resolution. In any event, the most prudent course of action for school board staff is to continue to deal with parents in a respectful manner at all times and, most importantly, to continue to do the best they can for the student in question. While parents may continue to view school board staff conduct in a negative light, an unbiased third party who is removed from the situation will be able to form a much clearer picture of events.

The goal for school board staff — and parents — will be to establish and maintain respectful and open communications. For school board staff, this will involve keeping parents informed, including them in decision-making, inviting parents' advice and suggestions and engaging in meaningful "consultation". For parents, this will mean keeping school board staff advised of all relevant information concerning their child, understanding the pressures which school staff are under and remaining open to hear what school board staff have to say about their child.

In those rare circumstances where incidents between parents and teachers do occur, it is important that any school staff member who observed or was otherwise involved in the incident make a careful written record of it. In situations where

---

[1] By the same token, several Tribunal decisions have been critical of conduct on the part of parents.

there are ongoing disagreements between home and school, it may be wise to keep a journal which records any events that cause concern

PREPARATION AND PRESENTATION AT THE IPRC

Meeting with the Parents in Advance of the IPRC Meeting

Whether or not a "pre-IPRC" process is followed, it is wise to ensure that parents do not hear anything for the first time at the IPRC. Meetings between school staff and parents in advance of the IPRC may be arranged to advise parents what will be happening, what the school staff will be recommending and why. Taking the mystique out of the process for parents and advising them in advance of what school staff is thinking will go a long way towards establishing the open communications which will be important in the long term.

Some school boards hold "pre-IPRC" meetings where school staff and parents work out together what will be presented at the IPRC meeting. Where parents and school staff are in agreement at the end of the pre-IPRC process, the IPRC meeting will represent a relatively short culmination of what has already been agreed to. Where there is no agreement between parents and school staff through the pre-IPRC process, a more formal IPRC meeting will be held in which the issues outstanding can be fully canvassed.

The school's presentation to the IPRC will normally involve the principal and the teachers or consultants involved with the student contributing information to the IPRC's discussion, as well as providing relevant documents to the IPRC.

Parents similarly will provide information and documents to the IPRC.

Documents

The first step in preparing to present a case to the IPRC will be for school staff to pull together all documents which are relevant to the issues to be considered by the IPRC (*i.e.*, identification and placement, or a review of one, the other or both). These documents will include:

- educational assessments;
- medical reports;
- psychological reports;
- other professional assessments;
- any reports prepared for the IPRC (*e.g.*, observations of staff);
- samples of the student's work;
- report cards;
- IEPs in the case of a review, provided that a parent has given written permission;[2]

---

[2] *Identification and Placement of Exceptional Pupils*, O. Reg. 181/98, s. 23(2). See Chapter 7 for further discussion of IEPs.

- articles or excerpts from texts, etc., which are relevant to identification or placement issues.

In most cases, both parties will want to submit all documents which they believe to be relevant to the IPRC in order that the IPRC may make its determination with all relevant information before it. This will include pertinent documents from the Ontario Student Record ("OSR"). On rare occasions, a parent may decline to consent to the disclosure of OSR documents. As noted in Chapter 6,[3] while there is some question whether OSR documents can be produced to the IPRC without parental consent, a reasonable legal argument, buttressed by common sense, supports the conclusion that the student's teachers or principal may nevertheless produce OSR documents to members of the IPRC who are school board employees. Moreover, the *Education Act*[4] itself supports the view that the student's teachers, principal and supervisory officers may disclose relevant information from OSR records to the IPRC.

In addition to relevant documents, it can be helpful for the committee to have a chronology setting out all relevant events, including the date of birth of the student; the date of enrolment of the student in school (and, if the student has attended several schools, the dates of enrolment at the various schools); the dates of medical or other assessments; in the case of a student with a behavioural exceptionality, the dates of any major disciplinary actions; the dates of any prior IPRCs and so on. A chronology can assist in providing an historical context to the decision which the IPRC must make.

School staff must also keep in mind that the documents which they submit to the IPRC will form part of the IPRC's record. Should there be an appeal by the parents, that record will be forwarded to the SEAB.[5]

Documents should be organized by subject-matter — that is, all medical reports should be grouped together, all psychological reports should be grouped together and so on. Within each grouping, documents should be ordered chronologically, from earliest to latest. The documents, once organized, can be put together in a binder (a "brief of documents"). An index of the documents in the binder should be prepared and each document should be individually tabbed so that it is easy to locate. If the documents are numerous, a list summarizing all or some of the documents might be prepared or a table of contents provided at the front of the binder. The chronology should also be inserted at the front of the brief of documents.

In putting together the brief of documents, at the outset, it is wise to consult parents and obtain their input on what they feel should be included in the documents brief. Encouraging parental input into the process will start the process out on a more inclusive footing. Where there is a dispute about the relevance of

---

[3] In particular, see the discussion under the heading "Information to be Considered".
[4] R.S.O. 1990, c. E.2 (as amended), s. 266(10)(a). See also O. Reg. 181/98, s. 15(1).
[5] O. Reg. 181/98, s. 27(6).

specific documents, school staff and parents may submit their documents separately.

Whether a joint set of documents or separate sets of documents are submitted, a set of the documents should be provided to the parents in advance of the presentation of the documents at the IPRC meeting.

Preparing for and Making the Oral Presentation

Where there is agreement between parents and school staff on identification and placement, either as a result of a "pre-IPRC" process as described above, or because it is clear in discussions that school staff and parents are in agreement, any presentation by either the parents or school staff will normally be quite short. The situation will not be the same if agreement on all issues has not been reached prior to the IPRC meeting.

Ideally, school staff will have an opportunity to meet in advance of the IPRC meeting to review the information which they will contribute to the IPRC's discussions and to agree who will present what information. It is best that those contributing information speak to what they have personally observed, rather than providing second-hand information.

One person should be chosen to lead the presentation of information to the IPRC. This person might introduce the school staff and summarize the staff's position at the end of the presentation.

Care must be taken to ensure that events and observations are described as accurately and neutrally as possible. Where possible, objective rather than subjective language should be used. Those contributing to the discussion should prepare speaking notes to ensure that they stay on track during the presentation and have a record of what they said for later reference.

Care must also be taken to avoid "teacherspeak" as much as possible or to translate technical terms being used. Parents can become overwhelmed by staff presentations which are punctuated with technical pedagogical terms which the parents are not familiar with. Without being overly pedantic, every effort should be made to make sure that the parents understand what staff are saying.

On occasion, there may be disagreements between staff and parents during the IPRC meeting. In such a case, school board staff should attempt to ensure that a respectful atmosphere continues to prevail at the IPRC meeting.[6]

PREPARATION AND PRESENTATION AT THE SPECIAL EDUCATION APPEAL BOARD

Although the SEAB meeting is to be held in an informal manner, the proceeding is likely to be more formal than an IPRC meeting since the SEAB

---

[6] See, also, Chapter 6 under the heading "Procedures" .

members will not likely be known to the parents or to the school board staff. Generally, SEAB hearings last about one day.

The position of school board staff before the SEAB will normally be to support the IPRC's decision. However, on occasion, school board staff may also be prepared to "table" a compromise position which they could support.

Documents

The IPRC must maintain a record of all the documents which it has received in its meetings surrounding each student together with its decision.[7] All of these documents must be forwarded by the chair of the IPRC to the chair of the SEAB.[8]

If school board staff have put together a brief of documents in the first instance, this brief can be used as a starting point. If this brief was submitted to the IPRC, then it will form part of the record which is forwarded to the SEAB. Nevertheless, for purposes of convenience, if additional relevant documents are to be added (*e.g.*, documents omitted in the first instance or new documents that have come into existence or have been created for the SEAB), an "updated" brief can be put together for the SEAB. Care should be taken to update the index and chronology. Even if there are no new documents added to the brief, additional copies of the brief should be made to ensure that all members of the SEAB have one.

If no documents brief was prepared for the IPRC, then a brief should be put together for the SEAB in the same manner as outlined above with one possible proviso. Consultation with parents may be more difficult at this stage as a result of the disagreement which prompts the appeal. However, if possible, parents should be invited to consider putting a joint brief before the SEAB.

It should be remembered that OSR documents (including the IEP) cannot be provided to the SEAB without the consent of the parent (or student if aged 18 or older).[9] However, it would appear that if OSR documents were properly presented to the IPRC,[10] then they will form part of the record which is sent to the SEAB by the IPRC. Accordingly, school board staff should ensure that any document which they wish to put before the SEAB has been presented to the IPRC.

Copies of whatever documents school board staff intend to provide to the SEAB should be provided in advance of the SEAB meeting to the parents.

---

[7] O. Reg. 181/98, s. 27(6). This record will include any reports, assessments and other documents considered by the IPRC, as well as the IPRC's decision.

[8] *Ibid.*

[9] *Education Act*, s. 266; *Municipal Freedom of Information and Protection of Privacy Act*, R.S.O. 1990, c. M.56 (as amended to 2000, c. 26, Sch. J) ("MFIPPA"), ss. 53 and 54(c). It should be noted that while s. 266 of the *Education Act* stipulates 18 years as the age at which a student gains control over his or her OSR, s. 54(c) of the MFIPPA sets 16 years as the age at which students gain the right to control their personal documents, which would include OSR documents. Accordingly, it is arguable that a student may consent to the disclosure of OSR documents at age 16.

[10] See Chapter 6 under the heading "Information to be Considered".

Preparing for and Making the Oral Presentation

Although the conduct of an SEAB process is intended to be informal,[11] it will be important for school board staff to present its case in an organized fashion. It must be kept in mind that, unlike the IPRC members, who may have had some understanding of the case before they considered it, the SEAB members will come to the case with no prior knowledge of either the case or the parties. It is helpful to think of the process of presenting a case as being akin to relating a story which has a beginning, middle and end. If you start in the middle instead of at the beginning, the person to whom the story is being related will not fully understand the story.

One person should be selected to lead the presentation by school board staff — usually this will be a superintendent with the responsibility for special education. This person will introduce the school board staff present and will link the presentations which are to be made by school board staff together into a cohesive whole. In order to facilitate this, all staff who will be involved in the presentation should meet in advance and determine what information must be presented and who will present it.

A presentation to a SEAB by school staff might follow this format:

- An opening statement should be made which includes a clear outline of the position being taken by school board staff on the appeal. The opening statement should outline the topics which staff will touch on during the presentation and identify who will be delivering which parts of the presentation.
- An outline may also be provided setting out the historical context, touching on any relevant points (*e.g.*, how long has the pupil been with the board, significant incidents, etc.). The chronology and brief of documents will assist in this regard.
- The observations of the student's most recent teacher regarding the student's strengths and weaknesses, the student's performance in class and, if socialization is an issue, on the student's interaction with peers and others, will provide critical information.
- The presentation should include a clear explanation of the school board's position on the issue in question. If the issue is placement, a description of the placement which the IPRC decided was appropriate should be provided to the SEAB as well as an explanation on why the placement is appropriate. It should also be explained why school board staff disagree with the parent's position.

The order of speaking and what will be said by each presenter should be worked out in advance of the SEAB hearing so that there are no surprises for other members of the school board staff who are providing information to the SEAB. School board staff should be prepared to answer any questions which members of the SEAB may wish to ask them about the parents' case or any allegations being made by the parents.

---

[11]   See Chapter 9, "The First Stage of Appeal".

On occasion, parents may have questions for members of school board staff during the meeting. In the event that a question asked by a parent or an SEAB member cannot be easily answered, a brief recess might be requested to consider the question. Should the school board have any questions for the parents or any "guests" who the parents might bring, these might be put to the parent or guest through the chair of the SEAB.

Written submissions are not necessary, but may be helpful, particularly in a complicated case. Written submissions may be as simple as a brief outline of the presentation by school board staff. If a written submission is to be presented to the SEAB, an advance copy should be given to parents, if possible.

As a final note, it will be important that throughout the SEAB meeting that school board staff maintain a respectful demeanour towards the parents and anyone contributing information on their behalf, despite any disagreements which might arise. This means that, should parents make comments critical of school board staff, it will be important to ensure that body language remains neutral. At the point that school board staff are given an opportunity to reply, they will be able to present their arguments to rebut those of the parents.

PRESENTING YOUR CASE BEFORE THE SPECIAL EDUCATION TRIBUNAL

The hearing before the Tribunal is, as noted in Chapter 10, much more formal than the meetings conducted before either the IPRC or the SEAB.

Historically, most school boards have retained legal counsel to represent them in Tribunal proceedings. This is prudent because the *Statutory Powers Procedure Act*[12] applies to the Tribunal's proceedings, as do more formal rules of evidence, including the rules which apply when examining and cross-examining witnesses. Accordingly, the prime responsibility will rest with counsel to ensure that proper presentation is undertaken.

Documents

Assuming that the documents have been assembled as suggested above for the IPRC and SEAB meetings, the starting point will be to review these previously assembled documents to ensure that all relevant documents have been included. Any additional relevant documents created since the SEAB should also be assembled for presentation to the Tribunal. However, where legal counsel is involved, the inclusion or exclusion of documents should be discussed with the lawyer acting for the school board.

Documents are usually entered into evidence through witnesses and in particular, the witness who created the document. Accordingly, documents should

---

[12] R.S.O. 1990, c. S.22.

be organized by witness and sufficient copies should be made for the three Tribunal members, the Secretary of the Tribunal and the parents.[13]

School board witnesses may expedite their testimony if they prepare curriculum vitae setting out their qualifications and experience. Each witness's "C.V." can be entered into evidence at the outset of their testimony.

Witnesses

It will be necessary to identify the witnesses who will testify on behalf of the school board well in advance of the hearing. This may include "expert" witnesses from outside the school board. For example, a recognized expert on a particular exceptionality might be called as a witness to give evidence on the issues in dispute or a psychologist may be called to discuss the results of psychological testing.

Counsel will meet with witnesses in advance of the hearing in order to review the process which will be followed during the Tribunal's hearing and the evidence which each witness will provide. Counsel will decide the order in which the witnesses should be called.

As with the presentations to the IPRC and the SEAB, it will be important for those attending the Tribunal to maintain neutral body language and a respectful demeanour while attending the proceeding despite any disagreements with evidence which a witness might provide. This might sound self-evident, but sometimes attendees at hearings do react to hearing a witness or counsel say something they very much disagree with and this can prove to be distracting and unhelpful to the overall presentation.

Law

At the Tribunal, legal arguments are much more likely to be made than at the levels below. It will be necessary to review decisions of the Tribunal dealing with similar cases, as well as the court decisions on the standards which will be applicable in making the decision in the particular case. Again, it will be the responsibility of legal counsel to locate these cases.

---

[13] As noted in Chapter 10, "The Final Appeal", normally parents do consent to the disclosure of OSR documents to the Tribunal. See Chapter 10 for a discussion on the issue of dealing with OSR documents where the parents do not consent.

13

"Hard to Serve Students" and Other Legal Issues

INTRODUCTION

In this chapter we deal with a number of diverse issues which arise in the provision of special education programs and services to exceptional students.

"HARD TO SERVE" STUDENTS

Bill 82 introduced for the first time a requirement that every school board must provide, either directly or by way of purchase of services from another school board, a placement with appropriate special education programs and services for any student enrolled with the board, who was found to be exceptional. However, one exception to this requirement was included in Bill 82: where it was determined that, because of a mental or a mental and one or more additional disabilities, an exceptional student would be unable to profit from instruction offered by the board, a school board could determine a student to be "hard to serve". In this case, the school board was required to assist the parents to find a suitable placement for the pupil and the province would pay the cost of the placement.[1] This provision was removed in 1993.[2]

While the designation of "hard to serve" and the accompanying cost transfer provisions have now been removed from the *Education Act*, there remain students who are extremely difficult to serve and in some cases may even meet the criteria of "hard to serve" outlined above. The number of exceptional students who exhibit uncontrollable violent behaviour as a consequence of their disabilities is increasing. As well, the number of very medically fragile students attending school is on the rise. Both of these situations generally involve students who have mental disabilities and it is often a question whether such students are capable of profiting at all from curriculum, no matter how modified. Even where such students are able to profit from instruction, they pose special challenges to educators not just from a pedagogical perspective, but from a legal perspective as

---

[1] *Education Act*, R.S.O. 1980, c. 129, s. 34.
[2] *Education Statute Law Amendment Act*, S.O. 1993, c. 11.

179

well. In the case of exceptional students who exhibit violent behaviours as a consequence of their disabilities, the legal rights of these students to attend school must be balanced with the rights of staff and other students to work and learn in a safe environment. In the case of medically fragile students, legal questions arise about the rights of these students to medical care while attending school.

Dealing with Exceptional Students Who Exhibit Violent Behaviours as a Result of Disability

An exceptional student who exhibits violent behaviours as a result of disability has the same rights as other exceptional students:

- to be enrolled in the district school board where he or she is a resident pupil;[3]
- to be provided with a special education placement appropriate to the student's needs and, where those needs can be met in a regular class with appropriate special education services and the parent prefers this placement, to be placed in the regular class;[4]
- to be provided with appropriate special education programs and services;[5]
- to be provided with a safe learning environment, without undue disruption by other students.[6]

At the same time, students have a right to a safe learning environment without undue disruption from others and school staff has the right to work in a safe environment. (As a corollary to this, the school board has a duty to provide a safe working environment.[7])

All students have the right to expect that a school board and school staff will exercise a standard of care towards them which a prudent parent would exercise.[8]

---

[3] *Education Act*, R.S.O. 1990, c. E.2 (as amended), s. 32.

[4] *Identification and Placement of Exceptional Pupils*, O. Reg. 181/98, s. 17. Where the student's exceptionality results in behaviours which threaten the safety or disrupt the learning environment of other pupils and special education services to remove such threat or disruption cannot be provided, then it is questionable whether the student's needs can be met in the regular class.

[5] *Education Act*, ss. 8(3) and 170(1), paras. 6 and 7.

[6] *Ibid.*, s. 170(1), para. 10, s. 265(a) and (j).

[7] *Occupational Health and Safety Act*, R.S.O. 1990, c. O.1 (as amended to 1998, c. 8).

[8] *Thomas (Next Friend of) v. Hamilton (City)* (1994), 20 O.R. (3d) 598, 85 O.A.C. 161 (C.A.); *Walsh v. Buchanan*, [1995] O.J. No. 64 (QL), 52 A.C.W.S. (3d) 800 (Gen. Div.); *Durham v. N. Oxford P.S. Bd.*, [1960] O.R. 320 (C.A.); *Myers v. Peel County Board of Education*, [1981] 2 S.C.R. 21, 123 D.L.R. (3d) 1, 17 C.C.L.T. 269, 37 N.R. 227; *Plumley v. North York Board of Education*, [2000] O.J. No. 2636 (QL) (S.C.J.); *Long v. Gardner*, [1983] O.J. No. 268 (QL), 144 D.L.R. (3d) 73 (H.C.J.). This standard of care includes consideration of the age of the student, how severe any potential harm may be, and how likely it is that the harm will occur: *D.H. (Public Trustee of) v. S.A.H.*, [1998] B.C.J. No. 1388 (QL) (B.C.S.C.). See also *Lelarge v. Blakney* (1978), 92 D.L.R. (3d) 440, 23 N.B.R. (2d) 669 (C.A.), in which it is noted that as the age of the child increases, the expectation that the child will conform with adult standards of behaviour will also

This means that students and their parents have a right to expect that every reasonable step will be taken to ensure that while students are in the care of the school, they will be protected from situations which would foreseeably result in injury to them.

Where an exceptional student demonstrates violent behaviours as a result of disabilities, a conflict may arise between the rights of this student and the rights of staff and other students in the school. In this case a school board will have to balance the rights of all. Some of the steps which might be taken are outlined below.

Provide Staff and Students with Adequate Information

School staff should be provided with information and appropriate training to deal with exceptional students who exhibit violent behaviours as a result of their disabilities. Information may be obtained from the student's parents, from associations dealing with the particular disability, from the local SEAC member who represents the association concerned with the student's exceptionality and from medical professionals. Where necessary, students (and their parents) should also receive information or education on how to deal with the exceptional student. Where the parents of the exceptional student agree, students (or at least the exceptional student's classmates) may also be provided with instruction about the nature of the student's disability in order to assist them in understanding why the student behaves as she or he does.

The principal should meet with the staff who will be working with the student as soon as possible at the start of the school year in order to advise them of the circumstances and to discuss with them the safety measures which will be put into place. This can include a review of the triggers which instigate the violent behaviour and manner in which the behaviour manifests itself, if these are known. It may include a review of the protective equipment which may be used by staff who come into contact with the student and of the physical conditions of the classroom in which the student is placed to ensure that any items which might be a factor in the behaviour have been removed. Further, it should include a review of the training which staff have received to ensure that all staff are properly trained for dealing with the particular problem. It may be appropriate to invite to such meetings other school board staff with expertise in these issues. In addition, the student's parents might be invited to attend meetings to contribute information about the types of events that could precipitate a reaction so that they will understand the school's response to these reactions. The meetings might also review how staff should react to violent behaviour on the part of the student. If necessary, further meetings and training updates may be scheduled through the school year to review the situation.

---

increase, with a resultant decrease in the parental duty to control and supervise the child's activities. Of course, the opposite applies to students whose conduct is foreseeably risky.

Provide Staff with Protective Equipment

Staff who are dealing with exceptional pupils with violent behaviour must be provided with appropriate protective equipment. This is a requirement under s. 25(2)(a) of the *Occupational Health and Safety Act*. Equipment may be as simple as sports protective gear (*e.g.*, hockey shin pads).

Develop a Protocol for Dealing with Violent Behaviour

A properly designed protocol can ensure consistency in approach while also allowing flexibility in dealing with unique situations. Protocols can give school staff a process to follow if a violent incident does occur, which has been thought out in less stressful circumstances. Moreover, the development of an appropriate protocol and training in its application may give staff and parents a sense of confidence and encourage staff to react and be pro-active from an informed position, not an emotional or frightened one.

The protocol may set out guidelines which advise staff what to do immediately upon the occurrence of violent behaviours on the part of an exceptional pupil: for example, to immediately ensure the safety of the exceptional student and the safety of other students. It may be appropriate to remove the exceptional student to a different location in the school. (In some instances, schools may have a designated safe area into which to withdraw such students.) The protocol might also identify when and from whom to seek assistance and when to apply restraints.

The protocol should require that an immediate report be filed when a violent outburst occurs and should require a meeting of the principal and the staff who work with the pupil to review the situation. Appropriate and reasonable flexibility should be built into the protocol. For example, if violent conduct is a daily occurrence, the protocol may require meetings only where someone is injured or some new conduct is observed which necessitates a review of how the matter has been handled to date with a view to determining whether changes are needed.

If the situation worsens, the pupil's placement might also be reconsidered. The matter can be referred back to the IPRC for review of the placement if placement is a factor in the outbursts or if it appears that a different placement would work better for the pupil.

It is wise for staff working with the student to document the violent behaviours of exceptional students, and the responses of staff to those behaviours, in order to create a record of what has occurred. This record may prove useful in tracking the behaviours, determining triggers and the responses that work best. A record may also prove useful should any question be raised about actions taken by the school in dealing with the situation.

The protocol should also provide for notice to parents and, when meetings are held to discuss the student's behaviour, that the parents will normally be invited to attend.[9]

---

[9]   Parental involvement in such meetings is desirable whether the meetings are a preliminary step in an IPRC review which parents are entitled to attend, part of a

Utilize Appropriate Special Education Programs and Services and Individual Education Plans ("IEPs")

A student whose exceptionalities or disabilities involve violent behaviours should have an IEP which reflects appropriate programs and services which address these behaviours. If the violence continues, these programs and services should be reconsidered and the IEP amended if it is determined that other appropriate supports and programs might be provided.[10]

. A Last Resort: Remove the Exceptional Pupil from the School

Very rarely, where an exceptional student's violent behaviour puts others at risk, it may be necessary to remove the student from a school. Depending on the circumstances, there are several ways in which this may occur.

Suspension and Expulsion

At the time of writing, those provisions of the *Safe Schools Act, 2000*[11] which amend the existing *Education Act* provisions pertaining to discipline are expected to be proclaimed into force at various points during 2001. These amendments, which will be fleshed out by regulations promulgated by the Minister of Education, will change quite substantially the nature of suspensions and expulsions. While a full examination of suspensions and expulsions is beyond the scope of this book, it is appropriate to touch briefly on some of the issues which may arise for exceptional pupils.[12]

Under the *Safe Schools Act* amendments, two of the circumstances in which a suspension will be mandatory which have a particular impact on exceptional students whose disabilities lead to inappropriate behaviours are:[13]

- where a student "utters a threat to inflict serious bodily harm on another person"; and
- where a student swears at a teacher or "another person in a position of authority".

---

discussion about school rules about which parents are entitled to be informed, or as part of the parental right of access to educational information.

[10] See Chapter 7, "The Individual Education Plan".

[11] S.O. 2000, c. 12.

[12] At the date of writing, s. 23(1) of the *Education Act* permits, but does not require, a principal to suspend a student because of "persistent truancy, persistent opposition to authority, habitual neglect of duty, the wilful destruction of school property, the use of profane or improper language, or conduct injurious to the moral tone of the school or to the physical or mental well-being of others in the school". Similarly, s. 23(3) permits, but does not require, a school board (upon the recommendation of the principal and appropriate supervisory officer, notice to the parent or adult student, and the conduct of a hearing into the matter) to expel a student on the ground that the student's "conduct is so refractory that the pupil's presence is injurious to other pupils or persons".

[13] *Education Act*, s. 306(1) (not yet proclaimed in force).

An expulsion will be mandatory in certain circumstances which might directly impact on some exceptional students, including the following:[14]

- where the student commits a physical assault on another person which "causes bodily harm requiring treatment by a medical practitioner";
- where the student uses "a weapon to cause or threaten bodily harm to another person";[15] or
- where the student commits a sexual assault.

Questions have been raised about whether the mandatory suspension and expulsion rules will have a disproportionate impact on students with certain disabilities which influence behaviour. Some advocacy groups have suggested that these rules may raise issues under the *Canadian Charter of Rights and Freedoms.*[16]

However, it is hoped that any disproportionate impact which the mandatory suspension or expulsion rules may have on exceptional pupils will be rectified through regulations, policies and guidelines issued by the Minister of Education. The *Safe Schools Act* empowers the Minister of Education to establish regulations, policies and guidelines respecting the conduct of persons in schools and respecting discipline of pupils,[17] this includes the power to establish different rules for different classes of persons[18] — for example, exceptional pupils. Further, the Minister of Education may issue policies and guidelines to assist in the interpretation of ss. 306 and 309.[19]

---

[14]　*Ibid.*, s. 309(1).

[15]　It is to be noted that "weapon" is not defined by the *Safe Schools Act* amendments with the result that objects such as books or rulers might become weapons if used to inflict injury.

[16]　Being Part I of the *Constitution Act, 1982*, being Schedule B of the *Canada Act 1982* (U.K.), 1982, c. 11. A challenge might also arise under the Ontario *Human Rights Code*, R.S.O. 1990, c. H.19, against any school board which implements the Safe Schools legislation in a way that discriminates directly or indirectly against students with disabilities.

[17]　*Education Act*, s. 301(5) and (6).

[18]　*Ibid.*, s. 301(8).

[19]　In respect of mandatory suspensions, regulations may: (1) vary the length of minimum and maximum suspensions and set different standards for different circumstances or classes of students (s. 306(2)); (2) define those circumstances which constitute exceptions to the statutory requirement that a mandatory suspension be given in certain situations (s. 306(5)); and (3) specify the factors, apart from the student's history and other matters which the principal considers appropriate, which the principal shall consider in determining the length of a mandatory suspension (s. 306(9)). In respect of mandatory expulsions, regulations may: (1) define those circumstances which constitute exceptions to the statutory requirement that a mandatory expulsion be given in certain situations (s. 309(3)); (2) vary the limitations of a limited expulsion and specify different limits for different circumstances or different classes of persons (s. 309(15)); (3) specify the factors, apart from the student's history and other matters which the principal considers appropriate, which the principal shall consider in determining the length of a mandatory expulsion (s. 309(19)); and (4) vary the minimum duration of mandatory

At the time of writing, O. Reg. 106/01 and O. Reg. 37/01 had been put in place to define circumstances in which the mandatory suspension and mandatory expulsion provisions will not apply to a student when the *Safe Schools Act* amendments come into force. The circumstances are where the student does not have the ability to control his or her behaviour, the student does not have the ability to understand the foreseeable consequences of his or her behaviour, or the student's continuing presence in the school does not create an unacceptable risk to the safety or well being of any person. While neither regulation specifically excludes exceptional pupils from the application of the mandatory suspension and mandatory expulsion provisions of the *Safe Schools Act* amendments, it is clear that the regulations were designed to address the concerns which had been raised about the impact of the provisions on exceptional pupils.

In addition to the mandatory suspensions and expulsions defined by the *Safe Schools Act* amendments, the amendments permit school boards to define additional circumstances in which mandatory suspensions or expulsions may be imposed on a discretionary basis.[20] In exercising this power, school boards may define different rules for different classes of persons. School boards should take care in defining the circumstances in which suspensions and expulsions will or may be imposed, to ensure that they are not putting in place policies which result in unequal treatment towards exceptional students whose behaviours result from disabilities, since this may violate the Charter rights of these students to "equal treatment" without discrimination because of disability.

The Minister has the power to require school boards to provide programs, courses and services for students who have been suspended or expelled.[21] In the case of students with exceptionalities, it will be necessary that accommodations be made to these programs, courses and services to meet their special needs.

Exclusion

A principal may refuse to admit a person to the school or a classroom where the principal believes that the person's presence in the school would be detrimental to the physical or mental well-being of the pupils.[22] Depending on the circumstances of the particular case, this section may be used where the exceptional pupil's conduct has endangered other students, whether or not the student intended to do so.[23] While a student who has been excluded from a school is excused from

---

expulsion and prescribe different standards for different circumstances or classes of persons (s. 309(18)).

[20] *Education Act*, ss. 307 and 310.

[21] *Ibid.*, s. 312.

[22] *Ibid.*, s. 265(m). This power is subject to an appeal to the board of trustees.

[23] Note that, historically, s. 265(m) was intended to apply to trespassers rather than students and that its applicability to students has not been tested in court. At the same time, s. 21(2)(f) of the *Education Act* excuses a child from attendance at school if "the child is suspended, expelled or *excluded* from attendance at school under any Act or under the regulations" [emphasis added], thereby suggesting that students can be excluded under s. 265(m).

attendance at school,[24] if the student has been excluded because of behaviour which is the result of a disability and which the student is unable to control, it may be discriminatory for a school board not to provide some sort of appropriate instruction for the student. This may be done by providing home instruction to the student or by locating the student's placement in a different location within the school board.

A Placement in "Home Instruction"

Home instruction is not home schooling. Students receiving home instruction, usually for health reasons, have their instruction delivered by the school board.[25]

The Special Education Tribunal has approved the placement of an exceptional pupil in what was called a "home instruction program" for seven hours a week.[26] In *Eady v. Dryden Board of Education*,[27] the student displayed aggressive tendencies including violent outbursts. These violent outbursts apparently interfered with the ability of the school board to provide educational services to the student in school.

In the *Eady* case, the school board had included in its Special Education Plan a "home instruction" placement. This placement was defined in the Special Education Plan as a modified school day with individual instruction that could be carried out in a location other than school. In this case, the particular home instruction placement proposed by the school board was to be provided in one of the school board's buildings. A teacher's aide would be with the student all day (the school board offered to hire the parent to act as an aide for two and one-half hours per day and another aide would work the remaining three and one-half hours per day). A home instruction teacher would provide seven hours per week to assist with the academic program. The principal of the secondary school the student otherwise would have attended was to be responsible to supervise the placement.

---

[24]　*Education Act*, s. 21(2)(f).

[25]　*Operation of Schools — General*, R.R.O. 1990, Reg. 298, s. 11(11), permits a principal, subject to the approval of the appropriate supervisory officer, to arrange for home instruction to be provided for a student where the principal receives medical evidence that the student cannot attend school and the principal is satisfied that home instruction is required. In contrast, children receiving "home schooling" are not students of the school board. Their parents have assumed the legal obligation of providing appropriate instruction. Section 21(2) of the *Education Act* excuses a school-aged child from attending school where the child is "receiving satisfactory instruction at home or elsewhere".

[26]　"Home instruction" appears to be a misnomer since this placement, approved by the Tribunal, was a school board placement entirely under the responsibility, supervision and control of the school board. The provision of instruction at home would interfere with the school board's ability to control the safety and appropriateness of the learning environment and may, therefore, undermine the board's legal obligations to ensure the safety and well-being of all of its students.

[27]　(unreported, January, 1998) (Tompkins).

Dealing with the Medically Fragile Student

Increasingly, school boards are facing the challenge of dealing with students who are extremely fragile from a medical perspective. Inevitably, these students are exceptional since such conditions will interfere with the student's ability to benefit from the regular curriculum delivered in the regular manner.

Section 21 of the *Education Act* excuses attendance where a student is unable to attend school by reason of sickness or other unavoidable cause. In this event, the principal may arrange for home instruction of the student, subject to the approval of a superintendent.

Where a medically fragile student is able to attend school, s. 265(j) of the *Education Act* requires a principal to give "assiduous attention to the health and comfort of the pupils". At the same time, the common law standard of care imposed on school boards and their staff is that of a reasonably prudent parent — albeit a reasonably prudent parent with a large number of children.

Where there is any issue as to the safety of a medically fragile student in attending school, it may be prudent for the school to request the parents to provide a medical assessment of the student which indicates the effect of attending school and school activities on the student.[28] Where the medical report suggests that there is a risk to the student in attending school, it will be necessary for the school board to assess, in consultation with the principal, whether the risk can be adequately dealt with by the school. This will include a review of the nature of the risk, the ability of staff to respond to the risk and whether it is feasible to hire additional staff to attend to the student (including an assessment of whether it would constitute an undue hardship to the school board to be required to hire such staff).

The school board will be obliged to make whatever accommodations are required, short of undue hardship, to permit the student to attend school.[29] In some circumstances this may include providing a nurse so that the student can attend. This may be a reasonable accommodation required under the *Human Rights Code* even if the Intensive Support Amount grant[30] for the pupil does not cover the cost of a medical attendant. On the other hand, it also may be possible for the school board to argue that such an accommodation is unreasonable because, for example, the cost consequence would pose an undue hardship on the school board (assuming that compelling financial evidence can substantiate this assertion).[31] If

---

[28] Since the presumption is that a student may attend school, the cost of any assessment which is done for the benefit of the school board, should be borne by the board.

[29] See also, B.J. Bowlby and J. Wootton Regan, *An Educator's Guide to Human Rights* (Aurora: Aurora Professional Press, 1997).

[30] See Chapter 7, under the heading "Mandatory Individual Education Plans".

[31] In *British Columbia (Superintendent of Motor Vehicles) v. British Columbia (Council of Human Rights)* (1999), 181 D.L.R. (4th) 385 at p. 401, [1999] 3 S.C.R. 868, [2000] 1 W.W.R. 565, 214 W.A.C. 280, 70 B.C.L.R. (3d) 215, 36 C.H.R.R. D/129, 47 M.V.R. (3d) 167, 249 N.R. 45, the Supreme Court of Canada held that "one must be wary of putting too low a value on accommodating the disabled". The Court stated that cost arguments will be critically scrutinized, particularly when they are advanced by Government. In the Court's words (at p. 401): "Government agencies perform many

the condition of the student is such that the student is unable to benefit from any educational services, no matter what accommodation is provided, this may support an argument that the accommodation required to permit the student to attend school is an undue hardship based on cost, if it can otherwise be established that cost is a prohibitive factor in providing the accommodation.

If the school cannot safely and adequately deal with the risk which is occasioned to a medically fragile student in attending the school, then a principal might legitimately exclude the student for his or her own health and safety. However, in this circumstance, arrangements should be made for home instruction for the student.

If the student's medical condition is such that the student is unable to attend school on a full-time or regular basis or if the student's medical condition otherwise results in the student missing school on a regular basis or tiring as the day or week goes on, then the school board may reduce the length of the instructional day for the student. Regulation 298, s. 3, sets out a minimum requirement of five hours daily for the instructional program for pupils of compulsory school age. However, the same section also permits the board[32] to reduce the length of the instructional program on each school day to less than five hours for an exceptional pupil in a special education program. The board could thereby also reduce the number of days on which the student was obliged to attend school.

TRANSPORTATION

Section 190(1) of the *Education Act* does not oblige school boards to provide transportation. Rather, the issue of whether to provide transportation for "resident pupils" is left to the discretion of each school board.

The Act specifically permits school boards to provide transportation for persons who are qualified to be resident pupils:

---

expensive services for the public that they serve" — the implication being that they can be expected to absorb greater costs with respect to accommodation than private parties. This approach is problematic in application to broader public service entities, like school boards, which must operate within a fixed funding envelope. Nevertheless, it signals the obstacles school boards face in making undue hardship arguments based on cost. There are at least two reported Canadian decisions — one involving a university and one from the health care field — in which a broader public sector service-provider has been ordered to fund the cost of an attendant — in both cases an interpreter for the deaf — as a form of accommodation: *Howard v. University of British Columbia (Re)* (1993), 18 C.H.R.R. D/353 (B.C.H.R.C.) and *Eldridge v. British Columbia (Attorney General)*, [1997] 3 S.C.R. 624, 151 D.L.R. (4th) 577, [1998] 1 W.W.R. 50, 155 W.A.C. 81, 38 B.C.L.R. (3d) 1, 46 C.R.R. (2d) 189, 218 N.R. 161.

[32] The reduction in instructional time must be for the benefit of the student, not for the convenience or administrative benefit of the board. The reduction prevents the student from being charged with truancy.

- to and from the Ontario Schools for the Blind and the Deaf, or Ministry demonstration ("provincial") schools for students with severe communicational exceptionalities;
- a centre classified as a Group K Hospital under the *Public Hospitals Act*;[33]
- a facility designated under the *Developmental Services Act*;[34]
- a psychiatric facility designated as such under the *Mental Health Act*;[35] and
- a place where an agency approved under the *Child and Family Services Act*[36] provides a child development service, a child treatment centre or a child and family intervention service.[37]

The *Education Act* also provides that school boards may assist in the provision of transportation for children who are qualified to be resident pupils of the school board, to and from centres operated by a local association that is affiliated with the Ontario Association for Community Living, although this provision would appear to be a provision which relates to the pre-Bill 82 era when "schools for the mentally retarded" were operated by local Associations for Community Living.[38]

Once a school board has decided to provide transportation services to pupils, it must do so without discrimination based on any ground prohibited under the *Human Rights Code*, including handicap. This means that where, because of handicap, a student is unable to access the normal means of transportation, accommodation to a point short of undue hardship must be provided in order to transport the student. This may mean providing a taxi or leasing a specially modified vehicle to transport the pupil.[39]

---

[33] R.S.O. 1990, c. P.40.

[34] R.S.O. 1990, c. D.11.

[35] R.S.O. 1990, c. M.7.

[36] R.S.O. 1990, c. C.11, s. 8(1).

[37] *Education Act*, s. 190(3).

[38] *Ibid.*, s. 190(4).

[39] In one case, not decided in the school board context, the British Columbia government was even ordered to contribute to the costs of vehicle repairs for a disabled recipient of social assistance benefits where the recipient was able to establish that, because of her medical condition, it was "medically necessary" for her to use her personal vehicle for transportation purposes: *Chipperfield v. British Columbia (Ministry of Social Services)* (1997), 30 C.H.R.R. D/262 (B.C.H.R.T.).

Index